THE ELGIN MARBLES

THE
ELGIN MARBLES

Dorothy King

HUTCHINSON
London

First published by Hutchinson in 2006

1 3 5 7 9 10 8 6 4 2

Copyright © Dorothy King 2006

Dorothy King has asserted her right under the Copyright, Designs
and Patents Act, 1988 to be identified as the author of this work

Hutchinson
The Random House Group Limited
20 Vauxhall Bridge Road, London SW1V 2SA

Random House Australia (Pty) Limited
20 Alfred Street, Milsons Point, Sydney
New South Wales 2061, Australia

Random House New Zealand Limited
18 Poland Road, Glenfield
Auckland 10, New Zealand

Random House (Pty) Limited
Isle of Houghton, Corner Boundary Road
& Carse O'Gowrie, Houghton, 2198, South Africa

The Random House Group Limited Reg. No. 954009

www.randomhouse.co.uk

A CIP catalogue record for this book is available
from the British Library

ISBN 0–09–180013–7

Papers used by Random House are natural,
recyclable products made from wood grown in sustainable forests.
The manufacturing processes conform to the environmental
regulations of the country of origin

Typeset by Palimpsest Book Production Limited,
Polmont, Stirlingshire
Printed and bound in Great Britain by
William Clowes Ltd, Beccles, Suffolk

For my parents
Urszula and James T King

Contents

Illustrations

Acknowledgements

Years ago, whilst digging at Sparta, Guy Sanders first interested me in the Byzantine town of Mistras on the hill above, and in Slavic Greece. Later Andrea Nanetti and I went on a tour of the Venetian and Frankish Peloponnese. In 2001–2, thanks to the Onassis Foundation, I spent a year in Athens, living opposite the tenth-century Moni Petraki Monument, and enjoying many wonderful chats with Pierre MacKay about Ottoman Athens. I am particularly grateful to these people for fostering my interest in areas other than Classical Athens.

Alexander Lesk has written a history of the Erechtheion, and helped when I started this book, the two structures having had a parallel history. Peter Schultz is one of the great scholars of Greek sculpture, and could not have been more generous in sharing information. Michael Vickers, Judith Binder, and many other scholars made this book possible through their encouragement and help. Professors Tanoulis and Korres, who work on the Acropolis, went beyond the call of duty to give me access to material on the Acropolis. Many other archaeologists were helpful with information, and rather than naming them individually, I should thank all those who have added to the field over the years, through research and publication.

Anthony Whittome of Hutchinson first suggested writing a book. The next day I ended up sitting next to Sir Peter North, who had advised the government on the Elgin Marbles; many such encounters seem almost serendipitous. Tony and all those at Hutchinson have been very patient with me. Rosemary Scoular, Sophie Laurimore, and Simon Trewin at PFD are wonderful agents. Georgina Capel and Andrew Roberts were very generous with their advice. Michael Daley, the director of ArtWatch UK, deserves special thanks for his support and encouragement, as well as his suggestions and help with technical questions. Sean Kingsley of Minerva was supportive despite disagreeing with my views.

Joanna Mackle and Dyfri Williams of the British Museum, and Freddie New of the British Committee for the Restitution of the Parthenon Marbles, all answered the many questions I put to them. Evangelos Venizelos tended not to answer my questions, but politicians rarely do.

Prof. Michael Vickers is a great advocate of using familiar English names rather than unrecognisable pseudo-correct ancient ones, and I follow him. I have also followed Setton in using Castilian rather than Catalan names, so Pedro rather than Pere, and hope that Spanish is familiar enough not to have to translate it into Peter.

The Medieval year began on Lady Day rather than the first January, so to a Frank January 1208 would therefore be in our 1209 under the New System (NS); similarly there can be a little confusion with ancient dates, since the year started in the summer. We rarely know birth dates for many of the great historical figures, so dates given are reign dates rather than dates of birth and death.

All measurements are in metres rather than feet, although I sometimes give the measurements in ancient feet, where it seems relevant.

Prelude

Millions of years ago, during the Mesozoic Age, when dinosaurs still walked the surface of the earth, the African tectonic plate crashed into the Eurasian one. Where these two collided, they formed first the basin around the Mediterranean Sea, and eventually great mountain ranges such as the Alps. In the small area of Greece called Attica three great mountains were formed: Hymettus, Parnassus and Pentelicon. In the centre of this ring of mountains a smaller, lower mound, only 150 metres above sea level, was formed. It would be around this mound, which later came to be called the Acropolis, that one of the great world civilisations would briefly flourish. That civilisation would in turn build what was the ultimate expression of all that it stood for: the Parthenon.

Man is known to have first clustered around the Acropolis during the Neolithic period (Stone Age). As each generation succeeded the next, they began to tell tales of their ancestors, the early inhabitants of the area. These tales grew with each retelling, sometimes developing morals and lessons, and so the early history of these peoples became intricately interwoven with their mythology. In time, the history and stories of those peoples would become the mythology of the Athenians, and they would become the heroes of the classical Greeks. When they found the bones of the long-extinct dinosaurs, they added those creatures to their historical narrative, making them the great mythological beasts, the dragons their heroes slew, the creatures their gods had fought to gain control of Olympus.

Mount Lycabettos, a little to the north, was much higher than the Acropolis, but less hospitable to man. Only the flat surface of the Acropolis was conducive to building, and the mound formed of sandstone, limestone and schist was more stable. The surface measured a little more than seven acres, leaving plenty of space for settlement, and its sheer sides were easily defended. It also had springs that ran through it which could supply water, all of which made it an ideal place on which to build a new settlement. The geological make-up of the Acropolis made it hold water, and this water was welled from the Neolithic period by the citadel's first inhabitants. Other wells dating from the Bronze Age also survive. The availability of water was important and so wells continued to be dug, those wells becoming increasingly elaborate and more monumental as time went on.

To the west, the Acropolis sloped gently downwards towards the Areopagus and the Pnyx, making that the only easily accessible entrance to it. The Acropolis is, however, a natural structure, so over the years pieces of it have come crashing down on to the plain below. Occasionally, bits of the rock broke off, and boulders fell down on to the city, making the gods' displeasure clear to the Athenians.

Most cities in ancient Greece were centred around an acropolis, but Athens' is the best example. The term acropolis literally means 'high city'; the Athenians referred to it as that, or sometimes merely as the 'Polis' (city). The first Neolithic inhabitants of Athens cannot be described as 'Greek', for they did not speak the language. The language arrived towards the end of the early Bronze Age. Where the Greeks came from is not certain, but it is likely that they were Indo-Europeans who arrived in the middle Bronze Age, and led to the civilisation we describe today as Mycenaean.

Greeks, defined as those that spoke the language, appear to have arrived in Attica a little before they migrated to other parts of Greece, settling there in waves rather than in one migration. The Athenians are not aboriginal as they liked to claim, but rather a result of the intermarriage of these two peoples. Despite this, the

Athenians were arguably 'racially purer' than the citizens of many other Greek states, and they emphasised this regularly in their mythology. Both peoples lived on top of the Acropolis, where there are signs of habitation dating to the period.

The Acropolis of today has been excavated down to bedrock. In antiquity its polygonal top was covered in earth, trees grew there and plants were abundant. This bedrock is not even; it slopes down towards the south so that the Greeks would have to create platforms to make the surface horizontal and suitable for building on. The earliest surviving fortification walls belong to the Bronze Age; the Acropolis continued to be fortified and used as a fortress from that time until well into the nineteenth century. Later walls continued the lines of the sheer perpendicular cliffs of the Acropolis, the two blending into each other so that both nature and man ensured the impregnability of the Acropolis. The Acropolis was easy to defend and had a plentiful supply of water; it was high up and also flat enough to build on easily. All these features made it an ideal fortress, home to rulers and gods, and the focal point of the city.

The next generations of the Mycenaean era (Bronze Age) were the Greeks later heroised by Homer in the *Iliad* – those who had fought at Troy. Attica, however, was not yet unified, and remained a series of separate towns and states. One of these independent states was centred around the coastal village of Marathon. Athens was very much a state of the second rank, far behind Sparta and Mycenae. The honour of uniting these various towns would later fall to King Theseus.

The large number of later building phases at Athens has left us with almost no Mycenaean remains in the city, although some have been found apparently at the site of the New Acropolis Museum. The sixteenth century BC is the period in which Cecrops reputedly reigned over Athens. Cecrops' Mycenaean town probably centred around the Acropolis, with houses to the south and east of it. The town's cemetery was kept clear from the houses, located in what later became the Classical Agora. His own tomb became a shrine, eventually part of the complex called the Erechtheion on the Acropolis. Some remains on the Acropolis have been identified as his 'palace', but this was modest by the standards of other Mycenaean states.

Massive walls were built around the top of the Acropolis in c.1200 BC; these walls were called Cyclopean, because the giant Cyclops was said to have built them. An alternative Athenian tradition ascribed them to the Giants, who had been forced to construct them as punishment for their attempt at overthrowing the Olympian gods. Until the time of the Persian Wars these walls were the principal fortification of the Acropolis, greatly admired by contemporary Athenians who could not imagine who on earth could possibly have lifted the colossal boulders from which they were made.

Athens was now the most powerful city in Attica, and soon it became inevitable that she would draw the other cities first into her orbit, and then incorporate them into her state. Later Greek historians regarded the unification of all the Attic cities into one state as having been the work of Theseus. All became Athenian citizens, and they held a great festival to commemorate the event, and to celebrate the unification of these many peoples, the Panathenaia. Athenian myth and Athenian history collide once more.

Historically, this unification of Attica can be dated to around the same period as the Cyclopean walls of the Acropolis and can be dated archaeologically to c.1200 BC. The Athenians contributed relatively few ships to the Greek navy that sailed to Troy. King Theseus of Athens was not one of the leading Greek kings; his estate was relatively poor compared to others in the Mycenaean period, although later mythologising by the Athenians, after the other cities had fallen, would of course make him one of the great kings of Greece. In fact, although Theseus plays a role in Greek mythology, there are few other Athenian heroes whose tales feature.

The first kings of Athens, who historically lived between the fifteenth and the eleventh centuries BC, were, according to legend, born of the earth. This claim of autochthony was an important component of Athenian myth, since if the Athenians were descended from these early semi-human kings their line could not have been tainted by intermarriage with other races or the people of other cities. Towards the end of the Mycenaean period a people known as the Dorians had migrated to mainland Greece, but they do not seem to have settled in Athens, and this is reflected by the myth of Erechthonios and Athenian kings being born of the

4

earth. Erechthonios was autochthonous, literally springing from the earth. He was not, however, the child of Mother Earth like the Giants, but rather the product of the seed the god Hephaestus had in a moment of excitement dropped on Athena's thigh. The goddess brushed it off on to the ground; later this king was born and she adopted him. In this way the Athenians made their first king the son of Athena, while preserving her virginity. Erechthonios and Erechtheus are often confused in myth, and may be two alternative spellings of the same king. Although some scholars treat them as different kings, for the sake of clarity I treat them as being the same man.

Poseidon, according to legend, had given the city water, during the time of the first king, when he and Athena had competed to be the principal deity of the city. The fact that two gods competed for the city, according to its mythology, shows how highly the Athenians thought of themselves. We do not know what the early inhabitants called themselves or their city, but the name of Athens is in the plural, and would seem to reflect the amalgamation of several towns that all saw themselves as being under the protection of Athena. The myth of the contest between Athena and Poseidon may represent other towns, perhaps those closer to the sea, which were under the patronage of Poseidon before their amalgamation with the towns of Athena. In any case, this was considered an important enough episode of Athenian history for them to later depict it in the Parthenon sculptures.

Homer's *Iliad*, which tells the tale of the Trojan War, reflects the glory of the many Mycenaean states in Greece. The fall of Troy would also be depicted in the sculpture of the Parthenon. Unfortunately, the glory lasted only a couple of centuries, and from around 1200 BC the various states seemed to crumble. The reason for this is not certain, but a vacuum was created and the Dorians managed to step into it.

This period saw the beginnings of literacy in Greece, although this literacy was limited to the scribes of the elite. Early Greek writing, Linear B, was used to record possessions; this is comparable to the first use of writing in Sumeria, which was also used for administrative records, although in Egypt the first forms of writing were used to record history.

Historically and archaeologically, the centuries that followed the Mycenaeans are ones of decline. Mythologically, they were the golden age of Athenian history, where heroic kings ruled and fought fabulous beasts. The arrival of the Dorians in Greece coincided with the final fall of Mycenaean civilisation in much of the Greek world. Whether the Dorians were fought off by the Athenians and so never settled there, as the later historians of the state would claim, they certainly bypassed the city, and the Acropolis was never taken. Although scanty, and therefore far from conclusive, the archaeological evidence of the period does not contradict later legend; the Acropolis was never sacked and there are linguistic differences between the language spoken by the Athenians and that spoken by other mainland Greeks.

In these following centuries the Bronze Age gave way to the Iron Age, as that metal came to be the one most used for weapons. This era is sometimes described as the Dark Age, because we have no records of any events that took place then; we are literally in the dark when it comes to the history of the period. However, this is misleading, as in the archaeological record one can see that Athens soon began to flourish once again, as did the city's commerce. This is seen in pottery most clearly, as styles in pottery can easily be attributed to communities, and dated more accurately than other items.

Athens soon became a prosperous city once again, although prosperity led to an explosion in the population, which in turn led to migration. According to later legend, Ion, the son of Apollo, led the Athenians to the west coast of Asia Minor, where he founded many colonies. By the fifth century BC these cities were known collectively as Ionia. Although not all the colonists were from Athens, the Athenians emphasised their links with the new cities above all others. This would eventually lead to a crisis, in the form of the Persian Wars.

One of the earliest references to the town of 'Athene' is in the *Odyssey,* and is the exact same word Homer used to name the goddess Athena. The Acropolis also seems to have been called Athene at that point in time. Rather like the stories of the chicken and the egg, it is not certain which came first: was the city named after the rock, or the rock after Athena, or was Athena given her name because she was so closely linked to the city? Later Greek writers claimed that the city was named after the goddess, yet etymologically the word is pre-Greek and may well predate the cult of the Olympian gods. The mystery will probably never be solved, and in many ways, since the cult of Athena and the development of the city of Athens are so inextricably linked, it doesn't really matter.

Primitive societies may or may not have been matriarchal, but most worshipped an earth mother or goddess. The cult of Athena may well have been a continuation of that cult.

Other states included Athena in the cult of the gods, but it was in Athens that she was most venerated and that her cult and iconography became fully developed. Athena Polias (Athena of the City) was so named because she guarded the city, and because she lived on the Polis (the Acropolis). This was the prime aspect of Athena who was worshipped on the Acropolis, and to whom a great temple was built in the sixth century BC. Different aspects of the goddess were emphasised when she was given different epithets, making her Athena the founder, Athena the leader, Athena the protector, Athena the victor, Athena the fighter, and Athena the virgin, who would all come to be represented on the Acropolis. Athena's virginity, and therefore her purity, was an important aspect of her cult – this caused problems when the Athenians wanted to claim descent from her. Athena could also be the goddess of work, of horses, of health – her cult could be adapted to suit any purpose the Athenians needed.

In this way Athena invalidated the need for other gods, although the Athenians of course made sure they paid homage to her kin, the other Olympian deities. Almost everything on earth could be brought under the guardianship of Athena. Only the sea was beyond her reach. At that early point in Athens' history the sea was not of such great importance, although it would later become the source of her wealth and power after the Persian Wars. The cult of Poseidon had always been honoured in the city, but would become increasingly important over the centuries as the Athenian navy increased in size.

Although Poseidon was also god of horses, in Athenian myth

Athena had invented the bridle, and so the means to tame them. The Centaurs, symbolising lack of civilisation and depicted in the Parthenon sculptures, would serve as a warning to those who did not appreciate this gift of the goddess. Horses were an important status symbol in Classical Athens, and many of them would be depicted in the Parthenon frieze. During the Trojan War Athena's cunning had been put to good use. It had been Athena who had suggested that Epeios create the hollow wooden horse that would trick the Trojans into opening their gates. The Trojan War would also be depicted on the north side of the Parthenon, and this episode almost certainly featured in one of the metopes. Athena had helped Perseus slay Medusa in another myth; the Gorgon's head subsequently decorated the goddess's shield.

In Antiquity the Erechtheion was referred to as 'the temple on the Acropolis in which stood the ancient statue'; it housed the cult of Athena in the Classical period. From the few descriptions' we have, it is possible that the cult statue was an ancient one, perhaps from the Bronze Age, and venerated more for its great age than for any great skill that went into carving it. The statue was small enough to have been removed when the Athenians abandoned the city in 480 BC. Although the statue later created for the Parthenon was much grander, this statue remained the centre of Athena's cult. It was the terminal point of the annual Panathenaic procession, and the recipient of many dedications from Athenian citizens throughout the ages. Those dedications would later be kept in the Parthenon.

In Athenian mythology the story of the Labours of Heracles are often confusingly similar to the Athenian myths relating to Theseus. When Peisistratos, in the sixth century BC, became the tyrant of Athens, he too was faced with the task of reuniting all the small towns into an Attic state. Peisistratos' propaganda was thus that he was reuniting and recreating the Athenian state of Theseus. Although Theseus had always been part of Athenian mythological history, he now became one of its leading protagonists, and the myths that were part of his story became a major part of Athenian iconography.

It was said that Theseus' ghost later appeared during the Battle of Marathon, and helped the Athenians to their surprising victory against the Persians. This event may well be represented on the frieze of the temple of Athena Nike (Athena of Victory). In 475 BC Cimon brought the bones of Theseus back from Skyros, and arranged a great shrine to the heroic king to be constructed in Athens. That shrine may well be the building we now call the Hephaisteion. Well into the fifth century the myths relating to Theseus were emphasised by the Athenians. Heracles was a hero from the Peloponnese, and so too closely linked to Sparta, a rival for the Athenians. Theseus was a home-grown Athenian hero.

Although Theseus, as a king, might not seem as suitable a hero for democratic Athens, a little tinkering with his myths soon sorted that out. Theseus, just like Heracles, began to have an increasing number of Labours associated with him. According to these myths Theseus civilised the world, including subduing barbarians such as the Amazons and killing many mythical beasts, and this suited the Athenian state, because the Athenians perceived themselves to be the most civilised of people. Theseus, for example, slew the Minotaur, and destroyed King Minos' ships before he returned to Athens and became king. Crete and the Minoans had once been the dominant naval power in Greece. That had been many centuries before, in the Bronze Age, and in the fifth century the Athenians dominated the seas: this myth served to explain the transition of power from one state to another.

After the so-called Dark Age of Greece we move into the proto-historic period known as the Archaic Period. Geographically Greece was by then made up of a series of city states, the largest of which was Sparta, followed in size by Athens. Ancient Greeks would not have seen this as the state, or 'polis of Athens', but would rather have described it as the 'state of the Athenians'. A man would identify himself as Athenian or Spartan, but not as Greek.

There was no such thing as 'Ancient Greece', but rather a plethora of separate states, each with their own individual cultures. The mainland of what is now Greece was in Antiquity made up of around two dozen main states, with hundreds of smaller ones dotted between them which were independent, or at least nominally so – usually they followed the lead of their stronger neighbours. The people of these 'city states' had certain similarities in the religions they practised and spoke more or less the same language but had little else in common.

Although these city states shared many myths, others varied considerably. Heracles, for example, is well known today for having performed Twelve Labours, but these Labours varied considerably from area to area depending on that state's history. The states united at times of crisis, for example for the Persian Wars and before that for the Trojan War, but they varied greatly politically, both in their policies and in the form of government they had. The citizens would have concentrated on their differences in terms of creating their own identities. Greece only became a geographical whole when it was conquered, first by the Macedonians and then by the Romans, becoming a Roman province, a Byzantine province and finally a province that made up part of the Ottoman Empire.

Certain sanctuaries were pan-Hellenic, meaning that they belonged to all Greeks. These were religious sites such as Delphi and Olympia, and when these hosted games citizens from all around the Greek world competed in them as individuals. Cities could also host pan-Hellenic festivals and there were several in Athens, the most important of these being the Great Panathenaia held every four years. A lesser Panathenaia was held annually but this was usually attended mostly by people living in Attica. Perhaps the greatest expression of pan-Hellenism in the Classical period was the Delian League formed by the Athenians. Although it united many Greek states, its main aim was not to foster brotherly relations but rather to fight their enemies, the Persians. Arguably there is a greater level of homogeneity between the Greek states under Philip II and Alexander the Great, but this was not pan-Hellenism by choice but rather one that was imposed on them through conquest.

Xenophobia also united the Greeks, who were generally rather racist, and almost all looked down on what they considered to be barbarians. Chief among these barbarians were the Persians to their east, of whom the Greeks made fun and whom they considered both effeminate and only suitable for slavery. The intermarriage of aris-

tocrats from various Greek states also helped to create bonds. This
ended, however, when Pericles pushed through a law on Athenian
citizenship, which stated that to be an Athenian citizen one had to
have both an Athenian father and an Athenian mother.

This Athenian state covered Attica, with people living in smaller
towns at least in theory being equal to those that lived in Athens
itself, and all landed men were citizens. Athens retained close links
with her colonies, and saw herself as their guardian and protector.
By the time of the Persian Wars there were around a thousand of
these Greek city states, many of them small, mostly dotted around
the Mediterranean but some also extending to the coast of the Black
Sea.

The rule by a 'tyrant' in Greek simply meant rule by one man; it
did not imply any of the negative, despotic elements we associate
today with tyranny. In the Archaic Period various Athenians tried
to set themselves up as autocrats, tyrants. Few of these were successful
but the period can be described as alternating between these tyrants
and brief periods of democracy. In 594 BC, to deal with some unspec-
ified crisis, Solon was elected archon.

Solon gave the Athenians a constitution for the first time, for
which he is often acclaimed the father of Athenian democracy.
Ownership of land was a requirement for Athenian citizenship, and
by setting a maximum amount of land any one man could own,
Solon increased the numbers of Athenian citizens. His political
reforms also began to codify citizenship and the citizen's role in politics. All citizens could take part in the assembly, but a council of
four hundred, selected at random rather than elected, was in charge
of day-to-day affairs.

He also encouraged skilled workers to settle in Athens, which led
to a boom in manufacturing, and then in trade. Before Solon
Athenians had been subjects; after him they became citizens, with
rights within the community. In this way Solon set Athens on the
road to democracy, this institution being arguably Greece's greatest
gift to the world; although his reforms were of dubious immediate
success, for the city continued to alternate between democracy and
dictatorship.

The most successful of those who tried to seize power was

Peisistratos, who achieved it through a combination of wealth and charisma rather than military might. His rule, between 547 and 528 BC, was seen by later Greeks as one of Greece's golden ages, democracy not necessarily having been seen by the ancient Greeks as superior to tyranny. Peisistratos was a political reformer, and in his times Athenian culture flourished. He rebuilt much of the Acropolis, including the Temple of Athena, and rebuilt temples all around Attica. Another achievement for which he is known was the reorganisation of the Panathenaia, the main Athenian religious festival, including incorporating games into the Great Panathenaia. If he did not found it, Peisistratos at least considerably enlarged the festival of Dionysus, held every spring, during which plays were performed. Plays themselves were developed in the later sixth century BC, and since drama needed actors, thespians were born, named after Thespis, one of the first.

The main achievement, however, was the creation of the Athenian drachma, one of the first standardised coins in the ancient world. These coins were stamped with an owl, which guaranteed their weight and their purity. Because of this they became the ancient equivalent of the dollar, one of the only coins accepted by other states.

Peisistratos was succeeded by his eldest son, Hippias. The younger son, Hipparcus, was a playboy, and his antics insulted a certain Harmodius who, with Aristogeiton, assassinated him in 514 BC during the Panathenaia. These two men had hoped they would start an uprising against Hippias, but the Athenians, generally happy with his rule, did not eject him. All golden ages must unfortunately come to an end, and the assassination of his brother made Hippias paranoid, which in turn led to tyrannical behaviour in the modern sense of the word. Eventually the Athenians, with Spartan help, removed him from power. Hippias sought refuge on the Acropolis, but seeing that he had lost the city he surrendered, and went into exile at the Persian court. The Athenians, not averse to a little revisionism, immediately declared the slain Harmodius and Aristogeiton tyrannicides – heroes who had delivered the city from tyranny. Statues of the two were erected in the Agora, statues that would later be stolen by the Persians and then returned to Athens by Alexander the Great.

Democracy was not immediately reinstituted. Instead, the aristo-crats tried to make Athens an oligarchy, a city ruled by the few, as opposed to a democracy which was rule by the people (the *demos*). The oligarchy ultimately failed and a form of democracy re-established. Cleisthenes instituted yet another series of reforms. In theory democracy meant that any Athenian citizens (these were all of course men) that had come of age could take part in the running of the government. In practice it meant that only the rich, who had the time to do so, were able to take part.

By the Archaic Period, the Acropolis was no longer the residence of the city's rulers, although the Peisistratids may well have lived in a palace there. Under the kings the ruler had lived on the Acropolis and governed the state from it. When the Athenians ceased to be ruled by kings, the Agora became the location of the new demo-cratic government and of all institutions related to it. The Acropolis housed the main state cults and continued to be used by the Athenians as both a sanctuary and a fortress in times of need, where gods' and men's lives ran side by side. More and more cults came to have their homes in shrines there. The first stone temple on the mound was constructed in the Archaic Period, and by the mid-sixth century BC the sanctuaries came to be more important than its role as a fortress. The Acropolis was given over to religion.

The size of the ramp leading up to the west entrance had been greatly increased in the first half of the sixth century, probably to make space for the larger reorganised Panathenaic procession (566 BC). Around the same time the Athenians built the first large-scale, monumental temple to Athena on the Acropolis. The temple domi-nated the Acropolis, although by the standards of the day it was not particularly colossal. Doric columns ran around the exterior of a building that measured twenty metres by just over forty metres. The architecture was of limestone, as was the sculpture – one of the first monumental examples of elaborate architectural sculpture in Athens. The metopes were carved with relief figures, and the gables filled with sculptures.

The whole was highly decorated and coloured. Much of this colour survives; when the temples were destroyed by the Persians, the elements were buried, possibly for religious reasons, by the Athenians. These conditions helped preserve them. Several sets of sculptures are preserved, and it is not always possible to be certain which building they originally adorned. One of the sculptures may well have represented the chthonic Cecrops; if so, here his human legs were replaced by snakes, while later on the Parthenon he was depicted as human. Snakes in general featured prominently among these sculptures. Another temple, called the Old Temple of Athena Polias, was constructed later in the sixth century.

Until then, for the Greeks, as for many ancient peoples, history and mythology had blended together. The Archaic Period was a time of greater literacy, when the first historians began to record the city's history. Homer's epics, written in the eighth century, are the first great semi-historical Greek writings. In the *Iliad*, Athens is mentioned only twice in passing; even these brief entries may be later additions. Homer mentions Athena going to Athens, to the house of Erechtheus, the early king of the city. The fifty ships the Athenians supplied to Troy may also have been inserted later for reasons of propaganda. By Homer's day the Athenian kings were in the past, and the city was a fledgling democracy. By 632 BC we know that, as in the *Iliad*, there was both a statue to Athena and a temple to her on the Acropolis mound, that the Athenians were firmly in the historic period and the age of heroes was left behind.

Although in the sixth century the use of the Acropolis as a sanctuary came to the fore, the mound never lost its importance as a fortress, a citadel in which one could take refuge. Those who wanted to control the city usually had to control the Acropolis; this would prove as true in the nineteenth century as it was in antiquity.

The Persian Wars

Meanwhile, to the east, the Persians were conquering new lands and increasing their power. Macedonia and Thrace, regions of what is now modern Greece, became Persian vassals, offering the Persian king earth and water as symbols of their submission. In 506 BC there was a crisis in Athens, when the Spartans tried to establish another tyrant in the city. The Athenians panicked and sent an embassy to the east to try to form an alliance with the Persians, to gain their protection and military assistance against the Spartans. The Persians would of course only help their vassals, so the embassy agreed to this, and briefly the Athenians technically became Persian vassals. As soon as the political situation in Athens was resolved, and the threat of war with Sparta had passed, the Athenians equally quickly repudiated this alliance.

In 499 BC Miletus revolted against Persian rule, and soon many other Greek cities of Ionia in Asia Minor followed their lead. The Ionians asked the Spartans for help, Sparta being the pre-eminent state of the time. When the Spartans declined to help, Athens stepped in. After the overthrow of the tyrants, and the re-establishment of democracy, the Athenians became arrogant, thinking there was nothing they could not achieve. Rather than concentrating their efforts at home, they interfered in foreign affairs. The Athenians claimed a link to the Ionian Greeks through Ion, whose mother was the daughter of Erechtheus, their early king. Although the Ionians, assisted by twenty Athenian ships, had some early successes – winning a few initial battles – they lost the war.

The Athenians and the Ionians launched an attack on Sardis, one of the Persian capitals. The Persian king Darius, on being informed that the Athenians had tried to invade his territory, was surprised since he had never heard of those particular peoples. He was, however, determined to exact revenge. By 494 BC Darius had put down the Ionian revolt and recaptured all the Greek cities in Asia Minor. He enslaved many of the Ionian Greeks, and razed some of their cities. Mardonius, Darius' son-in-law and one of his most able generals, launched an expedition against Greece in 492, but this failed due to bad weather, and the ships had to return to Persia.

Another fleet was assembled at Samos in the summer of 490 BC and launched against Greece. It is unclear whether Darius had intended to try to conquer the whole of the Greek mainland, but certainly he planned to exact revenge on the Athenians, destroying their city and making it a vassal of the Persian state with Hippias as a Persian puppet tyrant. As they made their way down the coast-line, the Persians sacked Greek cities. Eventually they landed at Marathon, a small village in Attica. Marathon was one of the first villages in Attica that had been settled. Hippias, the exiled tyrant of Athens, and son of Peisistratos, was with the Persians at Marathon.

Faced with a common enemy, the various factions in Athenian political life immediately united to fight for their country and to preserve their way of life. The battle was an astonishing victory for the Athenians, who lost only 192 men, routing the much larger Persian army, which fled after 6,000 of their number had been slain on the field. The great victory changed the course of Athenian history, and arguably that of the entire world.

Athena and Heracles had stepped in to assist the Athenians at Marathon, appearing on the battlefield to fight side by side with the Athenians. After the victory the goddess and the hero were accorded special honours by the city. When the Persians panicked just before they fled, this panic was seen to have been caused by the god Pan. Pan's assistance was recorded by the Athenians after the battle, and he was given a sanctuary in the caves on the northern slope of the

Acropolis, where offerings were made as well as sacrifices. The bronze sculpture of Theseus and the Marathon bull, still to be seen on the Acropolis in the Roman period, may well have been a dedication linked to the battle. Theseus is said to have caught the dangerous bull, brought it to Athens and sacrificed it to Athena on the Acropolis. A statue of winged victory was also dedicated on the Acropolis by Callimachus to commemorate the Athenian victory. The battle was one of the major Athenian successes on the world stage, and the citizens made sure they commemorated it with dozens of sculptures and monuments.

Soon after the Battle of Marathon the Athenians began to clear space for and to construct a colossal monument on the Acropolis, a building which was to be the precursor of the Parthenon. It was funded using loot seized after Marathon, and intended to commemorate the Athenian victory there. Progress on this pre-Parthenon was not swift, and it was never finished. Many of the architectural elements were later reused in the foundations of the Parthenon. This older Parthenon had been planned as the biggest temple in mainland Greece, to be constructed entirely of marble. A new gateway to the Acropolis was also begun at that time, lined up with and emphasising the old temple of Athena. Unfortunately, in 480 BC, during the course of their construction, the Persians invaded again and sacked the Acropolis. The first Parthenon anticipated the Periclean Parthenon in its plan, and also had Ionic features. The Athenians were clearly attempting to differentiate themselves architecturally from the pure Doric temples of the Dorians in the Peloponnese, and to emphasise their own eastern, Ionian heritage.

When Xerxes succeeded his father in 486 BC, he was determined to punish the Greeks for the embarrassing defeat they had inflicted on Darius. Darius had apparently sworn revenge on the Athenians, a servant reminding him every day by whispering in his ear 'Remember the Athenians'. Just before he launched his army to invade Greece, Darius sent ambassadors to the Greeks in 491 BC giving them the choice of submitting to him rather than being annihilated. As a sign of allegiance the states were asked to give the Persians gifts of water and of earth. Although these demands seem trivial – nothing compared to handing over bags of gold – to the

Greeks this was an insulting demand, since they valued their freedom above all. Athens was a democracy, but most other Greek states were monarchies or oligarchies, and so for most of their inhabitants transferring rule to the Persians would have made little difference to their actual freedom, but their pride meant that they did not wish to be ruled by those they saw as effeminate barbarians. The Athenians provided earth by throwing the Persian ambassadors into a deep pit; the Spartans chose instead to give the gift of water, casting the Persian ambassadors into a well.

After the first Persian War, the Athenian constitution was amended, and from then on real power could only be exerted by generals, ten being appointed each year for a term of one year. All other positions were chosen by lot, but the generals were elected, and so this was the only position those who wanted to make politics their life could try to achieve. Since poorer citizens could not afford to devote themselves to politics, this meant that once again the exercise of political power in Athens became the domain of the rich and the aristocracy.

The leading politician at the time was Themistocles, a foresighted man who was able to strengthen Athens in preparation for the inevitable invasion of the Persians. He moved the city's harbour to the much more suitable site at Piraeus, strengthened the city's walls and made it easier to defend. He also, most wisely, persuaded the Athenians to use their wealth to build ships. Huge quantities of silver had been found at an Athenian mine and the Athenians had wanted to distribute this wealth among themselves. He persuaded them to invest it instead in their navy, a navy that would become decisive in the fight against the Persians at the Battle of Salamis.

In 481 BC a Persian invasion became inevitable, and some of the Greek states chose to form a coalition, led by the Spartans. The most famous episode of this war was the stand that three hundred Spartans under the leadership of Leonidas, their king, made against the Persians at Thermopylae. The Spartans were eventually slaughtered, but they became martyrs, admired for their dedication to Greek freedom, even if they had done little to stop the Persian advance southwards through Greece.

The Athenians sent to the oracle at Delphi for advice. The oracle, never known for its clarity, replied that they would be saved by wooden walls. Some Athenians assumed this meant they should seek shelter on the Acropolis, but Themistocles persuaded them that the wooden walls were the walls of their ships, and that the Athenians should abandon Athens and seek shelter elsewhere. The wooden walls would save the city, but these turned out to be the wooden walls of her ultimately victorious navy. The Persians marched on to the city, taking it without any resistance, and sacking it.

Only the ancient and venerable cult statue of Athena Polias is known to have survived the Persian destruction of the Acropolis. Common sense suggests that movable treasure and gold was probably taken by the Greeks before they fled. The priests who remained fought valiantly to defend the Acropolis, but the Persians soon set fire to it, a fire that swiftly took hold due to the large amount of timber present because of the construction work. Every building was destroyed, ravaged by fire, and came tumbling down. Mardonius sacked Athens for a second time in 479 BC. Scorch marks can still be seen on some of the blocks of the old Parthenon that were reused within the later one. Nothing survived. Marble was smashed and bronze melted down for reuse. The heads were deliberately knocked off statues of maidens, and the Greeks when they returned buried these figures in the ground of the Acropolis, where they were found in the nineteenth century. The monuments the Athenians had erected to commemorate Marathon, which had stood on the Acropolis for less than a decade, were pulled down.

The Persians moved on to Salamis, where they fought a naval battle against the Greeks. The Greeks won, but not as decisively as they had at Marathon. Xerxes returned home, leaving Mardonius in charge of the army and of a war that looked increasingly won.

The Greeks united under Spartan leadership at Plataea and drove out the Persians, forcing them out of their last stronghold on the Greek mainland. Thousands of Persians were killed. Athens lost fifty-two of her citizens, but made up for this by seizing arms and armour from the Persian leaders, treasures that would be displayed on the Acropolis for many generations to come.

The Greeks defeated the Persians again at Mycale, an even more humiliating defeat for them since it was within their own territory in Asia Minor. Athenian generals had fought valiantly, and played a major part in forcing the Persians to withdraw from Greece. Their leadership during the second Persian War was soon converted into leadership of a league of nations who united to protect themselves against any future Persian invasions.

The Athenian playwright Aeschylus took part in both the Battle of Marathon during the first war and the Battle of Salamis during the second. These wars influenced his writing, and in 472 BC *The Persians* was produced, one of the few plays set in contemporary times rather than the mythological past. By one of those coincidences that make history so interesting, we also know that the production of this play was funded by Pericles, in one of his first public acts as an Athenian citizen who had come of age.

The sacred olive tree on the Acropolis, given to the Athenians by Athena, had been destroyed during the Persian sack, burned to the ground. A few years later, apparently without any human intervention, the tree miraculously began to grow again. The Athenians drew parallels between the tree and their state, which had risen out of the ashes stronger than ever, and determined to become the leaders of the Greek world.

The Delian League

The golden age of Athens lies between the attempted Persian invasions and the later successful Macedonian invasion in the fourth
century BC. The Athenians almost immediately began to prepare for
future wars and invasions, building new walls around the city and
fortifying the Acropolis to cope with any eventuality. Although the
threat from Persia was the more obvious, the Athenians also knew
that the Spartans, the only power that could rival that of Athens,
might invade. As the two vied for power and for territory this could
lead to a conflict of arms.

The Acropolis itself was bare of buildings, the temples having
been burned and razed by the Persians. All the remains were ritu-
ally buried in the soil of the Acropolis. Dedications, often statues,
by individuals continued and many are attested on the Acropolis,
but the temples in Athens were not rebuilt immediately after the
war. When Athenians went about their business in the town below,
they could look up at the Acropolis and see nothing. This devastation reminded them of the recent Persian sack of the city, and that
they needed to take action to prevent another invasion.

After the second Persian War, Miltiades was commemorated in a
number of Athenian monuments. Pheidias, the leading Athenian
sculptor of the day, created a bronze group of the general and the
gods which was dedicated by the Athenians in the Sanctuary at

21

Delphi. One of his earliest major commissions, the group was paid for by booty taken off the Persians at Marathon. Elsewhere, in the Agora, the administrative centre of the city, Miltiades and the Greek generals were represented in the company of gods fighting the battle. Since Miltiades' son Cimon wielded a great deal of political power at the time, he is likely to have been instrumental in arranging these commissions.

In the decades after the end of the war, Athenian influence spread to encompass much of the Greek world in terms of political power, and the state became richer than ever. This makes it all the more surprising that they did not rebuild the temples on the Acropolis which the Persians had destroyed.

At Plataea the Greeks allegedly swore an oath before the battle not to rebuild their temples until the Persian threat had been erad-icated. This oath is preserved in Diodorus (11.29.3), although some scholars dispute its authenticity, believing it might have been a later invention; nevertheless, the temples were not rebuilt, and whatever the truth of the oath, the archaeological record supports its exis-tence.

In the past the Greeks had reacted to the Persians, but now they realised that they had to be more proactive, to prevent another Persian invasion. The Athenians went on the offensive, founding an alliance of 140 Greek states in 478/7 BC. In theory, at least initially, these states were equal partners.

In 477 the Athenians reorganised the alliance, and officially formed what became known as the Delian League. It became a confederacy of states from both sides of the Aegean, dedicated to protecting Greek cities from the Persians, and to freeing others that were still under their yolk. Members of the League provided ships or money, usually the latter, and the League's treasury was on Delos, an island that was a sanctuary of Apollo, whose son Ion was the eponymous founder of the cities in Asia Minor. The idealism of this alliance, where Athens was merely the first among equals, soon disin-tegrated, and the League turned instead into an Athenian Empire. Athens soon began to compel other states, particularly those that were strategically important, to join the alliance. States that tried to leave it were often besieged, and forced to remain within it.

The Athenians had always taken the leadership of the League, but when their general Cimon won a battle at the River Eurymedon in 469, overwhelmingly defeating the Persians, the Athenians began to see the League as potentially their instrument in an expansion which became an Athenian empire. That the whole concept of having an empire seemed to be incompatible with the idea of democracy did not bother the Athenians. They were happy to practise democracy at home, while using the funds of their empire to build monuments to it.

The Athenian democracy was not universal but rather it was restricted to men born of both an Athenian father and mother, who also owned land. Women, slaves and foreigners who had settled in Athens could not vote; despite this, the Athenian democracy enfranchised far more of the population than any other government anywhere else in the world. It allowed a substantial portion of the population to be involved in governing the state, in a world where states were usually ruled by only one man, or at most only a few members of its aristocracy.

The Athenian love of freedom and democracy is easy for us to admire today, but it is less easy for us to condone the way they oppressed many of their allies in an attempt to win this fight to free themselves from potential Persian tyranny, as they saw it, and more likely to increase their own power. The land in Attica is fairly rocky. They needed to exploit their colonies to increase the economic sufficiency of the Athenian state, and they did so with great skill: they were not exploiting fellow Greeks, but rather foreigners. The Aegean was filled with islands and each was independent; when the Athenians first formed their Delian League they had 140 allies. By the time it became an Athenian empire it comprised 300 individual city states.

Pericles the Statesman

This was also the time that Pericles became one of the leading statesmen in Athens. There were no political parties in the modern sense in ancient Athens. Rather, individuals helped shape the city, whether through laws or policies. Occasionally these individuals continued the work of a predecessor, creating a sense of continuity, but they cannot be divided as easily as we can divide politicians nowadays as belonging to either the left or the right, as having liberal tendencies or traditionalist ones.

The age of Pericles, the time when he was the leading statesman in Athens, was probably the most glorious in the city's history. Great playwrights staged plays at the festival of Dionysus, great philosophers taught in Athens, and the leading artists and architects of the Greek world were brought to the city to help beautify it. Culture had flourished under Peisistratos but then waned. Now that the city was rich again it attracted the best, brightest thinkers, artists and intellectuals.

Pericles' family was a landowning one, from the deme of Cholargos, now a northern suburb of Athens, and the tribe Akamantis. His father Xanthippos, because of universal military service, probably fought with his tribe at the Battle of Marathon in 490 BC. Pericles, the second son, was born between 495 and 492 BC, most scholars putting his date of birth in 493 BC.

His elder brother Ariphron was active in politics; we know this not because any records of his activities are preserved, but because a handful of *ostraka* with his name have been found, showing that he was sufficiently successful to have been a candidate for ostracism, the system of decade-long exile the Athenians used as a check against those they felt had become too powerful. Xanthippos himself had been ostracised c.484 BC.

Ostracism is named after *ostraka*, the small shards of pottery on which Athenian citizens would write the names of those they wished to send into exile. Exile was not necessarily a punishment for having done something wrong, but was used more as a safety valve to prevent any one person gaining too much power. Many of the leading Athenian politicians, some of whom we now see as the great men of the period, were sent into this exile when it was felt they had become too self-important. Ostracism is one of the curiosities of Athenian democracy, where leading politicians were sent away for ten years, although this was not a punishment that involved loss of any land or of any rights in the city.

Xanthippos prosecuted Miltiades, the Athenian leader at

Marathon, after that general's subsequent disastrous venture against Paros, an island which had remained a Persian ally. Cimon paid his father's fine after Xanthippos' prosecution, Miltiades having meanwhile died in prison. This rivalry would continue to the next generation, with Cimon and Pericles on opposite sides politically.

Cimon, older than Pericles by some twenty years, was instrumental in Athens' continuing attacks against the Persians after Salamis, and helped move Athens into a pre-eminent position in the anti-Persian alliance that would become the Delian League. One of the first places the League captured was Skyros, and from there they repatriated to Athens the bones of Theseus, their legendary early king. A shrine to the hero was built in Athens, where his bones were reburied, and the Athenian king joined the Delian god Apollo as protector of the League, another step towards the Athenians gaining control of it. Theseus was prominent in the decoration of the Athenian treasury at Delphi, and he probably took part with Heracles in the battle against the Amazons that would later be depicted on the Parthenon.

Pericles' first act of public service as an adult Athenian citizen, in 472 BC, was as the financial backer (*choregos*) to Aeschylus for three tragedies and a satyr play. The tragedies included *The Persians* and were put on as part of the annual festival of Dionysus. *Choregoi* were chosen from the wealthy Athenians, and this was considered one of their public duties, a sort of wealth tax on a par with outfitting a ship, but one which could also bring a great deal of prestige if the play and *choregos* won at the festival. The play can be read as a political statement in support of Themistocles and his actions in the recent war. If so, it failed; Themistocles was ostracised, probably in 471/0.

In 454 BC the Athenians demonstrated their power over their so-called allies in the clearest possible way: they moved the League's treasury, about 8,000 talents, from Delos to Athens, to be kept on the Acropolis. After the disasters in Egypt and the first Peloponnesian War, Athens probably felt she needed to tighten her control over what had become a de facto Athenian empire. Once the treasury had been moved, the Athenians behaved rather like mobsters, demanding protection money from the various 'allies' who were now subject states, and punishing severely those who refused to pay them tribute. A marble slab from the following year survives, listing the tribute that the states had to pay Athens. The one-sixtieth of their tribute, which was dedicated to Athena, was listed, and from these sums we can work out how much each of the so-called allies was forced to pay. Tribute by colonists and allies was paid at the festival of Dionysus. The Athenians and their allies also dedicated, for example, a percentage of their production of wheat and barley to Demeter and Persephone at Eleusis, showing how the Athenians actively and financially involved their 'allies' in the participation of their state cults. Other inscriptions record the various gifts the allies had to send to Athens during its many festivals.

Rates were standardised throughout the empire, based on the Athenian scales, and Athens' coins became the currency of the empire. Athenian tyranny grew over its allies, while at home democracy enjoyed a renaissance, with citizens gaining increasing amounts of rights. The period after the second Persian War marked a flowering of democracy in Athens, if not in the Delian League, and also in its culture. The Greek victories in the second Persian War were celebrated, but the Athenian victory at Marathon was still considered the most important.

The Persians and the Greeks reached a peace in 451 BC, known as the Peace of Kallias, after the Athenian who had negotiated it. Whether it was a formal peace, or one artificially imposed by historians later, taking into account a period of peace, is uncertain and remains hotly debated, but it was probably a peace of tacit agreement by both sides to respect the status quo of lands and of non-aggression. By doing so, they were removing the ostensible *raison d'être* of the League. In fact, the Delian League did cease to exist. It was not disbanded because the threat of war was over, but turned instead into an Athenian empire.

The Athenians now demanded ever greater tribute be paid by their allies, and since that money no longer needed to be spent fighting the Persians, they chose to spend it on the city of Athens instead. The Spartans and the Athenians had ostensibly signed a thirty-year truce, but when the Athenians started to expand to the west, war between the two great states of the Greek world broke out.

Kolophon, an Ionian city, tried to leave the League in the early 440s, but her attempt to revolt was crushed, and a democracy established there instead. In 446/5 Euboea then Megara, both mainland allies, revolted. A Spartan army tried to intervene, but Pericles bribed the king to retreat. Although the Spartans chose to replace their king, they also recognised a thirty years' peace with Athens. The Spartans returned home, the Megarians settled their differences with Athens, and the Euboeans were brought to heel by Pericles. A colony was established at Hesteaea, and the Euboeans paid Athens tribute. Interestingly, Chalcis at this time also paid tribute to Athens, and swore loyalty to her, though not to her allies, in exchange for which Athens guarded the cities.

Pericles may well have been able to persuade the Athenians that the Peace of Kallias meant the end of the war with the Persians, and so the end of the period in which they could not rebuild their temples under the Oath of Plataea. Pericles attempted to set up a congress of the Greek world to overturn the oath, but the Spartans refused to take part so it failed; this may itself be a later myth to make Pericles and his building programmes appear more pan-Hellenic.

Whether he consulted all the Greeks, or only his fellow Athenians, the decision to start rebuilding Athens' temples was certainly taken around this time. The great building programme that Pericles initiated was not restricted to the Acropolis. Plutarch lists its main buildings in chronological order: the Parthenon; the Telesterion, or home of the mysteries, at Eleusis; another wall linking the city and the port; the Odeion, or music hall, on the south slope of the Acropolis; the monumental gateway to the Acropolis; and the statue by Pheidias of Athena Parthenos.

The year in which work on the Parthenon began was 447 BC, although several years must have been devoted to organising its construction. By the time the Parthenon was completed Athens' fall from glory was beginning. She clashed with the Spartans, a dispute that would soon escalate into a full-blown war. By the time the other main buildings of the Periclean building programme were complete, Athens had lost the war against the Spartans; she no longer had an empire, no tribute from that empire, her navy was destroyed, and the Athenians themselves had surrendered their city to the Spartans.

The brief glory of fifth-century Athens can be compared to that of many of the heroes of mythology. The self-belief that made those heroes accomplish great things also led to their downfall. Achilles before the Trojan War had been offered a choice between a short but heroic life and a long but uneventful one. Achilles, like all other heroes, chose the former. Although the Athenians may not have been conscious that they had made the same decision, the history of the city shows that they did. The belief in themselves, and in their destiny, led them to found an empire, but that same self-belief led them to mistakenly believe they were infallible, and so brought about their downfall.

The same year that the Athenians began the Parthenon, they also fought their neighbours and allies both on land and at sea. Work on the Parthenon was briefly stopped because of this, although the peace treaty signed with the Spartans in 445 BC ensured that construction on it continued. The treaty bought Athens fourteen years of peace, enough time to build a monumental gateway to the Acropolis and to complete the Parthenon. During the same period Pericles' political career was at its peak, and each year he was elected one of the ten generals of the Athenian state.

Pericles is first recorded as a general in c.453 BC. He is recorded as having been elected a general every year from 443 to 429 (the year he died). Information is not preserved for the other years, but he could have been a general continuously from 453 to 429. He had, and would have been able to yield, a great deal of popularity and influence. As Thucydides (65.10) later wrote: 'Athens was a Democracy in name, but in fact power was in the hands of her Leading Man.'

The Acropolis Building Project

Before they could begin rebuilding their temples, the Athenians first had to clear the rubble from the Acropolis. The debris of temples, sculptures and pieces of other sacred offerings destroyed by the Persians were buried within its soil. It may well be that, as sacred offerings, they could not be thrown away, and so this solution was found. Archaic sculptures survived the Persians, to be seen on the Acropolis by Pausanias in the Roman period, but these were few and far between. Civic structures in the lower city had been rebuilt, and the institutions of the state were once again running smoothly. Before the Persian Wars the Agora had been to the east of the Acropolis, but Cimon moved it to a new location to the north-west of the mound. Some minor structures appear to have been erected on the Acropolis, but the rebuilding of the major temples did not begin until the Persian menace had been defeated.

Once rubble had been tidied away, the next priority was to rebuild the walls and refortify the Acropolis. The recent war had clearly demonstrated that it had potential as a citadel, and ironically Persian spoils funded much of the construction of these new walls. While most of the walls were plain, the north wall had a decorative band on its outer face, created using architectural elements from the temples that had been destroyed. By reusing these elements from temples, such as the old temple of Athena, the Athenians were commemorating their destruction, but also the subsequent victory and rebirth of Athens. The old gateway to the Acropolis, started before the war, was first repaired to ensure that the Acropolis could be made secure. This work appears to have been undertaken in the 460s, when Cimon was in power. The gateway was not a temple, and so its reconstruction was not forbidden under the Oath of Plataea. A temporary structure must have been built to house the ancient and venerable cult statue of Athena Polias, which had been saved from the Acropolis.

In the 'Papyrus Decree' now in Strasbourg, the anonymous author attests a suggestion, possibly dated to 450/49, made by Pericles. He wanted to spend the 5,000 talents accumulated in the Treasury of Athena on public projects in Athens. The building work on the Acropolis may have come out of this suggestion, and been funded by this money. The surplus of what had become by then their empire was thus used by the Athenians to beautify their city, through rebuilding of what was in effect the capital of that empire. History has shown us that this was money well spent, for it was for these monuments that Athens was admired in the Roman period, and is still admired by us to this day.

The building programme on the Acropolis probably cost around 2,000 talents, and half that amount again was spent on other sanctuaries in Athens and Attica. Inscriptions show that the building programme was funded from the Treasury of Athena, and from the one-sixtieth dedicated to the goddess by the Delian League. Since the money was dedicated to Athena, and was principally used to construct her sanctuary within the city, the Athenians were spending on the goddess money that belonged to her through dedications.

The whole project was overseen by a board. Pericles was only one, but the most influential, of the board that oversaw the creation of the Athena Parthenos. Pheidias, according to Plutarch, was *episkopos* – the overseer or supervisor of the Acropolis building programme. He was the creator (*dêmiourgos*) of the statue of Athena Parthenos, as well as in charge of (*epastatei*) all the workmen. Some dismiss this as Plutarch superimposing Roman ways of doing things, but others accept it, and common sense suggests that someone had to be responsible and so Pheidias became a sort of ancient Minister of Culture, in charge of the building programme. It is estimated that between 2,200 and 3,300 men were at any one point employed on the Periclean building projects, redistributing the wealth of her empire to Athens' citizens, foreign residents (*metics*) and slaves. The building accounts of the Erechtheion have preserved the names of most of those who worked on the construction. From these we can deduce that the workforce on this building, and presumably also on other Acropolis projects including the Parthenon, were half foreign-born workmen, one-fifth slaves and the rest Athenian citizens. If we wish to be more specific in assigning precise roles, then Callicrates seems to have been the contractor or builder, and Ictinus the architect of the Parthenon. Since the primary role of the Parthenon was to house the statue of Athena, Pheidias was in charge of the whole project. Mnesicles designed the monumental gateway to the Acropolis, and possibly also some of the other buildings. Callicrates was also responsible for the small temple of Athena Nike.

Pheidias had worked on the Acropolis a decade before, on a colossal bronze Athena, which later came to be called the Athena Promachos, and which had been funded specifically with the spoils from Marathon (Pausanias 1.28.2). Pheidias completed another Marathon memorial (Pausanias 1.20.1–2) that included statues of Miltiades, gods and Attic heroes.

Of the many monuments erected, perhaps the building whose propaganda value was the most obvious was the Odeion of Pericles. Built in the 440s on the south eastern slope of the Acropolis, the Odeion had a pyramidal roof supposedly based on the war tent of Xerxes that the Athenians had captured. Parts of Persian ships that had fallen into Athenian hands were used in the construction of the roof.

Any ruins from earlier periods were incorporated into the designs of the Periclean buildings, emphasising the great history and heritage of the city. This was most obvious in the design of the Erechtheion, although the monumental gateway was also slightly adapted to incorporate the old Cyclopean walls. Although earlier foundations were reincorporated within the foundations of the Parthenon, these would not have been visible.

* * *

The Periclean building that is most famous today, and that is the focus of this book, is of course the Parthenon. It was built between 447 and 438 BC, and the sculptures completed by around 434 BC. Demosthenes (*Against Androtion*, 76–7) saw the Parthenon as reflecting the glory of the Classical Athenians. He added cryptically that it had been built to honour the people of Athens. Presumably he interpreted it not as a temple, but as a symbol of the state of the Athenians.

A large quantity of the marble slabs on which the building accounts were inscribed were preserved when they were used many centuries later to repair the Parthenon. Because of this we know many of the details of the construction of the Parthenon. Although the accounts are not complete, they inform us of these exact years of construction, and give us some information about costs and various architectural details. Unfortunately, they are not particularly informative about the Parthenon's sculptural decoration.

The Parthenon was not a temple in the strict meaning of the term. The word 'temple' itself comes from the Latin *templum*, and we have artificially transferred a meaning with the use of a later word. The Greeks referred to many buildings, including temples, as *naos*, meaning 'the house'. Our earliest sources simply call the Parthenon '*naos*'. A lost book about the building called it the '*hekapompedon*' ('hundred-foot building'). The detailed financial accounts did not call it anything at all. This lack of a name is rather surprising. The building is first called the Parthenon by Demosthenes, and this name became popular during the fourth century BC. It literally refers to the fact that the structure housed the statue of Athena Parthenos, and shows that this statue was far more important to the Athenians than the building itself.

Lists of the treasures of Athena began to be inscribed on marble slabs in 434/3 BC and continued to be listed annually. These list treasures both in the *hekapompedon* and in the Parthenon: the former is here referred to as the large eastern room of the structure, in which the statue of Athena stood, and which measured approximately a hundred Attic feet. Now that we have identified the name for the eastern room, the Parthenon must by default be the smaller room at the back, on the western side. Treasures listed as 'in the opisthodomus' also seem to refer to the smaller back room, suggesting that it had two names. This opisthodomus could otherwise be simply the porch on the west end of the building.

The appellation of the 'hundred-foot house' continued to be popular for many generations, and it was even used in official inscriptions to refer to the Parthenon. By the Roman period the building's name had still not been clarified, and in the second century AD, the two authors who write about it call it different names. Plutarch decides it was the 'hundred-foot temple Parthenon', while Pausanias describes it as the 'temple they call the Parthenon'. The only sensible conclusion is that the building was called the Parthenon after the statue inside it, rather than the other way round. Although the Parthenon superficially looked like a temple, it was not used as one, and varied in many of its details – which may well have created some confusion about the naming of different parts of it.

Although the word *naos* was loosely used for the Parthenon, the building is never referred to as a temple of Athena Parthenos. There were never any priestesses of Athena Parthenos, nor did she have an altar. Dedications stored in the Parthenon seemed to have been made to Athena Polias rather than Athena Parthenos. The great statue by Pheidias was not used in the worship of the goddess, but rather as an ostentatious symbol of Athenian wealth, which later became a tourist attraction. The only evidence of worship or cult in the Parthenon comes much later, from the early Christian period, when the old cult statue of Athena Polias had turned to dust and so another one was needed.

The best way to describe the Parthenon is as a giant votive, a colossal version of the statues that individuals dedicated to Athena, and which dotted the surface of the Acropolis in Antiquity. It served as a symbol of Athens, and of the city's patron Athena, storing her treasures and depicting her legends in the sculpture that decorated it. The predecessor of the Parthenon, begun soon after 490 BC, had been designed as an offering to Athena, to thank the goddess for her help in securing the Athenian victory over the Persians at Marathon. The Periclean Parthenon was merely a modernisation of the previous building, built to a slightly larger scale, with an elaborate sculpture scheme to decorate it. The new building also commemorated Marathon, as well as all the subsequent victories of the Greeks over the Persians.

Plutarch gives us the names of the architects: Ictinus and Callicrates. Vitruvius, who wrote the only surviving book on ancient architecture, provides us with a bibliography in one of his chapters. This bibliography in turn allows us to work out who the architects of many famous ancient buildings were, since only the architect could write a book about the building he had created. Vitruvius lists the book about the Parthenon as having been written by Ictinus and Karpion, an otherwise unknown Greek. The name may well have been a corruption of Callicrates, which was distorted slightly at each retelling, like Chinese whispers – this happens quite often with ancient sources, where names are repeated and distorted over the centuries. Ictinus was clearly a leading Athenian architect, who was able to design such a beautiful building as the Parthenon, and was involved in many other Athenian projects. Strabo also lists Ictinus as the architect of the Parthenon.

Vitruvius also provides us with a guide to, and instructions for, creating the ideal temple. The Doric temple he describes has only recently been found to be based on the Parthenon. All Greek temples were built according to formulae, where the size of one element governed the size of all others. For years the unit of measurement of the Parthenon was a mystery, though Greek archaeologists tried, but failed, to discover it. Then one day Mark Wilson Jones, a British architect, solved the mystery: the unit of measurement for the Parthenon was based on the metope, as described by Vitruvius. Vitruvius wrote during the reign of Augustus, and many made the mistake of thinking he wrote about Roman architecture. In fact, he was a great lover of Greek culture, and so the temples he had described were Greek. The unit of measurement on the Parthenon was the Attic foot, which measured the equivalent of thirty-two centimetres, or one modern foot plus one inch. The frieze was thus three Attic feet high, while the metopes were four feet high.

The entire building was created of white marble from Mount Pentelicon, a quarry on the Attic Mountain; even the roof tiles were made out of thin slabs of marble. The rest of the building was elaborately decorated, with even its door carved out of expensive woods inlaid with gold and ivory. The architectural elements and the sculpture were both painted, although wind and rain have long washed away all traces of this. Athens' empire meant that, as well as cash tribute, she was able to get her hands on raw materials; these included gold mines in northern Greece, in territory she had seized. Large quantities of timber, which were necessary for any construction work, but which did not grow in Attica, could also be obtained from her 'allies'. Although built by the Athenians, the Parthenon was funded by many states, including such cities as Byzantium (Istanbul in modern Turkey).

The Parthenon was unique when it was built. It was one of the largest Greek structures, and the only octostyle peripteral temple-like structure built using the Doric order of Greece. This means that it was the only 'temple' with eight (*octo-*) columns rather than six across the front, and which also had a free-standing colonnade (*peripteros*) running all the way round it.

The large number of 'refinements' within the design is also often cited as part of its unique nature. These so-called refinements are where the architects tinkered with the building's design, creating minute variations within the architecture, in theory to make it more pleasing to the eye through the use of optical illusions. In theory, columns seen against the sky appear to be thinner in the centre, slightly concave, even if they are carved in a straight line. The refinement used to 'correct' this is called entasis, where the lower third of the column is slightly thickened to counteract this and create the optical illusion that the column is straight.

The steps and platform of the Parthenon all curve lightly upwards towards the centre rather than being entirely horizontally flat. The columns all lean in; in theory, if one drew a straight line through them, the lines not being parallel they would meet a few kilometres up. All these many features mean that no two blocks of the Parthenon are identical, and this caused problems when Nicholas Balanos tried to rebuild it in the 1930s. He did not pay enough attention to the individuality of these blocks, and so placed many of them in the wrong places. The Greek Archaeological Service have spent the last few decades undoing much of that so-called restoration, and putting blocks back in the correct place.

Nowadays these refinements are greatly praised, and seen as a sign of Athenian sophistication in the field of architecture. The sad truth is that they can be better described as gilding the lily and are largely superfluous. Most other Greek temples do not have these refinements, but even without them, they do not have all the 'flaws' that should in theory appear without them. Some refinements, such as the curvature of the platform and steps of the Parthenon, were common sense: they allowed the rainwater to roll off. Although one can interpret the refinements as corrections to what the naked eye sees, undertaken for aesthetic reasons, one can also interpret them as the Athenians demonstrating to the world the many tricks they could play, and the virtuosity of both their architects and masons. Creating these refinements was a huge undertaking, and in theory made the building look less 'heavy' and added interest to the design. In practice it was not necessary and an architectural ostentation.

One has the visual image today of the Parthenon crowning the Acropolis, and seen from almost everywhere in Athens, but the vision in antiquity would have been quite different, with walls, structures, buildings and dedications all around the Parthenon, obscuring large parts of it and preventing anyone from seeing the building in its entirety. Even today, one has to have passed through the gateway, and crossed the threshold of the Acropolis, before one can see the Parthenon itself.

The Periclean Parthenon was considerably wider than its planned predecessor had been. The main reason for this was almost certainly to accommodate the colossal statue that they planned to place inside it. The Parthenon is an important building in terms of Greek architecture now, because so few large buildings are preserved, but it was not an important building to all Greeks. In Antiquity the sources praise and mention the statue of Athena within it, not the structure that housed it. This statue was the most important element of the Parthenon, and the architects had to adapt their plans to accommodate it. On three sides, around and behind the statue, Ictinus designed a colonnade made up of two levels of Doric columns. This colonnade was largely decorative rather than structural, but it was also an innovation in the design of Doric temples.

The subjects depicted in the sculptures of the Parthenon celebrate Athena as patron of the city, and even more so the Athenians themselves. They underline the supremacy of Greek culture over barbarian disorder. Approaching the Parthenon from the gateway that formed the entrance to the Acropolis, one first came to the back of the temple, the western end. In the pediment above it, one could see the contest between Athena and Poseidon over control of the city. This location for the scene was appropriate since immediately to the left one would have been able to see the Erechtheion, which was not only the main temple on the Acropolis to Athena, but also housed the olive tree she had given the city in this contest and the cults of the early kings of Athens. The pediment on the eastern side of the building, over its entrance, depicted in sculpture the birth of Athena.

A series of square panels, known as metopes, ran around the exterior of the building just below the roof line. These metopes were carved in high relief, and depicted different battles on each side of the building. All of these battles represented the superiority of Greeks, especially Athenians, and their gods over their enemies and the barbarians.

Crowning the outer wall of the Parthenon, within the colonnade, ran a continuous frieze depicting a procession of Athenians and their gods. The use of a decorative continuous frieze was a feature associated with the temples of eastern Greeks living in Asia Minor, rather than the temples of mainland Greece. It was deliberately used on the Parthenon to recall the Athenians' links with Ionia, rather than the Peloponnese. The porches within the colonnade, at either end of the building and beneath the frieze, were created with Ionic rather than Doric columns to reinforce this link. The frieze was carved in low relief but demonstrates extraordinary virtuosity.

The metopes were carved by different hands, and show the progress of style in Athenian sculpture over the years. Originally, fewer metopes had been planned, to be placed within the colonnade. When the design of the Parthenon was altered, these were moved to the exterior of the building, and more had to be carved as a greater number of them was needed. The early panels are quite crude, with stiff figures, while the later ones are much more naturalistic.

Within the large internal room of the Parthenon (the cella) stood the colossal statue of Athena Parthenos designed by Pheidias. It depicted the goddess standing, her helmet almost scraping the roof of the temple. She held a smaller figure of Victory in her hand, representing the Athenian victories over all others. The giant statue was created on a wooden framework, which was covered in gold to represent the goddess's drapery. Ivory was used for her flesh, although only the face and arms were visible. The gold which was generally valued at forty talents (1,200 kg.) was part of the Athenian state's gold reserves. The statue was decorated with smaller sculpted themes which reflected many of those used in the architectural sculpture of the building; the birth of Pandora was depicted on the base, the battle against the Amazons inside her shield and the battle between the gods and giants on the outside of it; the battle against the Centaurs was even carved as decoration on her sandals.

Thucydides (1.10) pointed out that when future generations saw the Athenian Acropolis, they would immediately assume that Athens had been far more powerful than she was. When he puts in Pericles' mouth the famous funerary speech the statesman was meant to have given to commemorate those who had died in the Peloponnesian War (2.35–46), neither the Acropolis nor the Parthenon is considered important enough to be mentioned as being among the glories of Athens. No poems or great literature talk about the Acropolis, either praising its monuments or describing its ceremonies. Most surprising, given the current fame the Parthenon enjoys, is that there are only a handful of references to it in ancient literature.

An exceptionally brief description of the subjects of the pediments in a Roman travel guide written by Pausanias allows us to know what was represented there. This is the only ancient reference to the Parthenon sculpture to have survived. Nowhere are the themes of the other sculptures on the Parthenon identified. Although countless passages were devoted to praising, for example, the naked Aphrodite of Praxiteles, the Greeks in their literature seem almost to have ignored their temples, treating them as part of the landscape. The wonders of the ancient world, such as the statue of Zeus at Olympia, or the pyramids in Egypt, were all the subjects of lengthy descriptions. The Parthenon was not. This may be because the statue of Zeus was part of his cult and in an international sanctuary, while the Athena Parthenos, although also by Pheidias, instead personified the riches of Athens.

The opisthodomus of the Parthenon is mentioned in Aristophanes' play *The Wasps*. The term opisthodomus literally means 'the room at the back', and this is where Athena's treasures were stored. Although some try to locate the opisthodomus elsewhere, he was almost certainly referring to the room in the western part of the Parthenon. A few other Greek plays refer to monuments which were part of the Periclean building programme, but most classical literature is more noteworthy for the way it ignored them.

Just as today's tourists are kept away from the Parthenon, only being able to approach as far as the lower step, in the classical period the building also appears to have been inaccessible to Athenian citizens. Dedications to the goddess and her treasures were kept not only inside the west chamber but also in the colonnade. In Antiquity one could not walk in and out of the colonnade freely; grilles or fences were erected between the external columns of the building to prevent access to it. Entry to the main east chamber, where people could view the great statue of Athena, was possible, but again unlikely to have been open to all. The three-sided colonnade within the room that encircled the statue also allowed access to it from every side, so that privileged visitors could walk around the statue. The walls held shelves with yet more treasures to impress these visitors.

In myths of the Wonders of the World, the ancients named the temple of Artemis at Ephesus as the wonder, partly due to its size, rather than the Parthenon. It seems instead to have been the treasury-bank of one city state, rather than a temple of Athena of importance to all Greeks.

The Greek name for the monumental entrance to the Acropolis was the Propylaea. This is the plural of the Greek word for gateway, as there were five doorways of differing sizes allowing access to it. The slightly larger central passage had a rough floor rather than marble slabs and steps, and this is where animals being led to sacrifice would have passed. Humans would have used the steps and doors on either

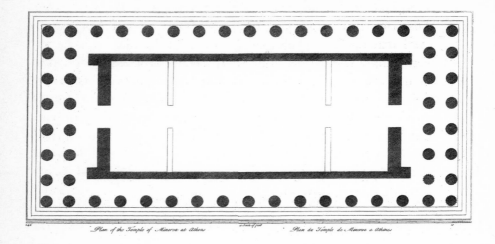

Dalton's 1759 ground plan of the Parthenon:
his reconstruction of the interior is no longer correct.

side, and once they passed through these gates, they were officially within the Acropolis. They could look up, and slightly to the right, and catch their first glimpse of the Parthenon; the columns were cleverly arranged so that one could not see the building until one had passed through them.

The Propylaea marked the official line which delineated the sanctuary of Athena on the Acropolis, sitting astride the boundary. The gate acted as an architectural link between the city below and the buildings on the Acropolis, creating the only passage to them. The sacred road that the Athenians followed during their processions ended at the Propylaea. The path they would have taken up to it is not the path we use today; the monumental steps were added much later by the Roman emperor Claudius. The building, designed by Mnesicles, had many of the same features as the Parthenon, and there are 'refinements' throughout the architecture. Like the Parthenon, it was a Doric building, but with Ionic columns and features within.

Because of the Peloponnesian War, and perhaps also lack of funds, the building was never finished. The projecting lifting bosses, used to lift the blocks into place, were never removed. Usually these were later smoothed off, but at the back of the Propylaea, on the Acropolis side, these are still clearly visible. This structure was probably begun after the Parthenon had been completed, using the same workmen, who were simply transferred from one project to the other.

Although the main part of the building was symmetrical, the two wings are of quite different sizes due to the slope of the land. This was partly deliberate, because of constraints made by the terrain, but may also have been influenced by funds slowly running out. To the left, as one approaches the Acropolis, is a large room. The door to the room is not placed centrally within the wall, but rather slightly to the right; this was because the room was a dining room. The Greeks dined reclining on couches, and so the door had to be slightly off-centre, to accommodate the arrangement of these couches against the walls. In Classical architecture doors that are positioned to one side always indicate that the room behind them was a dining room, just as buildings with outer walls created of two shells with a hollow space between them always indicate a library, the space acting as a safeguard against damp that would damage the scrolls.

Gateways had been monumental for as long as Greeks had been building, designed to create the illusion of strength and impregnability, and also to emphasise the city's wealth and to impress the visitor. Perhaps the most famous Greek gateway is the Lion Gate at Mycenae. Though the Mycenaean gateway to the Acropolis is unlikely to have been quite as grand, the gateway in the fifth century clearly continued the form that had started at that period, and which continued to be used in Greek history. The wing to the right of the entrance was shorter and shallower, partly to accommodate the ancient Cyclopean walls, respect for the past being shown by the fact that the Athenians chose to incorporate the early wall within the design. The fifth-century Athenian did not always show such respect to the past, nor did they preserve all ancient monuments, but here the walls still served their function to fortify the Acropolis, and so they were still useful.

The last preserved year for which we have accounts for the Propylaea is 443/2 BC. Work seems to have stopped soon after, although it is curious that when the city once again had funds to continue its building programme, it did not complete the gateway.

The Propylaea is mentioned many times in ancient literature, far more often than the Parthenon, partly because it was highly unusual to spend great sums on functional, utilitarian buildings such as gate-houses. It was the building, however, that was always cited as being the most beautiful, the most magnificent achievement of the Athenian building programme.

The Erechtheion

The Erechtheion was the last building designed and built as part of the Periclean building programme, but it was not completed until after Pericles had died. This was of course the principal temple to Athena in Athens. It housed her cult as well as that of other gods. It stood to the north of the Parthenon, and was far more important in terms of religion to the Athenians. The main cult within the building was that of Athena Polias, and the ancient cult statue of the goddess was housed within it. The important annual Athenian festival to Athena, where the statue of the goddess was presented with a new robe, is represented within the sculpture on the Parthenon. The real procession ended at the Erechtheion, as the centre of the Athena cult on the Acropolis. This was the most sacred spot on the mound.

The main body of the Erechtheion was shaped like a rectangular Greek temple, but with many porches jutting off it, and structures within. These additions, and the fact that it was built on a steep piece of land, and so had several levels, make it a difficult building to understand. Part of this confusion is that the architect was trying to unify a whole series of earlier structures, which had housed many different cults, into one architectural whole. The building is better known to visitors today for the Caryatid Porch attached to its southern side, where columns are replaced by figures of women, likely to have been intended as representations of priestesses of Athena.

The olive tree Athena had given the city grew within this complex, and it was this gift which had won her the city. Her contest with Poseidon for Athens was depicted in the west pediment of the

Parthenon, immediately to the south of the tree itself. Olives were of great importance to the Athenians and formed a substantial part of their economy. Olive oil was used for cooking and cleaning. It was used as fuel to provide light, and jars of it were awarded to winners in athletic contests. The episode of the contest between Poseidon and Athena for possession of the city was an important myth in Athens. Long before the Parthenon, the competition and the olive tree had been depicted in the pediment sculpture of one of the Archaic temples of the Acropolis that the Persians had destroyed.

Athena's Olive Tree, engraved onto an
Archaic pediment from the Acropolis

Visitors could also have seen cracks within the bedrock that had been made by Zeus when he threw the thunderbolt down to the earth, as well as the marks made where Poseidon had thrown his trident to make a saltwater spring. The tomb of Cecrops was located under the Caryatid Porch.

The solidity of the Caryatids' bodies and the way their drapery is represented, with the folds deeply carved, makes the figures quite similar in style to the women that were placed within the pediments of the Parthenon. The Erechtheion women are also heroic-sized, fully carved versions of the maidens from the Panathenaic procession on the Parthenon frieze. They could well have been high-born women who took part in the cult of Athena, figures from the annual procession that were for ever immortalised in stone. Since many priestesses of Athena were maidens appointed for fixed periods of time, these two identifications need not be contradictory.

Before the Periclean building programme, the temple of Athena had been located in a different spot on the Acropolis. Its location could be moved, meaning that it did not have to stay on exactly the same site.

The architect of the Erechtheion is unknown, but the innovative design and slender columns, as well as the elaborate ornamentation, all suggest that he was supremely talented. The similarities between the building and the Propylaea suggest that they might have shared the same architect.

An inscription dating to 408/7 BC records the creation of the Erechtheion frieze. Unlike the metopes or the frieze of the Parthenon, which were carved on to blocks in relief, the figures of the Erechtheion frieze were carved separately and later attached to the frieze blocks on the building by bronze pins. Most of the sculptors were foreign-born residents of Athens (*metics*), and we know from the inscription that they were paid for the sculpture by the piece: sixty drachmas per figure they carved. This is interesting because it differs from the way the sculptors were paid for their work on the Parthenon sculptures, where they were paid by the day. Perhaps the Athenians had not been satisfied with that method, as it had not ensured a satisfactory ratio of salary to work produced, and so they had changed the way in which workers were paid for this subsequent project.

One of the few undecorated areas on the Acropolis was the large, blank south wall of the Erechtheion. Since we know that almost every part of the Classical Acropolis was filled with monuments, dedications and sculptures, the huge empty space of this wall immediately opposite the Parthenon created a rather surprising vacuum, and an anomaly. Many explanations have been sought for it. The rest of the building was highly decorated, with architectural ornaments covered in gold leaf, and coloured glass inserted into many of the decorative bands to catch the light and create a jewel-like appearance for the whole.

The Parthenon and the Erechtheion were highly interconnected in their designs, both by their iconography, and by the cult of Athena which was housed in the latter but glorified by the creation of the former. The solid Doric mass of the Parthenon exterior and the ornate decoration of the Erechtheion contrasted to emphasise each other's qualities in architectural terms.

Hurwit emphasises the vacuum that this wall would have created, if it had been left plain. He comes up with the rather ingenious suggestion (p. 351, n. 136) that this problem could be solved if the walls were hung with the large *peplos* cloth embroidered with the battle between the gods and the giants, created for the quadrennial Great Panathenaia. He points out that *peplos* was used as a sail for the boat that was part of this procession; it must have been of colossal size, and so too big for the statue of Athena Polias. Therefore he suggests that it was hung on that wall, and displayed opposite the Parthenon. I find this argument highly appealing; presumably the *peplos* was brought in when it rained, and although there are no hooks to show where it could have been hung, that wall was largely rebuilt in the twentieth century.

Many of the heroes and legendary kings represented within the sculpture of the Parthenon had cults that were housed in the Erechtheion. The tomb of Cecrops was believed by fifth-century Athenians to have been the Mycenaean grave by the Erechtheion. Erechtheus, the king after whom the building is now called, also had a cult that was housed in it. Several of the gods on the Parthenon sculpture also had cults in the Erechtheion, as well as Poseidon and Athena.

Hades-Pluto had a cult in the building, and scholars have suggested that he might have been represented in one of the central metopes from the south side of the Parthenon, now destroyed, as well as among the east frieze gods. Others have tentatively indentified figures of him both in west metopes and the west pediment, where he was almost certainly represented. Hades, god of the Underworld, is almost a forgotten god these days, but he figured large in Greek myths and homage had to be paid to this one god that all Greeks knew they would one day meet.

The small temple to Athena Nike, or Athena of Victory, was built later in the fifth century, after the Parthenon. Several battles were depicted in the sculpture of its friezes. Some of them had taken place in what is now called the archaic period, and one, the Battle of Marathon, had taken place during the first Persian War. They can be described as historical battles, which we know took place and for which we have records. However, by the time the temple was built, they were long in the Athenian past, nobody who had taken part likely to have still been alive, blending in the thought of Athenians of the day as having taken place at a time when history and myth collided. In the 420s, when the Nike temple was built, those who had died at Marathon, defending Athenian society and democracy, were regarded just as much as heroes by the Athenians, as earlier Athenians who had died in the period of legend.

On the east frieze of the Nike temple, as on the Parthenon, one can see carved an assembly of the gods. Some are standing, others seated, and a few Athenian heroes might be depicted among their number. The central figure represents Athena, clad in full armour to emphasise her martial role, since the temple as a whole commem-orates Athenian military victories. Not all the frieze is preserved, and there was almost certainly a now lost figure of Nike, Victory herself, depicted wingless so that she could not fly away and abandon the Athenians. An interesting detail is the use, as in the other Nike friezes, of landscape elements; these developed later in Greek art, and are almost entirely excluded from the sculptures on the Parthenon. Aphrodite and her daughter Peitho, Persuasion, are carved at the southern end of the frieze, which was particularly appropriate since there was a shrine of Aphrodite immediately below the Nike temple.

Poseidon, in this frieze, is seated on a rock, which may well repre-sent the location of his shrine at Cape Sounion, a rocky windswept site where a new temple to him was constructed soon after the Parthenon. This god was to the right of Athena. On her other side one can restore the figure of Victory, and to the left of her, the figure of Zeus is depicted enthroned as the king of the gods. On the Parthenon frieze the gods were shown seated and in profile, while here they are seen from the front. This is partly because they face the location of their shrines, both on and around the Acropolis, pointing to a relationship between the themes depicted and the location of their cults. This relationship can help us identify many of the uncertain figures on the Parthenon, who may also have been depicted in relation to their sanctuaries, such as the reclining figure of Dionysus in the left side of the east pediment.

The Propylaea was impressive in its size and design, but not decorated with any architectural sculpture. The first thing the visitor would see, before he even went through this gate, was the parapet of the Nike temple. This parapet was carved with images of Victory, in her many forms. Sometimes she was depicted with Athena, at other times restraining a wild bull that was to be sacrificed to the goddess; in some scenes she is doing more mundane things, such as fastening her sandals. Together, these images of Nike, all creating a statement of victory, and particularly Athenian military victory, were the first images the visitor to the Acropolis faced.

This was not narrative on the parapet, but rather pure propaganda. The frieze is the ultimate illustration of how one first asked Athena for victory by making sacrifices to her, and then how this victory was commemorated, by the creation of trophies made of captured armour, also seen carved on to the parapet. To emphasise the images in the sculpture, arms and armour, both Greek and booty taken off the Persians, were attached to the parapet, and hung off it. On the south side of the parapet, immediately below the frieze depicting the Battle of Marathon, the trophies represented were ones that could clearly have been identified by Greeks as having been made out of piles of Persian armour.

The whole Acropolis, as shown repeatedly through its iconography, was a votive trophy to Athens' victories over the Persians, won with the assistance of Athena. Assistance from other Greek states is sidelined. Those approaching the Acropolis in antiquity, and seeing the Nike temple, a temple purely dedicated to victory, could not help but be aware that this was also the theme of the entire Acropolis, and all that it celebrated.

Several other temples were part of the Periclean building programme. The new temple at Cape Sounion to Poseidon, the god who had made Athens' navy victorious, has already been mentioned. A temple to Ares, the god of war, was also constructed in Attica. One can see that Athena, Poseidon and Ares were all associated with the recent war. The art of Hephaestus, the god of blacksmiths, was necessary to create the weapons the Athenians needed to fight these wars, and he was built a temple over the Athenian agora. Hephaestus was the catalyst for the birth of Athena, cutting open Zeus's head; without him the city's patron goddess could not have been born. Athena shared the temple with him; Pausanias tells us that they shared a statue group as the 'parents' of Erechthonios, and so the ancestors of the Athenians.

Athena Parthenos

According to Pliny, the Roman art historian, Greek sculpture reached its peak in the High Classical period of the mid-fifth century, and at the summit of the great sculptors practising then was Pheidias of Athens. Pliny gave the Athenian's flourishing as having been during the eighty-third Olympiad (448–444 BC), when the Parthenon was being constructed, and when Pheidias began the colossal statue of Athena Parthenos for its interior.

He had already made several other statues for the Acropolis, including the bronze Athena Promachos immediately opposite the Propylaea, and would later go on to create the giant statue of Zeus at Olympia which would become one of the Wonders of the Ancient World. All three statues were lost far back in our history, and the only original works we can now link to Pheidias are the sculptures he designed for the decoration of the Parthenon. Of the others, only small-scale copies and lengthy descriptions are preserved, but they give us enough information to allow us to reconstruct them on paper and in our imaginations.

The Athena Parthenos was a statue type called chryselephantine, a word whose first part means gold, and the second part indicates ivory coming from elephants. A wooden framework supported the structure of the figure, which was depicted standing within the interior of the Parthenon. Ivory was used for the goddess's visible flesh – her face, hands and feet – and describing skin as being 'like ivory' is still a compliment used to this day. Her eyes were also of ivory, with the irises and pupils of semi-precious stones. Gold was the material of choice for her drapery and armour, a soft metal which reflected the little light in the chamber, and which made up the city's treasury and gold reserves. Today we revere 'art'; although melting down the gold would have been an action of last resort for the Athenians, they had fewer qualms about doing so because of any artistic or 'sacred' nature of the statue of the goddess.

There is a story from the fourth century BC, possibly apocryphal, which illustrates the importance of not violating sacred spaces. Mausolus, whose Mausoleum of Halicarnassus became another Wonder of the Ancient World, was succeeded by his sister and widow Artemisia as satrap ruler of Caria. Like her namesake and predecessor, who had been at Xerxes' side at Salamis, this Artemisia proved to be a formidable warrior. She cunningly trapped the navy of the neighbouring state of Rhodes in the harbour of Halicarnassus, and annihilated it. To commemorate this victory, a statue of the queen with her foot on a fallen Rhodian was erected in the harbour. Years later, after Artemisia had passed away, the Rhodians captured the city. The statue still stood, towering over the harbour. Although an embarrassment to them, because it had been dedicated with a sacral nature, the Rhodians could not tear it down or destroy it. Instead, they chose to board the statue up, hiding but preserving it.

After the Persians had sacked the Acropolis, and destroyed many statues dedicated on it, the Athenians had buried those statues rather than using them as rubble for foundations of buildings. They did so because of the sacred nature of these dedications. There are countless other examples of the pains that were taken to care for sacred objects. The statue of Athena in the temple of Athena Polias (the Erechtheion) was washed, clothed and venerated. The statue of Athena in the Parthenon, however, was designed to be taken apart and melted down in times of need, and was never the subject of any sacrifices or cult.

The colossal statue was first made in pieces in a workshop, believed to have been on the southern part of the Acropolis. It was then put together inside the building; it certainly would not have fitted through the door in one piece. We know that it had been assembled and was inside the Parthenon in 438 BC because it was dedicated at the Great Panathenaia of that year.

Pheidias' Zeus became famous as it was the object of cult in a sanctuary at Olympia, which was shared and used by all those from around the entire Greek world. The Parthenos was a figure with a purely local significance, a symbol of Athens' power and wealth. Although over two hundred small-scale versions of the Parthenos survive, very few copies of the Zeus do; it seems that his statue could not be copied for religious reasons, while no such restriction applied to the Athena. Many of the copies of the goddess come from Athenian document reliefs, the official carved records of state business, such as treaties with other states, and which were displayed on the Acropolis. On them, the Athena Parthenos symbolised the Athenian state, with statue and state officially and for ever linked as one.

The same can be said of the official use of the statue on Hellenistic coins of Athens. The statue was an emblem of Athens' power in the age of Pericles and was used to emphasise the city's past, even if the reality of the Hellenistic city was less glorious. Although coins of Ephesus represented the temple of Artemis, and coins of Ilion (Troy) their temple of Athena, the coins of Athens never represented the Parthenon, leading further credence to the theory that it was not a temple. As an important and impressive statue of the goddess by a leading sculptor, the Parthenos became a model for later cult statues of Athena in temples in Asia Minor, but the original was never the object of such cultic activities.

Pheidias' most famous work was thus not the sculptures that decorated the exterior of the Parthenon, but rather the colossal statue of Athena Parthenos which stood inside the Parthenon. This was the statue for which he was celebrated in antiquity, which writers praised and which most visitors to the Acropolis came to see. We know that the gold of her drapery weighed approximately a ton, because of the various scandals and accusations of theft that were levelled against the sculptor. We know that moulds of the drapery were kept because occasionally in Antiquity, at times of great crisis, the gold was melted down and minted into coins. Since the gold drapery was always replaced, we can guess that Pheidias' moulds might have been preserved.

The Athena wore an aegis, a goatskin cloak, off which dangled snakes, and in the centre of which was the head of Medusa, the latter also in ivory. The goddess held a two-metre-high Nike in her outstretched right hand, and her shield, held in her lowered left hand, rested on the ground. Athena's spear rested against her left breast, by her shield, and she wore an elaborate helmet. In later copies, a column supported the raised hand that held the Nike, and a snake, representing Erechthonios, coiled behind the shield, but the column may be a later structural addition, the snake moved from beneath the Nike to make way for it, the column added beneath the outstretched hand to support it.

The rather trivial matter of whether the column had been there from the start, or added later, has over the years provoked many academic disputes. In the 1990s John Camp, the great archaeologist who works in the Athenian agora, found one of the earliest depictions of the Athena Parthenos. This terracotta image from the fourth century BC shows the Athena Parthenos, her right arm outstretched with the Nike in it, but no column supporting this arm; instead, a giant snake is depicted on the ground beneath it. When the column was added, this snake was moved to the other side of Athena, within her shield.

Ancient Greek shields were painted with images, as was this Athena's shield. On the inside of the shield, standing almost five metres high, a battle between the gods and the giants was painted, the same battle which was represented in the metopes above the east entrance to the chamber in which the sculpture was located. On the exterior of the goddess's shield, the Amazons were shown attacking a fortress on a hill, which can be identified as the Athenian Acropolis. The Amazon battle chosen was one specific to the Athenians, and part of their history. It depicted the Amazons laying siege to, and attacking, the Athenian Acropolis itself.

The myth was an allegory of the more recent sack of the Acropolis by the Persians. The Greeks fighting, and ultimately defeating, them are thus, of course, the Athenians themselves. This serves to locate the battle against the Amazons, also shown in the exterior metopes, as the particular battle that took place at Athens, and ties it to the Parthenon geographically. Panels with larger-scale reproductions of the figures from the shield were created during the Roman period, and some of these are now in the Piraeus Museum.

This mythical episode had many parallels with the more recent historical Persian sacking of the Acropolis, an association empha-sised by the fact that one of the Persian leaders was a woman, Artemisia of Caria. In the Hellenistic period a story made the rounds that Pheidias had included portraits of himself and Pericles among the Greeks; apparently this had been scandalous at the time, according to the story, although it is almost certainly untrue and a later invention.

The battle between the Lapiths and the Centaurs was shown on the goddess's sandals, carved in miniature on their straps. So the three main battles carved in the exterior metopes, apart from the Trojan War, were all included in the decoration of the statue of Athena Parthenos within the Parthenon. There was a great deal of such repetition of motifs in the sculptural programme of the Parthenon, and the Acropolis.

The base of the statue depicted the creation of Pandora, the scene set like the birth of Athena in the company of gods. This was a mortal counterpart to the birth of the goddess shown in large scale in the pediments. The birth of Athena was represented in the east pediment and celebrated, but the birth of this mortal woman had quite different implications. If one accepts the idea that the Athenians deprived their women of rights in order to appease Poseidon, after his contest with Athena, then the myth of Pandora could be interpreted as having been used to back up those actions. She was the woman who could not control her curiosity, and opened the box she had been given, so creating all the evil that is present in the world. The suffering she caused by this action was only partly mitigated by the last quality that emerged from the box, the notion of Hope.

In front of the statue Pheidias placed a rectangular pool of water. Although often explained as being necessary to increase the humidity of the chamber, and so prevent the ivory of the statue from cracking, the pool is more likely to have been there to reflect light and the image of the statue, thus emphasising it.

We know that the ancient Greeks and the Romans admired the statue a great deal, although it is sometimes difficult for us to understand this since most reconstructions make her look wooden and particularly unattractive as a work of art. The statue represented the goddess in her guise as a warrior, but would also have represented her booty, literally expressed through the use of the city's gold to create her drapery.

In addition, we have a description of the statue in the guidebook that Pausanias wrote in the mid-second century AD about Greece. The statue Pausanias saw was not the same one that Pheidias had created, because we know that the drapery was first melted down in the Hellenistic period, then damaged several more times in antiquity. Each time, however, the statue was repaired, as it was again by Hadrian in the second century AD. Pausanias first mentions that Pheidias had created the sculpture, although we know this from many other later sources.

The gold from which the statue was made formed part of the state treasury. It also caused problems for both Pericles and Pheidias, who were accused of trying to steal some of it and put on trial. The gold on the statue weighed between forty (Diodorus 12.40.3) and fifty talents (Thucydides 2.13.5). Philochorus, an Athenian historian of c.300 BC, who narrates the events surrounding the creation of the statue and the accusations made against Pheidias of embezzlement, gives a weight of forty-four talents. According to Philochorus, in a *scolia* of Aristophanes' *Peace*, Pheidias was tried for fraud and went into exile, presumably as he had been found guilty. He went on to Elis, to work on the cult statue of Zeus for his temple at Olympia. Plutarch picked up this story, but incorrectly has Pheidias dying in an Athenian prison. In other sources Pheidias seems to be subsequently executed by the Eleans, on a similar charge of embezzlement, suggesting that a pattern of theft emerges against the sculptor.

Diodorus also mentions the trial, in the context of accusations made against Pericles and his building programme (12.41.1). The League's treasury, when transferred from Delos to Athens in 454 BC, had consisted of 8,000 talents. A workman made an accusation against Pheidias of stealing, with Pericles' help and knowledge. In the winter of 430/29, when the war was going badly, Pericles appears to have been impeached, and was temporarily removed from office. One of the charges was of *klôpe* (embezzlement), presumably a revival of the earlier charges against him and Pheidias, who was by then working at Olympia. The charges again seem to have been linked to the gold used for the drapery of the Athena Parthenos and funds for the Acropolis building programme. Although Diodorus does not tell us the outcome of the trial we can guess from his subsequent reinstatement that he was not found guilty.

Thucydides, son of Melesias, an opponent of Pericles' and leader of what can be termed the traditionalist or Cimonian party, attacked Pericles over the vast sums being spent on the building programmes (Plutarch, *Pericles*, 14.2), notably the Propylaea, although he did not mention the Parthenon, and for his misuse of allied money (Plutarch, *Pericles*, 12.1). So many accusations made against Pericles would seem to suggest that many in Athens thought he may well have misused public funds.

Plutarch makes it clear that by attacking Pheidias – he names the accuser as one of his team of sculptors, a man called Menon – those Athenians were trying to get at Pericles. Plutarch also tells us that Pheidias had been able to remove the gold from the statue of Athena Parthenos, weigh it and thus prove that it was all there. Thucydides (2.13.5) also cites Pericles as saying that the forty talents of gold from the statue were removable. Both were acquitted.

Pheidias did not die in prison as Plutarch stated but went to Olympia, where he is archaeologically attested in the 430s and 420s (his workshop has been excavated). Apart from the cult statue of Zeus, he also created for the Eleans an Aphrodite Ourania (Heavenly) and an Athena Ergana (worker). He may have been indicted by the Eleans for embezzlement, as Philochorus states, but he certainly was in demand there for quite some time. Seneca (*Controversiae*, 8.2) seems to confirm that Pheidias was punished, by having his hands cut off for stealing some gold. One must assume that Philochorus conflates the Athenian stories with Pheidias' time at Olympia, as even into the second century AD his descendants had the honour of, and monopoly on, cleaning the statue (Pausanias, 5.14.4).

The Parthenon Sculptures

The West Pediment – The Contest between Athena and Poseidon

The visitor, climbing on to the Acropolis and seeing its monuments, would have first seen the rear and the west pediment of the Parthenon, before walking round to see the one over the entrance. Although visitors today see the west side of the Parthenon almost as soon as they pass through the monumental gateway leading on to the Acropolis, in antiquity many smaller monuments, various buildings and even trees would have blocked the view. Any Greek in classical times wishing fully to admire this end of the building would have had to come much closer, winding his way through the many structures to reach it.

The west pediment depicts the contest between Athena and Poseidon for possession of Athens and the right to be its chief deity. The contest between the two gods was celebrated annually by a feast in Athens. It was a local Athenian myth rather than one shared by all Greeks. The two gods continued to be worshipped in unison, or rather shared a cult, with the same clan providing priests and priestesses for them. Since Athena's victory disenfranchised the Athenian women, it is particularly appropriate that the battle represented in the metopes, immediately below the west pediment, was the battle between the Greeks and the Amazon women, showing the terrible things that could occur if women had power and took part in battles.

Athena's success in the contest she fought with Poseidon had won her the city of Athens. The contest had taken place when Cecrops was king of Athens, so he is represented in the pediment, having acted as a witness to it. The scene is the earliest known representation of this myth. Summary later drawings of it have survived, but it is hard to work out the details. Since the attributes the statues once held are lost, we cannot be certain which exact moment in the story is depicted: almost certainly it was the moment the two gods ended their race to the city on the Acropolis, or the moment when they presented the Athenians with their respective gifts of salt water and an olive tree.

Both gods wanted to own the city of Athens. Someone, perhaps the Athenian king, suggested that the two should offer gifts to the city, the one providing the most useful gift winning Athens. The contest took place on the Acropolis, where the Parthenon was situated, creating a geographical link between the myth and its depiction. Poseidon, god of the sea, hit the rock with his trident. A spring of water came gushing forth, but the water was salty, like the sea he ruled over. Athena, using her wisdom, presented the Athenians with an olive tree. The Athenians, rather crafty people themselves, realised that the olive tree was ideal to grow on their land, much of Attica being extremely rocky, and Athena's olive tree continued to grow for centuries on the Acropolis. It was destroyed during the Persian sack, but miraculously grew back a few years later.

In some versions of the myth, Poseidon was furious at losing the city, and flooded Attica. This myth was not considered suitable in Periclean Athens: much of the city's power was based on the strength of its navy, and so Poseidon as god of the sea had to be on the Athenians' side. The version of the myth represented on the Parthenon showed the two gods on friendly terms, engaged in a contest but not at war with each other. The olive tree represented agriculture, and the salt stream naval power. The Athenians of the prehistoric period had chosen the olive, which shows that their priorities at the time had been agricultural ones, rather than any desire to rule the seas.

The myth as represented in the west pediment seems to have depicted Athena arriving in Athens just before Poseidon. In the background, one presumably would have been able to see the olive tree she had granted the city. To the right of her was Poseidon, his trident in his raised arm, about to strike the rock and produce the salty water. The composition of the centre of the pediment is not preserved, although we can make out some of it from seventeenth-century drawings. Poseidon seems to stand just in front of Athena, and if a recent reconstruction of the figure by Peter Schultz is correct, he wore a burnished brass cuirass, which would have made him even more prominent.

Since Athena had won the contest, why was so much emphasis placed on the figure of Poseidon? Athena and Poseidon had been paired together in Greek mythology for almost as long as Greece had had mythology. Sometimes they fought each other, although at other times, as at Troy or against the giants, they fought side by side. When Plato wrote about Atlantis, he put the city under the protection of Poseidon; the Athenians, Athena's city, were those who fought against Atlantis. Poseidon had never been ignored by Athens, but after the Athenian victory at Salamis in 480 BC his powers, and his protection, became of prime importance to the city. In the fifth century the cults of both gods were housed in the same temple complex on the Acropolis, the Erechtheion. By presenting Poseidon and Athena as equally important, the Athenians arguably were trying to appease the god of the sea, and to ensure that he remained on their side.

All that remains of the figure of Poseidon is his colossal torso. It split vertically when it fell off the building, and is now divided between London (the back) and Athens (the rippling muscles of the front). A few fragments of his legs may have been found in the last few years. From Carrey's drawings we can see that the composition was once highly dramatic, filled with moving figures in convoluted poses. However, this drawing alone does not make the composition sufficiently clear enough for us to have been able to decipher the iconography, or the myth depicted. Fortunately, Pausanias preserved its title for us, and so we know that the competition between Athena and her uncle Poseidon for possession of the city of Athens was illustrated in the west pediment.

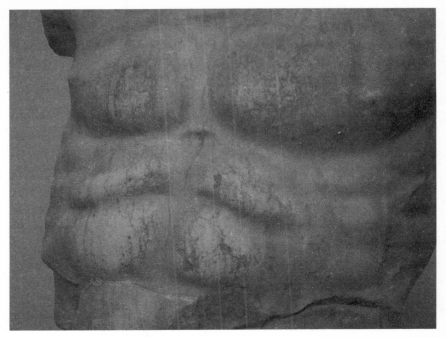

Detail of Poseidon's torso in Athens (original and cast)

From his recent work on the west pediment, Peter Schultz, probably the most brilliant and gifted scholar of my generation, notes that the musculature of the Poseidon is particularly developed; it is overpronounced, and unnatural. Although that can suggest that the figure was damaged and recarved at some point, a theory which fits the almost certainly restored Athena next to him, one wonders why the sculptors did not do a better job of his torso. Schultz's theory is to suggest that the torso was instead covered with a bronze breastplate. Breastplates were moulded to their wearers, and so the god's breastplate would almost certainly have been made in a similar fashion, placing softened wax against his torso and using the overcarved musculature as a template for it.

The figure of Athena is equally unusual, although her oddities cannot be explained by the addition of a breastplate. The goddess's torso has a number of features usually associated with later sculpture, and most of which are traditionally not seen on Greek sculptures until the fourth century BC, such as the use of a running drill to emphasise the grooves of the drapery. Her head was not carved out of the same block of marble as her body, but rather made of a separate piece, and inserted later. Probably the most unusual detail is the appearance of press-folds on the drapery across her breast. Such folds are also seen on the east pediment figure of Hera, but nowhere else on the Parthenon sculptures, and are generally believed to have first been depicted in sculpture c.375 BC, long after the Parthenon had been completed. The lines are not scratches, for if they were scratches these would run in one continuous line. Instead they are broken, following the line of her breast where a press-fold would have run through her dress. Because of this, we know that the Athena was almost certainly retouched at a later date, the sculptor subconsciously adding these details from his own period.

Otherwise the goddess is depicted in a conventional manner. She stands to the left of the centre, but turning towards it and her opponent Poseidon. She wears a long dress, and over it her habitual goatskin cloak. The cloak is decorated with a gorgon head, and snakes at the edges were added in bronze but are now missing. Her right arm seems to have been behind her body, and held a spear. On her head would have been a helmet, but like so much of the figure, it is now missing. She is an active figure, her pose designed to both complement and contrast with that of Poseidon, to create a V-shaped composition.

The figures were clearly visible from the ground below. Paint would have emphasised their various features, as would gilding on some of their attributes and bronze additions such as the weapons and the cuirass over Poseidon's torso. The wall of the pediment was painted bright red, to set off the figures that stood in front of it. The myth represented took place on the Acropolis itself, so that both the story and its representation shared a geographical location and space. The historical location of the events was a little to the north, where the Erechtheion was later built, and where Athena's olive tree could be seen.

The identities of the figures on either side of Athena and Poseidon are still the subject of much debate. One reconstruction has them as the Athenians, both male and female; the men voted for Poseidon in the contest, the women for Athena. Another theory sees them as the children of two gods and their supporters. The two interpretations both have merit, and need not be mutually exclusive – perhaps the group was meant to be interpreted on several levels.

Moving out from the centre, the two gods are supported by their own entourages. Immediately behind them, each has a horse-drawn chariot; Poseidon's driven by his wife, Athena's driven by Nike. The dynamism of the composition, the two main figures moving dramatically away from each other as if to use their weapons, led some to suggest that the moment depicted is the intervention of Zeus, who threw down a thunderbolt to stop the two from fighting. But since Poseidon's antagonism towards Athens could not be emphasised there in the fifth century, this is unlikely.

Poseidon stands slightly in front of Athena, his foot overlapping hers, so that the two figures create a Z-shaped composition; this Z-shape is considered typical of the design of Pheidias, and can be seen in some of the metopes, particularly those where the Centaurs and the Lapiths fight. In the corners are representatives of the city's history: heroes and kings, as well as mortals.

A male figure behind Athena's chariot appears to be Hermes, the messenger god. Further behind Athena is a figure seated, reclining backwards on a rock, who is identified as Cecrops, Athena's witness in the contest. His autochthonous nature, being earth-born, is represented by the snake coiled at his feet. He is depicted with his daughter Pandrosus, whose shrine was next to his to the north of the Parthenon.

A second autochthonous king may be represented in that half of the gable by another figure who does not have legs, and may originally instead have had a snake tail. Erechtheus, traditionally the sixth king of Athens, who also had a shrine to the north of the Parthenon, had been killed by Poseidon. Athena and Erechtheus had been associated for a long time in cult, and there was even a mention of them together in the brief reference to Athens in the *Iliad*.

Erechtheus had sacrificed his daughter to save Athens; some see this myth as having been represented in the Parthenon frieze but this interpretation of it is unlikely. Athena had adopted Erechtheus, who had been born of the earth, as his name indicates. The myth of Erechtheus was important to the Athenians as it emphasised that they as a people had sprung from the soil, rather than fighting to win the land. Athena had raised the future king on the Acropolis, the myth representing the Bronze Age palaces that had once stood on it. Various names have been suggested for the smaller, human figures: Herse, Aglauros, and so forth, but we will never be certain of their identifications, and they are less important to the narrative.

In the fifth century a strong link had developed between the cults of Erechtheus and of Poseidon, the two sharing priests, and later even a building in the form of the Erechtheion. It is therefore quite possible that Erechtheus was depicted in Poseidon's half of the gable, and some scholars see Erechtheus and his children as having been depicted in the right-hand side of the pediment, rather than in Athena's half. Since Erechtheus was raised by Athena, it is perhaps more likely that he was instead depicted in her part of the pediment. The figures in Poseidon's corner would therefore be his son Eumolpos, who ruled over Eleusis, and his followers who would later try to invade Athens, and have to fight Erechtheus.

The right-hand side of the gable was also of course filled with figures, the mortals in the corner, and again various Heroes. Behind Poseidon's chariot stood a winged figure which must be Iris.

The figures in the extreme corners fully recline and are usually identified as representing river gods; again one can argue for them being different rivers, although the Ilissos and the Cephissus, the two main rivers that run through Athens, are most likely. The Cephissus flowed to the north of the Acropolis, and so must have been depicted in the left-hand angle, and the Ilissos in the right-hand angle. The rivers, as personifications, would thus represent the real geography of the Acropolis, and the setting of this myth.

A fragment of an olive tree, around which a snake curls, has been found on the lowest slopes of the Acropolis, and is associated with this pediment. This tree would help to locate the myth within Athens, and indicate that the moment depicted was the moment when the two gods presented the city with their gifts. However, simplicity and clarity are gifts which archaeologists are rarely presented with. If the fragment had been found on the top of the

Acropolis, and if the details of its carving gave us a fifth-century date, it would of course clarify so much. Unfortunately the piece of marble was carved during the Roman period, and found in the city below; it may well be a Roman repair to the pediment, or a completely separate, unrelated sculpture. The original tree, or thunderbolt, or whatever was depicted in the centre of the gable, may well have been represented in bronze; this fragment may have been a Roman repair, or it may be a complete red herring.

The West Metopes – The Battle against the Amazons

Northern end of the metope frieze on the west side of the Parthenon

The metopes from the west end of the Parthenon were carved with a battle between the Greeks and the Amazon women. The Amazons, female warriors who lived without the company of men, had long been part of Greek culture and history. As the Greek world expanded, followed by the Roman Empire which encompassed ever greater amounts of land, the location of the mythical Amazon kingdom moved further and further outwards. To the north of the Black Sea, there seem to have been some tribes where women could be warriors, and the Amazons may be based on them.

These metopes were not the first on the Acropolis to depict Amazons; a late-Archaic metope with an Amazon riding has been found to the south of the Acropolis where it might have fallen during the siege. When the Amazons launched their attack, on the Acropolis, they used the hill below it, which was dedicated to Ares. Better known as the Areopagus, the hill was, under democratic Athens, the seat of the assembly, and so of legal government. This emphasised the Greeks as representing civilisation and government, fighting the Amazons representing effeminacy and barbarism. There were various myths that involved Greek heroes fighting the Amazons. Two in particular were important to the Athenians.

In the first of these the Amazon women try to besiege the Athenian Acropolis, and this myth was represented on the shield of the statue of Athena Parthenos within the Parthenon. Since the Persians had also recently invaded and sacked the Acropolis, it was easy to draw parallels between the two events. Although one event had taken place in recent history and the other in far-distant mythology, it is arguable that no great distinction was drawn between the two. In the second, the Athenian king Theseus fought the Amazons, and brought back as his wife their queen Hippolyta. Their son, Hippolytus, became the object of Theseus' second wife Phaedra's lust, and of a famous play by Euripides. An advantage of the Amazonomachy was that both Heracles and Theseus could be depicted within the same series of scenes fighting the Amazons.

The Amazons of course also represented female power, anathema to the Classical Athenians, and so also lack of civilisation. The Amazons' dress on the Parthenon was notably eastern; their clothes and headgear were designed deliberately to recall that of the Persians. Anyone who has ever tried archery will know that it is almost impossible to practise with breasts, and so according to legend the Amazons cut off a breast so their skills in archery would not be affected by their sex. Having only one breast is not as aesthetically pleasing as two, so in Greek art Amazons were always depicted 'whole' and anatomically correct.

As with the east metopes, the Amazonomachy in the west metopes was designed to be unchallenging, and to be 'read' in one glance so that it did not distract attention from the episode in the pediment above. Having the metopes carved with sculpture added to the whole sense of decoration of the Parthenon, to its lavishness, but they were also deliberately designed not to distract the viewer, who was obviously not thought to be able to appreciate both metopes and pediments at the same time, and on the same end of the building. Again, these sculptures were badly defaced by the Christians, and so are poorly preserved. Some of the Greeks appear on horseback, others fight on foot. In the end, they win against the women, and so civilisation is saved.

Although Athena was a goddess, and so female, she was not a woman, and Athenian women would not have been able to relate to her, or to see her as a potential role model for them. Athena as a female warrior was acceptable to the Athenians since she was on their side, but the Amazons were not.

The Athenians would have seen Artemisia of Caria, who fought with the Persians, as being an Amazon brought to life, and to their land, and so would have found her terrifying; this woman warrior came to conquer Greece, just as the Amazons had come to Athens in myth. She was queen of Caria, where interestingly there was also a sanctuary to the Amazons.

The Greeks feared feminine power; even great heroes such as Heracles could see their powers destroyed by feminine wiles. The prime example of this was when he fell in love with Omphale, queen of Lydia in Persia, and at her request began to wear women's clothes. The queen took on his lionskin cloak and club, and so his powers. This image was considered so shocking and repulsive by both the Greeks and the Romans, that later Augustus depicted Antony and Cleopatra as Heracles and Omphale to emphasise the fact that the Roman had fallen under the spell of an Eastern queen. Ares stole Aphrodite from her husband, and since the Renaissance we interpret their union as the triumph of love over war, of which he was the god. This is a modern interpretation, however, and the Greeks would have seen it as even warriors being potentially subject to women and so robbed of victory.

Situating the metopes with the battle of the Greeks and the Amazons, which depicted the potential of female power, was particularly appropriate on the west of the Parthenon. Immediately above was the pediment containing sculptures that illustrated the contest of Poseidon and Athena. According to one version of the myth, Poseidon, enraged that he had lost, flooded Attica with salt water, punishing the Athenians by ruining their land. In Periclean Athens the city's strength was largely derived from its navy, so this part of the myth was not emphasised. Poseidon had to be seen as Athens' friend, and so another myth arose; to appease Poseidon the Athenians promised to disenfranchise the women, allowing them no say in government, and no power. Women played very little part in classical Greek history. In fifth-century Athens women, even if well born, were almost always forced to lead rather sheltered lives, living together in a separate part of the house, and having no rights unless they managed to find a position as a priestess. Very few Greek women in any of the states were more fortunate. Even though Pericles played an important role in Athenian politics, the names of his wife and mother are not preserved.

Years later, when Pericles gave a eulogy at the funeral of Athenians who had died fighting the Spartans, he said that they did not need a poet such as Homer to glorify them. Instead, the Athenian soldier, who had fought battles to preserve their society and way of life, was glorified and eulogised in the sculpture of the Parthenon, particularly the procession. Athens' history began with a contest – that of Athena and Poseidon depicted in the west pediment – and competitiveness was a part of life that their society encouraged.

Just as women could not hope to compare themselves to Athena, so no Athenian would compare a woman he married or related to with the goddess, since Athena was goddess of war, in which they did not take part. Aphrodite represented marriage and procreation in the aspect of her cult that emphasised marital love, rather than the now more famous aspect of her that emphasised erotic love. Demeter also had connotations of marriage, although she produced a daughter and tragically lost her, just as Athenian women who produced daughters would lose them to the family of the men those daughters would eventually marry.

Maternity, from which women could derive power, and which was their contribution to society, is almost completely absent from the Acropolis. Although the east pediment represents a birth, it is not a birth in the human sense, and Athena's 'mother' Métis is not present. Only her father is depicted, and he gives birth to her. The Athenians themselves prided themselves on the autochthony of their first king, being born from the earth rather than a human mother. Pericles would say later that the greatest honour a woman could achieve and be accorded was not to be talked about, neither criticised nor praised. Athenian women would not put in much of an appearance in the state's history, and so one can read the Parthenon as a statement of Athenian misogyny. The east pediment, where a woman should have played a role since it depicted a birth, is notable for its lack of a mother.

The birth of Pandora, also born fully formed, and represented on the base of the statue of Athena Parthenos within the Parthenon, was the mortal equivalent of Athena's divine birth in the east pediment.

The Athenians also thought of themselves as superior to all other Greeks, for they claimed that they had always inhabited Attica, and had not arrived later as migrants, and so their race was the oldest. Athenian mythology is confusing, for it emphasises this notion of autochthony, and the lack of a human mother also of course emphasises how little the Athenians thought of women, and so we have not one king who sprang from the earth, but a whole series of them, so that a king almost didn't need a queen, or to bother himself with such trivial matters as procreation. Autochthony meant that the Athenians could claim they were purer, allowing them to see the other Greeks as pseudo-foreigners.

Man had always identified himself and his wider social group on the basis of contrasts and differences to others rather than similarities. The Athenians, for example, did not emphasise the common language and gods they shared with the Spartans, but rather stressed the different political and social structures of the two states, seeing themselves not as fellow Greeks, but as belonging to two different nations. The battles on the Parthenon emphasised these differences, the one against the Amazons emphasising the difference between male-dominated Athens and the female warriors. Amazon society was matriarchal, even those women having children being virgin warriors like Athena or Artemis. This element of course made them even more barbarous to the Athenians.

The battle against the Centaurs emphasised the differences between human Lapiths who were civilised and the Centaurs who were bestial. The battle between the gods and the giants emphasised the superiority of the developed and organised Athenian religion over more primitive cults. Although when we read Homer today we often think of the Trojans as being like the Greeks, the Trojan War ultimately emphasised the difference between Greek civilisation and self-control, and Eastern excess and depravity. It had been started by a man, Paris, who could not control his lust for his host's wife, seizing the woman, Helen, who as a woman of course had no self-control herself.

The North Metopes – The Fall of Troy

Although more rational Athenians might have been sceptical of the existence of Centaurs, most, including Herodotus and Thucydides, accepted that the Trojan War had taken place, and that it was part of Greek history. (Over a century of archaeology at Troy has confirmed that a great war did indeed occur there during the Bronze Age.) The Greeks would later see the Trojan War as having been the first great battle between the Greeks and the Persians, and the origin of all future conflict between the two races. The representation of the fall of Troy on the northern side of the Parthenon can be seen as emphasising the unity of the Greeks during that critical period of history, and creating an early parallel for the Athenians' unification of any Greek states in the form of the Delian League.

By the fifth century BC Athens had become one of the more powerful states, and so it decided to stake its claim within Greek history. The first great historical work we have preserved is Homer's *Iliad*. As mentioned above, Athens appears only briefly in it, and the two references to the city are believed by scholars to have been inserted later, when Pericles included reading of the two great Homeric epics as part of the Athenian festival. No great Athenian heroes took part, but Athens of course wanted to take some credit for Troy.

From the later description we have of a bronze Trojan Horse erected on the Acropolis, we know that it was colossal, almost twenty feet high, and that it held four figures of men depicted life-size, including two sons of Theseus, Nenestheus and Teucros. These two sons were relatively minor in mythology, and since enough Greeks hid in the horse it was possible for Athens to slip in a few of her own among their number. It was in this way that the Athenians managed to hijack Troy as belonging to their history, and so worthy to be represented on the Parthenon as one of the great Athenian events. The lie grew, as lies so often do, until it eventually incorporated Aethra, the maternal grandmother of these two young Athenians. Presumably these ancient Athenians were all depicted in the north metopes of the Parthenon, emphasising the link between Athens and the story.

To have all the metopes on the exterior of the temple carved with sculpture has become a cliché of Greek art, but it was in fact extremely rare. Although figured metopes could be fully decorated on small buildings, the only subsequent temple with all its metopes decorated was the temple of Athena at Ilion (301–280 BC), a building that deliberately copied the Parthenon. The scenes depicted on the four sides of the building were the same ones that had been depicted over a century earlier on the Parthenon. Ilion was the later Greek name for Troy, and the inhabitants saw themselves as Greeks; for this reason they did not see any contradiction in having the fall of Troy depicted on their temple. The classical Trojans created a Panathenaic festival in their city, deliberately modelled on the festival held in Athens. Since they had copied this manner of paying homage to their patron goddess on that of Athens, it is not surprising that they partly modelled their own temples to her on the Parthenon.

The west and east metopes had been quite monotonous in their design, designed to be read with one glance by the viewer. These metopes on the north flank of the Parthenon were far more varied and more interesting. This is because the north side of the Parthenon is the main side along which anyone visiting the Acropolis would have walked, whether to the front of the Parthenon or to other buildings. For this reason a story with many episodes, which could thus provide a narrative made up of interesting scenes, was chosen. Unfortunately, these metopes were badly damaged by the Christian Greeks, and much of the side was blown out during the explosion of 1687, so they are highly fragmentary.

Today we almost assume that the Trojans were Greeks, because they dressed in the same way, worshipped the same gods, and probably spoke the same language. In the Classical period, the Trojans were thought of as barbarians by the Athenians and other mainland Greeks, as foreigners who represented the uncivilised people of Asia Minor.

In the other themes represented on the sides of the Parthenon, it was possible to represent a battle by usually having two figures fighting in each metope. The episodes of the Trojan War presented a narrative, and so scenes sometimes had to be read over adjacent metopes, as an attempt was made at continuity of narrative. The emphasis on the historical events depicted there can be seen by the framing of the story with the sun rising in the first metope and the moon setting in one of the later panels.

In N25, we can see Menelaus and one of his Greek companions. He is rushing towards his wife in N26, where Helen is seeking sanctuary with a statue, the Palladion. To the left of Helen is Aphrodite; the figure is badly damaged but can be identified by the small figure of Eros floating above her right shoulder. The goddess acts as Helen's protector, since she had started the Trojan War.

The South Metopes – The Battle between the Centaurs and the Lapiths

For some reason the south metopes were not damaged to the same extent as the metopes on the three other sides of the Parthenon. Because of this, we know from drawings made in the seventeenth century how most of the panels were arranged. A few years after these drawings were made, most of the central panels from the south and north sides were damaged in the explosion. The south metopes may not have been as important in antiquity as the north metopes, since most people walking on the Acropolis did not walk by them. Although the space between the south side of the Parthenon and the edge of the Acropolis is empty today, it seems to have been filled by a number of small structures in antiquity.

The first metope on the southern side of the Parthenon

Because they had largely escaped vandalism, and were later brought to London by Lord Elgin, the few southern metopes that survive are by far the best preserved of the metopes on the Parthenon. This frieze can be divided into three sections, with the sections to the left and right depicting battles between the Centaurs, half-human half-horse, and the Lapiths. The Centaurs, being only half-human, were of course symbols of barbarity and lack of civilisation. The Lapiths were Greeks, and so naturally represented the superiority of Greek civilisation.

The link of the story to the history of Athens is rather tenuous. Theseus was a friend of the king whose wedding the Centaurs disrupted by their loutish behaviour. According to the myth, King Peirithoos and Hippodameia were celebrating their marriage, and because the Centaurs could not hold their wine – Greeks identified drinking undiluted as a sign of lack of civilisation – they disrupted the wedding. The Centaurs and Lapiths appear in most scenes fighting each other, with Greeks winning in some scenes, the Centaurs having the upper hand in others. A few Centaurs are depicted trying to kidnap Lapith women, the action which had spurred the Lapith men into fighting them.

The human figure in S32 is in the same pose as the famous group representing the Tyrannicides, which would have been recognisable to all Athenians. So if the Centaurs represent the barbarian Persians, one can also read into it a secondary meaning, this being the victory of democracy over the dictatorship of kings. The figure is often identified as Theseus, and he is represented in the same pose on the Hephaisteion sculpture.

The central metopes, S13 to S21, do not seem to represent the same story. These metopes were destroyed centuries ago, so we can only base our interpretation of them on drawings, but it seems certain that they depicted another myth. All the figures have human form, apart from the horses drawing a chariot in S15. The scenes are almost certain to have been a myth, and linked to early Athenian history, involving one of its early heroic kings. The most convincing explanation, so far, is that the scenes represented the myth of Ixion. An Athenian, he was the father of the Lapith king in the other metopes, and the grandfather of the Centaurs. The myth of Ixion encompassed greed, lust, madness and violence and had a link to the battle of the Centaurs on either side of it, filling in the historical background to the battle. One could thus see the story of Ixion in the centre, and the results of his actions a generation or two later on either side of it.

Ixion was the father of Peirithoos, who was marrying a Lapith bride. He was also, through an affair, the father of Centaurus, who was in turn the father and ancestor of the Centaurs, thus the Athenians and the Centaurs were related. The battle is therefore linked to Athens and represents the conflict between his human descendants, the product of marriage and civilisation, and his bestial offspring, the product of lust and lack of control. Killing one's family or kinsmen was a Greek taboo, although the killer could be expiated of guilt through ritual cleansing. The first time such purification apparently occurred was the purification of Ixion, and some scholars have seen this as being depicted within the missing central metopes of the battle, to show that the Greeks could be purified even if they killed each other. This, however, seems to be reading far too much into too few fragments, since the Athenians would not have seen the Boeotians or the Spartans as fellow Greeks or kinsmen, but rather simply as enemies.

In recent years Professor Alexander Mantis has found many fragments of the central south metopes. He points out that it is a pity the central north metopes were too damaged to be drawn in 1674, as we might similarly have had a secondary story represented in the central metopes. Mantis, one of the great Greek scholars working on the Parthenon, has now assigned thirty-five fragments to those central panels, many of them found within the later south fortification walls of the Acropolis. Many Classical archaeologists have difficulties with Carrey's drawings, which are post-Renaissance, and to which they cannot relate because they are so different in conception from ancient art. The fragments have shown that although there are some minor distortions and inaccuracies, the drawings overall are quite accurate in the way they represent the design of the missing metopes. We now have more of these south metopes than we did a few decades ago, though the fragments can still be interpreted in several different ways, to represent various different scenes.

Others have tried to identify a series of myths shown in pairs of metopes, such as the fall of Daedalus in S16, whose wings melted when he flew too close to the sun, represented in S15. None of these other interpretations, however, is entirely satisfactory. The central scenes on the north side depict Athena and the Trojan Palladion. It may well be that the central southern metopes represent something other than the myth of Ixion, probably an event that was intrinsically linked with Athena and the cult of the goddess in Athens. It is possible that the central scenes on the south side represent the arrival of the Palladion in Athens; this early image of Athena would thus be the statue represented in S21. According to Athenian myths, when the Palladion arrived in Athens a young man died, crushed beneath the horses pulling a chariot, and one could possibly argue that S15 and S16 represent the chariot and the young Athenian falling to the ground.

This interpretation would also see S19 to S21 representing weaving, making a *peplos*, and dressing a statue of Athena in it. Although the seventeenth-century drawings are good ones, the figures were already quite damaged by then, and to be able to iden-tify all this in the three panels is in my opinion quite creative, the evidence for it largely lacking. It would, however, provide the Parthenon with a representation of an event that was central to the cult of Athena in Athens, the robe that the Athenians presented to her at the Panathenaia, and which they also washed each year during the festival called the Paynteria. Each generation a scholar will almost certainly produce a new interpretation of these scenes, in an attempt to make his or her academic reputation, but as so often in archaeology we will never be certain of the meaning of those panels.

The myth of Ixion, which has a strong link both with the city of Athens and with the battle between the Lapiths and Centaurs surrounding these central metopes, still remains the strongest candi-date, and common sense suggests that that was the episode repre-sented.

The other south metopes are, however, well enough preserved for us to be able to comment on the general style of the carvings. Particularly notable in the panels in the British Museum is the great difference between the styles of the various metopes that all deco-rated not only the same building, but also the same side of it. Although the pedimental figures could be inserted into the gables later, and were, the metopes and the frieze had to be fitted within the architectural framework as the building rose towards its roof line, and so were an integral feature of it.

In some metopes the figures stand on carved ground lines, in others they do not. Although the Lapiths are always represented in an idealised way, the Centaurs vary: some are old, others are young and handsome, and others again seem almost to have deliberately ugly faces with exaggerated features. Some scenes have successful compositions, others are particularly crude in the way the figures are arranged. They vary from brilliant to disastrous, via mediocre.

This is usually taken to indicate that the metopes were the first sculptures carved for the Parthenon, with some sculptors working in the more old-fashioned style, and others rapidly adapting to the new trends of the time. During those central decades of the fifth century BC, Athenian sculpture was coming along in leaps and bounds, both in terms of technique and style. Although one can blame the carvings on different abilities among the sculptors, if Pheidias designed all the compositions, he must have been better at doing so on some days than on others.

The number of metopes executed in a more old-fashioned style suggests that they had originally been intended only to go across the two internal porches within the colonnade. When Pheidias decided instead to have a continuous frieze on the interior, and all the metopes of the exterior figured, he had to commission the execution of more of these metopes. Therefore the metopes carved in a more advanced style could well have been executed a couple of years after the others. The builders of the Parthenon were particularly concerned with economic matters. Reusing elements of previous building programmes in its foundation, and so using the first set of metopes, and adding metopes to these, seems likely.

The battle between the Lapiths and Centaurs had not been a myth that had featured prominently in the iconography of the Acropolis before the Parthenon. Its link to Athena is tenuous, although its link to the city of Athens is a strong one, since both sides were descended from Athenian kings. The battle was also depicted on the sandals of the Athena Parthenos. Towards the end of the fifth century, the Athenians seem to have commissioned a painting of this battle on the shield of the large bronze Athena Promachos which Pheidias had created earlier, and which stood opposite the entrance to the Acropolis as the first thing the visitor saw.

It is quite clear that the various mythological scenes chosen on the Parthenon were picked after a great deal of deliberation, and one can note that many of the battles on the metopes are also depicted elsewhere on the Acropolis, creating a giant web where various images were repeated in different locations, all creating a uniform image of the Athenians' history.

To have the battles against the Amazons and the Centaurs on the same building had many other parallels in the years after the Parthenon. The first of these were on the interior frieze of the temple of Apollo at Bassae and on the Hephaisteion in Athens. The two battles represented what the Greeks thought as the worst possible state, being either women or animals. These two battles were also represented on the friezes of the Mausoleum of Halicarnassus, although that building was constructed by a Carian ruler and so a Persian, whom ironically enough the Greeks would have seen as a barbarian. One can also interpret the two battles as showing women as enemies in the battle against the Amazons, and women who need to be protected in the battle against the Centaurs.

The East Pediment – The Birth of Athena

The Birth of Athena had been a popular motif for the decoration of vases in sixth-century Athens, although it does not seem to have been as popular during the first half of the fifth century. A small Archaic pediment might depict the birth of Athena, making it a precursor of the east pediment of the Parthenon, otherwise the scene is known mostly from vase paintings. In these early scenes Zeus was always shown on his throne, with a miniature goddess coming out of his head, which had been split open by Hephaestus with an axe. The story of the Birth of Athena was an ancient one, and is recorded in many surviving sources going as far back as Homeric hymns and the poems of Hesiod. The Birth of Athena did not take place in Athens. The Goddess was born on Mount Olympus, in the presence of the Olympian Gods. As the birth of the goddess who was the chief patron of Athens, it of course had a special significance for the city.

Métis, the name literally means cunning, and Zeus, the king of the gods, were lovers. Métis became pregnant, and the Fates predicted that her children would achieve great things. Zeus became jealous, lest one of these children take his place as the king of the gods, just as he had earlier replaced his own father Cronos in this role many years before. He turned Métis into a fly, and swallowed her. This should have been the end of her, but as this was a myth she continued to grow in his belly.

Eventually the child inside him grew so big that his head continually hurt. Hephaestus, his son and God of blacksmiths, cut open Zeus's head and out came Athena. The culmination of this event is depicted within the east pediment of the Parthenon: Athena has been born of her father, leaping out in full armour, and performing a dance.

Athena sprang from Zeus fully formed, and clad in gold armour, with both the wisdom of her mother Métis, and the military prowess of her father. She carried a shield and a spear, and at her birth she let out a mighty roar heard by all people everywhere, and she performed a military dance not unlike the Scottish sword dance. The Gods were frightened by her appearance, partly because Zeus had eaten her mother to try to prevent a prophecy being fulfilled, which had said that Métis' children might dethrone Zeus. Time stood still, as even the sun stopped moving in shock at the noise and did not cross the sky. The other gods panicked, as depicted by Figure G in the pediment, the preserved figure closest to the centre of the scene, who averts his eyes.

Athena, according to legend, then took off her helmet and armour and dropped her weapons, and so the gods heaved a sigh of relief, and peace once again returned to their midst as they realised that Athena would not try to replace her father. She assumed her more feminine nature as a peaceful woman and the daughter of Zeus, rather than the initial one of a warrior. These early moments following her birth would thus appear to have been depicted by the figures immediately surrounding the central group, who panic, the goddess literally filling them with dread and fear. The other figures in the wings, however, seem to be relaxed and happy and can be interpreted as representing the reaction of the fellow Gods once the Goddess had shown that she would not disrupt their equilibrium.

Athena could thus represent both war and peace, although her martial aspect was more important to the Athenians, leading them to victory, and this was how they represented her within the Parthenon. The more peaceful Athena they probably also associated with victory, although that victory for them was achieved through war. So we can see that the figures within the pediment would have represented two time-frames, and two separate emotions immediately after her birth, the threat at her arrival soon turning to joy.

The central figures were lost around 1500 years ago, when the Parthenon was turned into a Byzantine Greek church. To try to reconstruct them, we must thus look to other scenes of the Birth of Athena, to common sense, and to the scattered archaeological evidence. In earlier images Zeus was not only shown seated, but also almost always depicted in profile. It was possible to depict this in paint or in relief sculpture, but harder to do so in a group of free-standing sculptures within a pediment. The preserved images tend to depict the Birth itself, whilst the pediment illustrated the moment immediately after the Birth, when Athena had sprung to the ground.

The centre of the gable allows for a figure maximum 3.30 m high, and that would have fitted within the shelf that measured 0.90 m deep. We can however see from comparison with other figures that its back might have been shaved off to allow it to fit within this space. Iron bars had been inserted into the pedimental shelf to strengthen it, so that heavy figures could be supported without causing it to crack. Complex arguments can be made on the basis of the arrangement of these bars, and of patterns of wear on the floor of the pediment, that in turn allow us to deduce which figure stood where. The overwhelming concern in the design of statue groups set within pediments was one of symmetry, so Zeus standing, facing forward, is the only restoration that fits this criterion, and seems likely.

No fragments have been plausibly identified as having belonged to the figure of Zeus, nor have any later representations been conclusively shown to have been based on copying the Parthenon pediment. The God may have been represented seated on his throne, as Pheidias later carved him at Olympia, the larger scale of the chief god filling the centre of the gable, or since there is space within the frame for him to have been standing, this might also have been the way in which he was represented. In most other depictions of the Birth of Athena Zeus was shown seated on a throne, perhaps no longer having the strength to stand due to the terrible headache from which he was suffering.

Since the headache was caused by his daughter Athena being inside him, and the headache was cured when Hephaestus cut Zeus's head open with an axe, that God must also have been represented near the centre of the gable. His presence was necessary for the narrative of the story, and he could not have been omitted, so we must restore him within the centre of the gable. If Hephaestus flanked the central trio, another figure must have mirrored him on the other side of the gable, since the composition of pediments was always symmetrical. Poseidon, who was later to fight Athena for Athens, is a likely suggestion.

Even if we have all these figures in the centre of the pediment, this still leaves quite a large amount of space between those figures, and the figures that survive from the corners. Some scholars find an easy solution to this, filling the space on each side with chariots pulled by teams of four horses. The horses are restored as having been rearing, and so filling the frame. Personally, I find this unlikely as there were many Olympian gods, and Athens would have wished to honour as many of these as possible to avoid displeasing any one god and so incurring their wrath.

Two large pieces of a statue of a standing woman, one fragment covering the area just below her bust to the level of her hips, the other covering her legs from the knees down but excluding her feet, have been found. From their scale, we know that they belong to a statue that must have stood near the centre of the gable. She wore a *peplos*, and the way its folds are draped suggest a static, rather matronly figure, and so she has been identified as Hera, the wife of Zeus and queen of the gods.

Given that Hera, the wife of Zeus, was not Athena's mother it might seem surprising to see her at the Birth, but she was represented as having been present in other ancient depictions of this myth. Hephaestus was necessary to the narrative, as an integral part of the myth, whilst the other gods are there to welcome the new arrival, and to fill the space in the wings of the pediment. The surviving fragments of Hera are similar to a Roman copy of a Greek statue from Cherchel (Algeria) previously thought to have depicted Demeter. Because of this similarity, the Algerian statue is now believed to copy the earlier Hera, and so gives us an image for the Parthenon goddess. In recent years a head in the Acropolis Museum (no. 2381) has been associated with the fragments of Hera's body, and she has no longer lost her head at the Birth of Athena.

A highly unusual feature of the body is that press-folds are visible within the drapery. Although now we hang our clothes in wardrobes, until recently clothes were folded and stored in chests and trunks. When we look at portraits of Restoration Beauties, such as the mistresses of Charles II, one can often see the rectangles on their dresses, formed by marks left when they had been folded and stored. In the same way the dresses on ancient goddesses were made of pieces of cloth pinned into place. Statues of Greek women were carved with such press-folds, but they are generally seen as a feature which began in the fourth century BC. Similar press-folds, which were deliberate and certainly not later scratches, can be seen on the Athena of the west pediment; although the sculptors who worked on the Parthenon were technically very advanced, the features are too early for that date, and would seem to suggest later repairs to the pedimental figures.

Just as scholars like to come up with new interpretations for the Parthenon frieze, so they also like to come up with their own reconstructions for the missing central figures of the East pediment. Athena and Zeus are entirely missing, and only two fragments of the body of Hera survive. Because of the triangular shape of the gable there is a little more space in the centre, and this would have allowed the greater height for the figure of Zeus who needed to be represented as larger than the two goddesses, both because he was a man, and because he was the king of the gods. Possibly one of his toes, and maybe a hand holding a thunderbolt, belong to this figure. The consensus these days is that the god was represented standing, facing outwards, rather than seated on his throne as in Archaic art.

The surviving figures from the corners are quite static. Since the pediment represented neither a contest, nor a competition, it is likely that, unlike the figures in the other pediment, most of those represented here were quite calm, carved as serene deities witnessing the birth of one of their own. They were a large scale group, carved in the round, but otherwise similar in mood to the gods carved on the frieze below the pediment. The time of the birth of Athena is clearly sunrise, with Helios rising and his sister Selene setting.

Helios, the Sun, rising in the corner of the east pediment

Many of the figures from the sides of the pediment, which surrounded the missing central group, are still preserved. Beginning from the left, the extant figures include Helios, the Sun, rising in his four-horse chariot from the sea – represented by carved waves – which sets the time for the scene as having taken place at dawn. His sister Selene, the Moon, mirrors him by setting in the extreme right corner of the gable.

Then a reclining male figure, lounging on a lion-skin cloak, who is sometimes identified as Heracles. Since there were no mortals or even heroes present at the Birth, this makes it unlikely that the figure in the left pediment corner, immediately to the right of Helios and his chariot, was Heracles. Although later deified, Heracles was primarily a Hero rather than a god. Athena introduced Heracles to Olympus, so his deification cannot take place before her Birth; although concepts of time are quite fluid in mythology, and this minor anachronism might not have necessarily bothered the Greeks themselves, this would have been contradictory. The figure should therefore instead be identified as Dionysus. The figure is beardless, which would be unusual for both the god Dionysus and the hero Heracles at the time, since in classical art they usually had beards. Those who favour Dionysus point out that it is particularly appropriate that he should have been carved in the left angle, since that was on the south side, and his theatre lay just below, at the foot of the Acropolis on its southern slope.

Next were the two seated figures of Kore-Persephone and Demeter, daughter and mother. Although the citizens of Athens saw Athena as present all year around, other gods were only present on earth in certain months of the year. Figure D, if he is indeed Dionysus, was a newer god imported from Thrace, which bordered Persia. As the god of wine, he encompassed drunken revelry, although by including it within a cult the Greeks hoped to be able to control its potential chaos. When Dionysus came to Greece he went to Delphi, the sanctuary of Apollo. In later years the two shared the sanctuary, having it each for half the year, and so two gods were represented in the sculpture of the gables of the temple at Delphi on either side of the building.

Demeter, goddess of the harvest, was also on earth and providing its inhabitants with her fruit for only half of the year, the rest of which she spent mourning for her daughter Kore-Persephone, who had been kidnapped by Hades and so spent half the year in the Underworld; those two goddesses are figures E and F in this pediment.

The next and last figure preserved from the left wing of the gable is a standing female figure, who seems to be, if not running away from the centre, then at least turning away from it in horror. She is usually identified as Iris, the messenger of the gods, although other female deities have been suggested. The central figures are missing, but the figure that we have which survives nearest to them, figured G, seems to be moving, almost as if surprised; this fits the idea that she recoils in shock at the sight of Athena springing from Zeus fully-formed.

In the right side of the gable, starting from the extreme right outer corner, were the heads of the horses that drew the chariot of Selene, the setting moon; she was no longer on the building in 1674 when Carrey drew the figures in situ, but she has since been excavated and is now in the Acropolis Museum in Athens.

Selene, the Moon goddess, would have been shown with the horses that drew her chariot, in the right corner of the gable; mirroring the Sun on the left, and helping to create both a physical and a temporal frame for the scene which took place at dawn. The scene took place not on earth, but rather in the heavens. Both the sun's and the moon's horses had to be re-cut when they were first inserted into the gable to fit within the space, projecting out from and beyond the physical pedimental frame. Recutting can be seen on the backs of many of the figures; they were carved on the ground and later raised into the gable, but sometimes proved to be too large for the shallow space and so needed trimming. These two figures, the Sun and the Moon, which frame the scenes in many of the metopes as well, are the two figures from the East Pediment whose identity is accepted by all.

A female figure reclines on the lap of another woman; her drapery clings to her every curve sensuously. The reclining figure is identified as Aphrodite. The other figure, in whose lap she lies, continues to cause problems of identification but is probably her mother. In the frieze below, Aphrodite and Artemis are represented side by side, but the eroticism of the figures does not seem appropriate for a depiction of the chaste goddess of hunting. Therefore the prevalent identification is Aphrodite's mother Dione, although she seems a rather minor figure of Greek mythology in general to be depicted in such a prominent place, too minor to be represented in this grouping, where only the great Olympians are shown. Although Aphrodite had an active cult on the northern slope of the Acropolis, and was the goddess of marital love as well as of erotic love, her mother did not play a great role in Athenian history.

The pairs of figures E and F in the left wing, and L and M in the right wing, the groups furthest away from the central scene, are almost entirely static and relaxed, reclining as if nothing has bothered their peace. Figures L and M seem to be Aphrodite and her mother, the Greek gods not being seen within a conventional chronological framework, so Aphrodite could be a woman representing marital love as well as a child. Although the poses of the figures are highly innovative, compared to say the temple of Zeus at Olympia created a few years earlier, the figures are also arranged more or less symmetrically in the conventional way in which figures were arranged within a triangular pediment. Figures D and N, on either side of the pediment, are reclining in roughly the same pose, mirroring each other. The sun rising and the moon setting in the extreme corners also mirror each other.

The east pediment is in appalling condition, and only the figures in the outer sections of the triangular space survived the destruction by the Christian Greeks of the centre. The surviving figures are in poor condition, and their identification has led to many heated arguments. A reclining figure in the left corner of the pediment, for example, has been identified as both Dionysus and Heracles on the basis of the lion-skin rug on which he reclines.

Because of the poor state of preservation of the other figures, some large fragments are associated with the East pediment, although again they may or may not belong to it. A figure known as H, all the figures in the gables having been assigned letters as well as possible identifications, may or may not be from the pediment. A head in the Louvre in Paris, known as the Laborde Head, is traditionally said to come from the Acropolis, and may well have been the head of one of the goddesses in the pediment. On the other hand, the pediment and its sculptures are so fragmentary that the head may not be related to them.

Although there are some later depictions of the Birth of Athena, and whilst at least one of those may have been influenced by this pediment, there are no copies that can provide us with the missing central group. A small shrine of the first century BC at Eleusis, the sanctuary of Demeter near Athens, had miniature copies of the pedimental sculptures of the Parthenon in its gables. These are now on

THE EAST FRIEZE WITH THE PANATHENAIC FESTIVAL

The central block of the East frieze, showing the culmination of the Panathenaic procession with the presentation of a *peplos* to the statue of Athena. The Greeks removed this block when the building was converted into a church, and it was excavated from the soil of the Acropolis by Elgin. This meant that whilst the block was not damaged by the explosion, years of exposure to the elements have made it very worn.

The seated Gods and standing Eponymous Heroes of Attica, who flanked the presentation of the *peplos* on the east end of the Parthenon.

(*Above left*) Chariot racing was part of the games during the quadrennial Panathenaic Festival, rather than part of the procession itself. The charioteer held onto the reins whilst a hoplite in full uniform leapt in and out of the chariot.

(*Above right*) Only female animals were sacrificed to Athena at her festival. They would provide the main source of meat for many Athenians who could not afford to eat meat except at festivals. This scene is believed to have inspired Keats' *Ode On a Grecian Urn*.

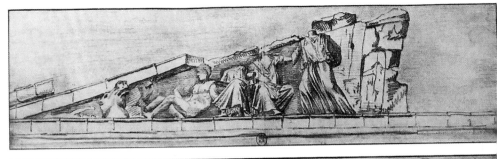

(*Above*) Carrey's drawings of the Parthenon pediments, executed before the 1687 explosion in which many of the figures were destroyed, are the best evidence we have for the original arrangement of the figures.

(*Below*) This young male god is sometimes interpreted as being Heracles, because of the lion skin rug on which he lounges, but is more likely to be Dionysos, god of wine and theatre whose sanctuary lay just below the Parthenon.

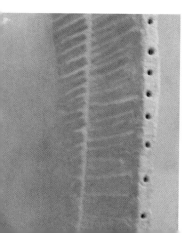

(*Top*) Three goddesses recline at the Birth of Athena. The pose is surprisingly sensuous to the modern eye, but the figure whose dress is falling off her shoulder is Aphrodite, goddess of love, reclining in the lap of her mother Dione.

(*Above*) The far right figure in the pediment was the horse of Selene, the Moon, setting the time of the scene as having taken place at daybreak.

(*Left*) The close-up of the mane shows a series of holes into which bronze attachments would have been inserted, creating a halo of moonbeams.

Carrey's drawings of th
west pediment are less
detailed, but they still
provide us with icono-
graphic evidence that is
otherwise lost, such as tl
horses on either side of
the two eponymous god

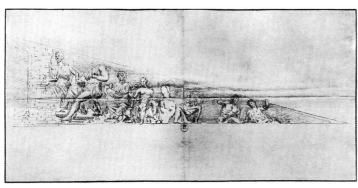

(*Left*) Athena's torso, all that survives
of the goddess. The hole in the centre of
her aegis once held a gilt bronze head of
the Gorgon Medusa.

(*Below*) A detail of Athena's breast,
showing the press folds, vertical lines
which were added during a later antique
restoration of the sculpture.

The torso of Poseidon, in London. The front is in Athens, seen here (right) attached to a cast of the BM piece. The overdeveloped musculature is not typical of the Classical period, so for years it was suggested that this was a later restoration. In fact, new research shows that it can be explained by the idea that it was covered by a bronze cuirass.

Cecrops and his daughter were left on the Parthenon by Elgin because they were thought to be Roman additions, depicting Hadrian and Sabina. They remained in situ until 1976, eaten away by acid rain, hence their appalling condition today. (Acropolis Museum, Athens)

A small shrine at Eleusis erected in the Hellenistic period was decorated with miniature copies of the figures from this pediment of the Parthenon. The figure of Cecrops and his daughter is amongst those that survive. (National Museum, Athens)

THE SOUTH METOPES

A Battle between the Centaurs and the Lapiths framing central scenes of uncertain iconography. Those scenes are now lost, but are preserved in the drawings of Carrey. The moral is simple. The civilized Lapiths represent the Athenians, and are superior to the Barbarian Centaurs, who represent foreigners.

(*Above left*) Carrey drawing of South 29, as preserved before the explosion that destroyed many of the Parthenon sculptures. (*Above right*) Metope South 29, today in the British Museum. A drunken Centaur tries to abduct a Lapith woman, which led to the battle between the two. Since the drawing was made, the woman lost her head.

(*Right*) Metope South 28, also in the British Museum, shows a Centaur who has defeated a Lapith, and is about to trample him underfoot. He is shown rearing up, his lion skin cloak draped over one arm, in a composition which would have been all the more dramatic when the panel was still on the building, 12 m above ground level. (*Below left*) South 10 is one of the few pieces Fauvel and Napoleon managed to get their hands on, and is now in the Louvre. (*Below right*) South 12 remained in Athens, and is now in the Acropolis Museum. Unfortunately it suffered badly in Athens, and is in extremely poor condition, with much of the panel lost.

Carrey also drew the Parthenon frieze. Before the explosion it was still on the Parthenon, high off the ground and hidden by columns and the architecture. For this reason the French artist was able to see less of it and his drawings reflect this. Some blocks had already been removed by AD 600 when the Parthenon was turned into a church.

(*Below left*) A rider from the west frieze in Athens. The figure is in poor condition as it was left on the building until 1993, then put into storage awaiting conservation for a decade. When the block was finally put on display in 2004, archaeologists were dismayed by its condition.

(*Below right*) Another block in the British Museum makes clear the difference in condition between the blocks that Elgin brought back and cared for, and those that were left on the Acropolis, whose condition declined sharply once Greece had attained Independence. These riders are represented as heroic, and may well have depicted the Athenians who fell at Marathon fighting off the invading Persians.

The Laborde Head in the Louvre

display in Athens National Museum (inv. 200–2), but unfortunately, just as on the Parthenon, only the outer figures survive – the central figures are missing.

A small statue of Athena, 0.70 metres high, was found at Epidaurus, and although we know from its inscription that it was dedicated as late as AD 304, it seems to represent an Athena, who turns towards the right, holding her shield in her left hand. An active figure, that might well be dancing, she is clad like a warrior (inv. 274). Some scholars sees her as representing the Athena from the east pediment, just as they see another small figure of Athena (inv. 275), of similar style and date, as perhaps representing the Athena that had originally stood in the west pediment. This second figure turns towards the left, with her shield also in her left hand, and the figure wears the goatskin aegis over her dress.

We know that there was a sculptural group below the east pediment, and slightly to the north, representing the Birth of Athena from the description of the Acropolis written by Pausanias. So we can see that motifs were repeated time and again on the Acropolis. On the other side of the Parthenon, again slightly to the north of it, there was a second group representing the same story as the west pediment; the two Gods are shown with their gifts, waiting to see which of them had won Athens. As with the earlier sculptures representing different episodes from the Trojan War, these two groups also represented different moments in the story of Athena. In the group on the ground Athena seems to have been shown literally climbing out of Zeus' head at the moment of her birth, whilst in the pediment she was almost certainly standing next to him, fully formed and full-size. In the group near the west pediment, however, the figures on the ground depicted an episode after the scenes in the pediment; the sculptures in the gable represent the competition, those on the ground the wait for a result based on that contest.

Above the pediments were acroteria, a modern term used to describe sculpture that stood on the corners and apex of the gable, located above the pedimental frame rather than within it. On the Parthenon the lateral acroteria, on each side of the pediment, were carved as marble figures of Victory (Nike), and those on the summit were more conventional stylised floral motifs.

The East Metopes – The battle between the Gods and the Giants

On the exterior of the building, the area above the columns but beneath the roofline was called the entablature. Within this entablature there was a frieze made up of more-or-less square panels divided by smaller rectangular panels called triglyphs; this literally meant three vertical lines. The square panels between them, which on the Parthenon measure 1.32 by 1.33 metres, were called metopes. There were ninety-two of these metopes in all on the Parthenon exterior, all carved with high relief sculptures where the figures projected up 0.26 centimetres from the surface of the panel. The term 'metopes' literally means 'between the eyes', and refers to their position between the triglyphs. The triglyphs themselves are so called because there were three lines (glyphs) carved into these vertical rectangles. The metopes on the Parthenon all illustrated the history of earlier Athenians, and their victories with the aid of Athena.

Immediately below the pediment that depicted the Olympian Gods attending the birth of one of their own, Athena, they are represented in the metopes as fighting the Giants. The battle is usually referred to as the Gigantomachy, the ending -*mache* meaning battle in Greek.

Athena, her father's equal in both strength and cunning, took part in the great battle between the Olympian gods and the giants, who were the sons of mother earth, Gaia. In later art these giants would be depicted with bottom halves shaped like snakes, to remind us of their earthly origin. At the time the Parthenon was created, they were depicted as having had human form. Heracles also took part in the battle, fighting on the side of the gods, since according to an oracle they could not win without a mortal fighting in their ranks. The various gods were almost always depicted as defeating the same giants: Athena is, for example, always represented killing Enceladus. The metopes on the Parthenon depicted pairs of figures, so when one can identify the god in the scene, one can then also deduce which giant is represented.

The myth of the battle between the gods and giants was popular in Athens and was depicted many times on the Acropolis in Athens. This battle was central to Athenian identity and iconography, woven into the very fabric of the *peplos* presented to Athena each year by the city, and vases decorated with the battle had been dedicated on the Acropolis in the archaic period. The battle was central to Greek history, and to the way the Greeks identified themselves and their beliefs, for it was in that battle that the giants, children of mother earth, were defeated by the Olympian gods, who from then on reigned supreme. It was the because of the gods' victory in the battle that the Greeks worshipped those gods and not the giants. Most scholars nowadays interpret the Panathenaia as honouring the gods' victory in this battle rather than the birthday of Athena, as had previously been assumed. The festival ended after all on the Acropolis, with a *peplos* decorated with scenes from the Gigantomachy being presented to the statue of Athena Polias.

The earliest images of the battle date from around the same time that the Panathenaia was re-organised, in 566 BC, on an Archaic black figure vase found on the Acropolis. The battle had also been represented in a pediment of the old temple of Athena on the Acropolis, which predated the Parthenon. Although the Gigantomachy had been depicted prominently in the gables of the main archaic temple and several smaller shrines, on the Parthenon it had to make way for the scene representing the birth of Athena over the entrance to the building. Therefore the battle moved below the pediment, and was represented in the metopes on the front of the temple.

Remains of metopes on the east side

The metopes, which were located over the main entrance to the Parthenon, and so its front, are in particularly poor condition, having been defaced by the Christian Greeks. The giants are barely differentiated, and can only be identified in relation to the gods fighting them, the pairings between certain gods and certain giants being

88

almost uniform in the entire history of Greek art. In the Hellenistic period, Pergamon based many of its buildings and much of its iconography on those of Athens, being a city built on top of a hill, and so having certain parallels to it. On the Pergamon Altar the battle of the giants was carved in a colossal scale on the exterior, and the gods were identified by having their names inscribed above the figures. The giants were identified by having their names inscribed at the bottom of the frieze, indicating their lesser status as the losers.

The metopes were deliberately designed to be unexciting in their composition, and to be easily 'read'. The viewer could glance at them, and immediately take in their narrative. This was done so that he would instead look up, and concentrate his attention on the more important pedimental group above, depicting the same gods present at the Birth of Athena. Because of this, many of the figures in the metopes are quite repetitive in pose. Combined with their highly fragmentary condition, this makes it difficult to work out who many of the gods represented are.

The identification of Athena in E4 makes the identification of the fallen giant beneath her certain: he had to have been Enceladus. A small figure of Victory hovers over Athena, crowning her with a wreath. This represents the concept that Athena won the epithet Nike, meaning victory, during this battle. The figure in E11 seems to have worn a lion-skin cloak, and thus is likely to have been Heracles, the mortal the gods needed to fight on their side in order to defeat the giants. At the right end of the frieze, in metope E14, Helios the Sun can be seen rising in his chariot, indicating that a new world order had been established by the victory of the gods over the giants.

Around 200 BC a Pergamene king would dedicate a bronze group in front of this end of the Parthenon. One of the figures represented a fallen giant, complementing the narrative of the metopes above it.

The Parthenon Frieze

The Parthenon frieze illustrated how the Athenians worshipped Athena and paid homage to her through their annual Panathenaic festival. This was the most important holiday in the Athenian calendar, at the start of the Attic year. The Great Panathenaia was held every four years, when the festival was celebrated on a larger scale, and the games for these were considered as important as the Olympic Games. People came from around the Greek world to take part. The prizes for winners were specially painted jars of olive oil, which was so prized that we have found several of these preserved in tombs as far away as Italy. The festival celebrated both the birth of the city's patron goddess and also the victory of the gods over the giants. The details of the festival are quite well known to us, and its great procession was represented on the frieze of the Parthenon.

The Panathenaia was supposedly founded by Theseus, and restructured by many statesmen over the years, including Pericles. Athenian colonies sent gifts and sacrifices, and by the mid-fifth century her 'allies' did too, reinforcing the nationalism of Athens and her empire through the festival. A small Archaic pediment, called the 'Olive Tree Pediment', may even have depicted the Panathenaic procession of the day, ending in front of the goddess's sacred tree on the Acropolis. The tree is one of the earliest depictions of landscape in Greek sculpture, and serves as a topographical marker giving the location as the sanctuary on the Acropolis.

In the frieze we see the Athenians participating in a festival during which they honoured the city's patron, Athena, and also glorified themselves and their city. The festival brought the Athenians into contact with the goddess, creating a link between the two through the form of sacrifices made to her, just as the Eucharist representing the sacrifice of Christ brings the Christian into contact with his God.

The ancient Athenians did not have regular days of rest, and so the many festivals would have allowed those who had to work time off. The festivals were such an important part of the calendar that many of the months were named after the festivals that took place during them. Although some festivals were exclusively for a particular group, such as women, the Panathenaia was the great occasion that united all the Athenians in celebration, and in which all could take part. All processed, citizens and non-citizens, male and female, the rich and slaves, of all different ages; they were differentiated by their dress and by the objects they carried, metics for example wearing red. Festivals played a large part in the lives of Athenians, but not all festivals were open to all, and there were so many that no one could hope to attend them all. The sacrifices did, however, provide an opportunity to eat meat, at a time when it was part of the diet of only the rich.

Each year the statue of Athena Polias was presented with a new robe, but at the quadrennial festival, which lasted nine days, the robe was larger and more lavish. The presentation of the robe was the main purpose of the festival, and since it was a gift of the entire population, everyone could take part in the procession that led up the hill to the Acropolis, where her temple was located. The robe had been woven over the nine months preceding the festival, crafted out of wool, and made by well-born maidens. The motif embroidered on it was the battle between the gods and giants, and seems to have been even more specifically the scene shown in the metopes in which Athena defeated the giant Enceladus.

It seems that only citizens could pass through the Propylaea during the procession, climbing on to the summit of the Acropolis and going to the temple of Athena Polias, where they would clothe the statue of the goddess in her new robe.

The use of the continuous Ionic frieze on the Parthenon, a Doric building, may not have been planned from the start. On the basis of small changes made to the architecture, it seems to have been an addition made after construction had begun, but is now considered one of the glories of the Parthenon. When we see it today in the British Museum – the Athenian portions having been mostly in storage until recently – one can admire the brilliance of the carving, where a procession up to four figures deep, with four riders represented side by side within a carved depth of centimetres, is miraculously carved into the marble, whose relief never projects more than a few centimetres forward.

The continuous Ionic frieze is often described as one of the unique features of the building. It was subsequently used on the temple of Hephaisteion, but otherwise it is assumed to have been an Ionian feature. The frieze is thus interpreted as symbolising Athenian dominance of the Aegean and Ionian Greeks who were by then part of her empire. The frieze may, however, be an Archaic Athenian feature. Part of a continuous frieze has been found on the Acropolis, stylistically dated to the later sixth century. Technical similarities, the coincidence of date and the lack of any other building with which to associate it, have led some archaeologists to assign it to the decoration of the old temple of Athena Polias. The three figures that survive from the frieze, a charioteer, a god, and a figure sitting on a stool, are all motifs also found on the later Parthenon frieze.

In recent years Ian Jenkins of the British Museum has done much research on the frieze, and has improved our understanding of it by correcting the order of the blocks. Because almost none of the blocks in the British Museum were taken off the building, we do not know where they were originally located on the Parthenon, and so their arrangement had not always been correct. We cannot move around the original blocks, but it has been possible to do so using casts thanks to the research undertaken by Professor Ernst Berger and the sculpture gallery in Basel, where a full set of casts of the Parthenon sculptures are held.

The background of the frieze seems to have been painted bright blue in antiquity, and the many figures represented would have been highlighted through the use of paint to assist clarity. Despite all this, one can question how successful the frieze was as a form of decoration. It was placed high on the outer wall of the cella, the main room of the Parthenon, behind the colonnade, in a dark space which the entablature in front of it on the exterior would have prevented from ever being lit by the sun, so casting it permanently in shadow and preventing it from being seen. If one walked around the Parthenon – itself unlikely to have been possible in antiquity due to the many buildings and structures dotted around it – one could still not have seen the entire frieze, since large sections of it would have been blocked and hidden by the columns in front of it. The columns broke it up visually, but also helped to break up the frieze into chronological episodes. One would also have had to start twice at the west end, following the frieze to its culmination at the east end, rather than simply walking around the building once. One would have to assume that Pheidias rather cleverly designed the frieze figures to be seen in groups, and for columns not to block the view of important figures. Although columns blocking certain figures such as riders or musicians along the north and south lengths might not have been a problem, to have deliberately designed the frieze so that some of the gods on the east side were covered by the columns in front of them seems almost a sign of impiety.

An optical illusion was used to make the frieze slightly more visible, by carving the figures a little deeper at the top of the frieze than at the bottom. And so perhaps the very fortunate, well-connected Athenians who could gain access to the colonnades might well have been able to walk around the frieze, perhaps followed by several of their slaves holding torches that would have lit the frieze and made it more visible. The vast majority of Athenians, even those who visited the Acropolis regularly, would not, however, have been able to see it.

Like the figures in the pediments, details of the figures on the frieze were added in bronze. Although these were lost a long time ago, the little holes into which the bronze attachments were inserted, or the holes for pins which held them in place, are preserved and so we can reconstruct them. On one figure bronze was used to represent the straps of his sandals, criss-crossing his ankles; elsewhere the Athenian men held spears and the horses had bridles and reins made of bronze.

One could argue that the Parthenon was created as a votive offering, a giant token of their appreciation by the Athenians for Athena. In that case, the sculpture was designed to be seen by Athena, rather than the Athenians, and so any lack of visibility of the frieze would have been irrelevant. Similarly, on large Gothic cathedrals we cannot see all the sculpture, but we know it is there, and this is impressive in itself.

The figures on the frieze were probably marked out on the marble slabs on the ground, and the primary carving done in the workshop, then finished once in place on the building. Finishing the carving *in situ* had two principal advantages; it meant that construction could continue on the architecture before the sculptures were finished, and so that architect was not delayed. It also meant that figures which were carved to overlap two blocks could join perfectly once those two blocks were in place, and additionally it meant that details in the carving could not be damaged as the blocks were hoisted up on to the building. The carving on all 119 blocks was pretty uniform, although one can note small differences in the way that, for example, the horses were carved, indicating the hands of several different sculptors. The blocks would have had to be on the building before the roof was added (c.438 BC).

Of all the Parthenon sculptures, we have more of the frieze than of any other category (the metopes or the pediments); the original frieze was 524 feet long, of which around 420, or 80 per cent, is preserved. The roof had not covered the colonnade from the late Roman period onwards, which although it improved viewing of the frieze, also meant that it was exposed to the elements, worn away by wind and rain for almost two thousand years. When Carrey visited the Parthenon in 1674 the building no longer had a roof between the cella interior room and the outer columns; this would have allowed sunlight to fall on the frieze, improving visibility. His drawings are confusing, and suggest that Carrey himself did not have an entirely clear view of the frieze, but they allow us to restore some of the missing sections.

The procession started on the western end of the Parthenon, splitting into two, and continuing down the north and south walls, culminating on the east front of the building over the main door. In the centre of the east side was a scene depicting priestesses of Athena carrying and folding her *peplos*. This scene was flanked by seated figures of the gods, who, being larger than mortals, would not have fitted the space had they been standing. Divided into two groups on either side of the central *peplos* scene, they must be conceptually understood to have been seated in a semicircular arrangement around the central and culminating episode of the procession, rather than as having physically 'broken up' the procession. To see the gods represented on the frieze would not have suggested to the Athenian viewer that they were on the Acropolis; rather he would have been able to identify their position as being on Mount Olympus, looking down at the Athenians below them.

The procession was always thought to culminate with this central *peplos* scene. Then the brilliant Greek archaeologist Manolis Korres, who has devoted his life to the study of the Parthenon, was able to reconstruct the architecture of the building using a computer. He worked out that the frieze continued within the pronaos, the small porch between the outer colonnade and the cella on the east. No fragments of this frieze have yet been identified, and they would almost certainly have been lost when the Parthenon was turned into a Greek church and that part of the building destroyed. So although we know that a frieze was planned for that area, we cannot be certain that it was ever carved, or know what had been intended to be depicted there. Given the amount of effort put into the construction of the Parthenon, and that it was one of the few buildings on the Acropolis that seems to have been finished, it is likely that the frieze was executed. This has led to a further debate: did the frieze continue the procession depicted on the exterior, or was another subject represented?

Visitors to the Parthenon approaching along the northern side would have seen more of the frieze than those who tried to view it from the south. The northern frieze began on the west end, and continued along the north side, ending in the middle of the east front; while the south frieze ran along the southern side and part of the east. Pausanias, our ancient source for the sculpture of the Parthenon, does not mention the frieze. This does not mean that he was unable to see it, but rather that he was not particularly interested in architectural sculpture, and rarely bothered to mention it; he mentions the pediments of the Parthenon, not the metopes.

At the beginning of the procession we can see figures still preparing, bending over to tie their sandals; to do this they rest their feet on rocks, early examples of landscaping within Greek sculpture. Elsewhere, figures are turning back, going against the general direction of the procession, to interact with those behind them and to emphasise the relationship between the figures, as well as to break up the monotony of the frieze. The procession began at sunrise, which was also the time frame of the scene in the east pediment above the culminating scene of the procession.

The longer northern procession on the frieze started with the depiction of twenty-six Athenians on horses, another eleven riders preparing to mount, two figures that are identified as marshals who supervised the procession, and two more young attendants. The riders are all young, probably men who also served in the Athenian army, and this is indicated by their lack of beards. Only two of the riders on the frieze have beards: one is represented in the centre of the west side, holding down the reins of his rearing horse; the motif of a figure and a rearing animal was common in Periclean sculpture, and implied the superiority of man over beast. This mass of men on horses, cavalry, are rich Athenians, since the poor could not afford the luxury of a horse. Although many might have owned horses in a country such as England, where there was a great deal of land for grazing, in Attica horses were a status symbol since the land was rocky. As some of the Greeks are already on their horses, and others only preparing to mount, so the procession is beginning on the west side, and preparations still being made. However, these first figures also cause our first problem, since we know that riders did not take part in the Panathenaic procession.

Most of these riders are naked, with the accentuated musculature of athletes; men familiar with physical activity, which formed part of the day-to-day lives of fifth-century Athenians. The Greeks equated a good body with a good mind, and so those who had physical deformities were often assumed to have mental deformities. Some wear hats known as Thracian caps, headgear usually associated with Amazons, Trojans, Persians and other eastern peoples. These caps may well be intended to be seen as having been taken off their recently defeated Persian enemies. A few riders appear in full armour.

In some ways the groups of riders are very similar, having almost identical faces and almost all facing the same way, with similarities in both their pose and design, but there are also notable differences in the details represented such as costume, gesture and stance. Despite the loss of most of their attributes, because they were originally added in bronze, these too varied to add interest, and are quite distinctive. The riders are in quite a loose formation as they congregate at the start, becoming more regimented and moving into ranks as they turn on to the long sides of the Parthenon where the procession is under way. They are tightly packed and so the bodies and heads of men and horses overlap repeatedly. Although there are enough superficial similarities between them to create a pattern and sense of rhythm, there is also no repetition of their variations, so that they are also all individuals at the same time.

In front of these riders were eleven chariots drawn by four horses each, with charioteers and armed soldiers. The chariots seem to be moving swiftly, with the athletes jumping on and off, a sense of speed created by the horses' flaring nostrils and their manes flowing behind them.

Chariots were not used in battle in Greek warfare at the time. These chariots instead represented a sport that was part of the Panathenaic Games, in which *apabatae*, or armed soldiers, jumped on and off the chariot until it had crossed the finish line. Horses were not as useful to the Greeks as they later were to the Byzantines, mostly because stirrups did not make their way from the east to the Mediterranean until the fourth century AD when they were introduced by 'barbarians' from Central Asia. Since the chariots represented a sporting event rather than part of the procession, marshals were needed to supervise the event, and these appear dotted among the chariots along with grooms.

In front of the chariots are sixteen men whose beards identify them as being among the older generation. Then eight musicians playing flutes and *kitharae* (a form of harp), four boys carrying jugs and three carrying trays of cakes are depicted. These walking figures would appear in the procession in front of the chariots, and are mostly represented in groups of four figures to help break up the frieze and to add interest to it by doing so.

The next figures are attendants who lead the animals to be slaughtered to Athena: four cows and four sheep. It seems that animals to be sacrificed to gods and goddesses were partly chosen on the basis of their sex. In the frieze female animals, such as heifers, are being led to their slaughter. Animals would then be sacrificed, roasted and eaten. As meat was not part of the daily diet for many Athenians, festivals provided an opportunity to eat it. The torch that lit the fire beneath these animals was important, and the fire came from a sanctuary of Eros located outside the Dipylon Gate.

The figures carved on the south frieze are similar to those carved on the north. The procession begins with ten rows of riders represented as processing six abreast. There is much variety in the dress of the riders, although those within each rank wore the same costume. As on the north, in front of these are ten chariots from the *apabatae* race. Then there are more elders, presumably also musicians, although those blocks of the frieze are missing. In front of them young boys carry water jars and other vessels on their shoulders. Again animals being led to sacrifice are represented, although on the south frieze only cows are depicted.

As both processions reach their culmination to the east, they turn the corner of the building and continue processing along the east frieze. It is here that the first Athenian women are represented; none appear on any of the other three sides of the frieze. Sixteen fully draped women are carved, in voluminous *peploi*, most of them also carrying ritual objects, such as incense burners and *phialai* (shallow silver or gold bowls from which oil was poured as a libation on to altars).

These women on the southern part of the east frieze are balanced to the north by a baker's dozen of women and four men whose identities are not certain, but who were probably officials involved in the organisation of the procession. One of the women passes a basket to one of the men. This identifies her as a maiden from a good family who has been awarded the honour of leading the Panathenaic procession, and of initiating the sacrifices to Athena that were part of it. The maidens standing behind her were called *canephorae* (*phorae* literally means 'carriers of', and *cane* means 'baskets'). Their dress differs slightly from that of the other women.

All these women would have been mortal well-born Athenian women who before marriage were permitted to take part in the cult of Athena. The objects they carried would often have been made of gold, and would later have been kept inside the Parthenon as part of the treasure of the goddess. As these women were all unmarried maidens from good families, one wonders to what extent festivals were used to 'show them off' to prospective suitors, rather in the way that 'the Season' in Britain was long used to introduce young women to society and to marry them off. Women rarely ventured outside the house, so festivals would have provided one of the few occasions for them to do so.

Next are male figures with staffs. They are carved on a slightly larger scale than the rest of the frieze. Since there are ten of these figures, and their size indicates that they are not human, but also not as important as the gods, we can identify them as the Ten Eponymous Heroes of Attica, the ten Athenians after whom the ten tribes into which Attica was divided were named. Staffs were symbols of authority, and legendary kings and heroes were depicted with staffs elsewhere in Athenian sculpture. These figures were heroes whose status fell between that of mortals and that of the gods, and served as a link between the two in the frieze, bridging the two meta-physically by acting as intermediaries through Athenian history, and also physically linking the two within the sculpture in terms of scale. Heroes were paid honours by living Athenians, who hoped that these would intercede on their behalf with the gods.

Next come seven gods on each side, the six more important gods seated on stools, and a lesser non-Olympian god standing flanking each group. To the left of the central scene is either Nike or Iris, the messenger of the Gods; on the right the standing male god is Eros, the son of Aphrodite. The gods interact with each other, but not with the heroes or with the humans; they are on Olympus watching the procession, not taking part in it. They are depicted in a rather gentler, more domestic, manner than is normal, as if at home on Mount Olympus they did not need to carry their armour and weapons. Athena can be identified by the aegis, the goatskin cloak, that rests on her lap.

The group of gods are there to set Athena within the context of the Olympian gods, to bear witness to the fact that the Athenians were properly practising her cult, and to represent the gods who also had cults on the Acropolis. The frieze – and also the other sculptures – represented the power of Periclean Athens, achieved thanks to the blessing of Athena as her reward for their devotion and sacrifices.

The first seated god's left arm is raised and would once have held a bronze staff topped by a pine cone, identifying him as Dionysus. Dionysus' sanctuary was almost immediately below this end of the Parthenon, to the south. He was linked through agriculture to Demeter, the goddess of grain, the figure to the right. Demeter is often represented in rather a pensive fashion, as here, where she is seen leaning forward to rest her chin on her right hand. In her left hand one sees a torch made out of bundles of wheat. This reflects the dual nature of the goddess who spent half the year mourning for her daughter in dark Hades.

Next is Ares, the god of war, whose attribute, the spear, was originally painted in, only its carved lower end preserved next to his left foot. The smaller standing woman behind him is Iris, who acted as a messenger to the gods without being an Olympian herself. Hera comes after Ares, her arm lifting up her veil, a traditional gesture used to represent a bride. She faces her husband Zeus to her right, who as the king of the gods is the only one represented seated on a chair rather than a stool. He is bearded, which indicates maturity rather than any great age, the gods being ageless. He holds a sceptre as a symbol of his power in his left hand.

To the right of the central *peplos* scene, the first figure we see is Athena, the recipient of the robe, and of course the most important goddess in Athens. Her aegis lies across her lap since she is represented in her feminine guise rather than as a warrior; just in case, she had a spear, again lost since it was originally created in bronze. She interacts and probably chats with the god to the right of her, Hephaestus, the blacksmith god who had cut open Zeus' head at her birth; he had a club foot which is diplomatically concealed by the leg of one of the stools, but one can still make out the crutch under his right arm. These two were the legendary progenitors of the first Athenian.

The gods are arranged in pairs, and the next pair is made up of Poseidon who taps the shoulder of the younger god in front of him, Apollo. Apollo's sister Artemis links her arm through that of her companion Aphrodite. These two goddesses wear elaborate robes, characterised by crinkly folds, which are associated with the style of Alcamenes, the pupil of Pheidias who had carved the pediments. Both also wear turban-like scarves that cover most of their hair, a deliberately archaising feature. The closeness between the two goddesses initially seems surprising since Artemis was known for her chastity, a virgin who killed any men who saw her naked, while Aphrodite we associate today with sex. In fact, Aphrodite as represented here was the patron of marital love, and Artemis was the patron of women in childbirth.

Aphrodite's and Artemis' legs overlap, and they echo each other in pose; a fragment of these is in Palermo Museum. When the Greeks thought that they had managed to convince the Italian government to return that fragment to Athens, the fragment was often described as depicting Peitho, Aphrodite's daughter and the personification of Persuasion. This was a misinterpretation. Aphrodite is accompanied on the frieze by one of her children, but this is her son Eros, clearly a boy rather than a girl since he is depicted naked, with most of his penis still preserved. Aphrodite's left arm reaches forward over his shoulder, to point to the maidens in the procession to the right of her. This emphasises the idea that the aristocratic maidens were paraded at the Panathenaia in preparation for finding a husband. Aphrodite's son in turn held a parasol in his left hand with which to provide her with shade, and to preserve her porcelain white skin, whiteness being seen as a sign of beauty by the Greeks.

The frieze is almost symmetrical on the east side of the building, with equal numbers of gods, then heroes and finally priestesses of Athena, all flanking and framing the *peplos* scene.

The central scene on the east, where the procession culminated, was the first block of the frieze to be taken off the building by the Byzantine Greeks, and so is the most weathered. This scene, which was immediately over the entrance that led into the Parthenon, is set once again in Athens, rather than among the gods, and so the size of the figures carved is smaller, as they represent humans, mortals. Two women on the left have folded bundles of fabric balanced on their heads and small objects in one hand, which we can no longer identify since the marble there has worn away. To their right are three figures, the first of which faces them in profile. Behind her back is another large figure, a bearded man, who unfolds the cloth that would be pinned into a *peplos* dress for Athena, helped by a young boy. The Panathenaic procession ended in the gift of a new dress to Athena, and this is the scene represented here.

As the central *peplos* scene is framed by the gods, and so set apart from the rest of the procession, it is possible to suggest that this scene does not represent contemporary events, but rather the mythological first festival and the folding of the *peplos* by Cecrops and Erechtheus. Or it could represent later Athenians re-enacting the folding of the *peplos* by these two kings, and each year the

Panathenaia did in fact re-enact this historical event, tying in the Athens of the day with the Athens of the glorious past. The scene could have both of these meanings, the two not being contradictory and illustrating the way that having one clear interpretation is a modern obsession that the Greeks did not necessarily share.

The importance of this scene is emphasised by the fact that it is flanked first by seated gods, then by Attica's Eponymous Heroes, and later at the ends of the east side by young women of marriageable age, who presumably would marry and reproduce, so creating future generations for the Athenian state. Those young women were the same girls who wove the *peplos* nine months before. Athena was the patron of weaving, and she had given this gift to her people, who in turn offered her a prime example of the art. Today we generally buy our clothes in shops. In the past spinning yarn and then weaving it was seen as a suitable activity for a woman, and practised by the highest born, although among queens that might well have been largely for show, to present a picture of virtue. Later, towards the end of the first century BC, when Livia claimed she spun the wool for the clothes Augustus wore, this was seen as an affectation.

We next have to work out where the events depicted took place. The procession takes place in a number of locations, beginning at the Dipylon Gate, and since the riders seem to be preparing to mount their horses on the west, the early part of the frieze was located there. The Athenians would then have wound their way along the road, through the agora. Although the *apabatae* are represented after the riders, these figures took part in the games associated with the festival rather than practising their sport during it. After the agora the road continued up the lower slopes of the Acropolis to its summit. This is where sacrifices, represented by the animals being led, would have taken place and where the *peplos* was presented to the statue of Athena in her temple. The frieze thus represents not one moment of the procession, but rather many episodes of the Great Panathenaia procession and games, beginning at the town gate and ending on the Acropolis itself.

The procession depicted on the Parthenon frieze is problematic in many ways. The procession could be either a mythological/

historical one, or a representation of the procession that took place in Athens each year, or even a blend of the two. We expect the images carved on temple-like buildings in Greece to be mythological, and so if the procession is also a mythological one, it would fit within this framework we have for Greek art. After the Persian Wars, however, the Athenians began increasingly to portray events from the recent past. A colossal fresco of the recent battle of Marathon had been painted in a public stoa (portico) in the agora, the commercial and administrative heart of the city. Later, we can also see that the friezes on the Nike temple would represent battles the Athenians had fought in the historical period, although by then those battles might have been seen as part of the glorious past that blended in with its mythological history.

If we identify the procession as a mythological one, the most obvious to have been depicted would have been the very first Panathenaic procession, which was the one instituted during the lifetime of Erechtheus. This king is also credited with having invented the chariot, which is given prominence in the frieze. Those taking part in the procession would thus be the early Athenians, those heroes and heroines that were by then part of mythological history. If the procession took place in the lifetime of Erechtheus, he would be the young man holding the first *peplos* in the central scene, and the older bearded man would be King Cecrops. The women on the left would be Cecrops' daughters, one of whom is carved next to him in the west pediment. If the bearded man were indeed Cecrops, one would assume that something would identify him, such as a snake at his feet, but no such attribute is present.

One can read into the ten rows of horsemen depicted the idea that these represented the Ten Tribes of Attica, and so must postdate the establishment of those tribes; the carving certainly does, and so if this is indeed a mythical early Panathenaia, arranging the figures in this way would be anachronistic, although not a clear argument against a depiction of the first festival as such historical anachronisms are a modern concept.

Since the Parthenon was a monument to Athenian superiority over the Persians, and their victories over these eastern neighbours in recent wars, particularly at the Battle of Marathon, Sir John

Boardman points out that the Panathenaia immediately before that battle might have been depicted. This interpretation is extremely appealing since it combines the images we have carved on the frieze with the greater meaning that we know the Athenians placed on the Parthenon.

Since the procession depicted cannot be identified as a specific mythological one, and indeed the attempt to do so was highly unsuccessful, the remaining options are that it depicted the contemporary Panathenaic procession, or a more generalised, generic procession. No other Greek architectural sculpture depicted a contemporary event, but the Battle of Marathon had already been depicted in a monumental painting in a civic monument not long after it had taken place.

Boardman draws a clear link between the procession and the Battle of Marathon. He points out that the battle took place in 490 BC, which was a year in which a Great Panathenaia was held, and that it was fought soon after the festival. The battle is usually believed to have taken place in September, although several scholars have recently argued that August might be the correct month, while the procession as part of the festival was held in midsummer by our calendar. Since the procession was intended to highlight every class in Athens, particularly the warriors and athletes, athletics being practised as part of military training, those that later fought at Marathon would have taken part in the procession and competed in the associated games.

The 192 men who fell in the battle on the Athenian side were later heroised and accorded honours by the city. Boardman has noted that in total 192 men, excluding male gods and the figures in the central scene, are represented on the Parthenon frieze. He thus argues that the Panathenaic procession represented in the frieze is the procession that took place in 490 BC, a procession set in the past and also one that pays homage to the Athenian heroes that died at Marathon. The flaw with this theory is that some panels are missing, and there might have been more men depicted on these, but one could still reach the glorious 192 through different calculations, such as excluding the older men and marshals.

If his interpretation is correct, then one can note that the Battle of Marathon was represented in the Agora stoa in the company of the mythological battle against the Amazons and the sack of Troy. Both those stories were also shown on the Parthenon, in the metopes, and within the Parthenon on the shield of Athena. Thus distant history, known as myth, is associated with recent history, the line between the two blurred and so the distinction – largely a modern distinction – lost. The procession representing the one that took place immediately before the battle would also be appropriate since the Parthenon replaced a building that the Athenians had begun after Marathon to thank Athena for the victory. Since men such as Demosthenes, writing a century later, described the Parthenon as a giant trophy to the Greek victory in the Persian Wars, paid out of loot taken off those Persians, it would be particularly appropriate if the supreme Athenians' victory was also commemorated on it. The battle itself would of course be carved a couple of decades later on the south frieze of the temple of Athena Nike.

To try to see the frieze as a procession of the mid-fifth century, one has to note the numerous times when the images carved contradict our many literary sources describing the festival. The figures carrying water jars on the frieze are male, while those in the procession were female. Although artistic licence and lack of space easily account for the things that are missing, such as the ship which was brought on to the Acropolis for the Great Panathenaia after Salamis, and the Athenian Hoplite soldiers, other elements are added that were not part of the procession, and figures seem mysteriously to have changed sex.

The strongest argument that the frieze is not a Periclean depiction is that the Delian League allies bringing tribute to the city are not represented. In Periclean times, since Athens had an empire, her allies brought gifts to the goddess of a cow and suit of armour. These allies could only be depicted after the creation of the Delian League, and after it they would almost certainly have been shown, since Athenian supremacy was important to its self-image, and since the Parthenon was the ultimate expression of this self-image. The lack of a ship is also rather telling in terms of date, since this was once again a great propaganda symbol, representing the Athenian dominance of the sea.

Discrepancies and outright contradictions between descriptions and the frieze suggest that this may not even have been a Panathenaic procession. The figures in the frieze are quite clearly processing, and chosen to represent the best of Athens. Rather than immediately dismiss it as not having been the Panathenaia, perhaps one should think of it instead as not being the Panathenaia in Pericles' day, but instead one from an earlier period, about which we have less evidence. The frieze would thus show excerpts of an older procession that took place in 'the past'. Contradictions do not seem to have bothered the Athenians when depicting this past. They were rather more interested in glorifying it, and presenting it in the best possible light. If one can accept this, then we should turn next to trying to find which particular age the procession was set in.

Since somebody went to a great deal of trouble to incorporate the frieze in the building, first changing the design of the Parthenon to accommodate it and then spending a great deal of money on the carving, it seems more likely that they intended it to have a specific meaning, and to represent a festival that was central to Athenian life, epitomising all that was great about the state, rather than a mishmash of various minor festivals. The central scene quite clearly depicts the folding of the *peplos*, and so places that scene not only physically on the Acropolis but also temporally within the Panathenaia. If the frieze were placed on the temple of Athena Polias, one could be certain that it represented the Panathenaic procession which terminated there. Since it was not, one can see problems with it if one wishes to. The frieze was instead located on the Parthenon. Although not technically a temple to Athena, the building was designed for a colossal statue of her, and all the other sculptural decoration on it is associated with her myth and cult. Given that all the other sculpture was associated with Athena, one can assume the same for the frieze, and so it must be seen as depicting a procession in her honour.

Some of these soldiers wear armour, and can be understood as idealised soldiers, whether contemporary or semi-historical, but others are naked, nudity being acceptable for mythological Heroes, like the battles represented elsewhere on the Parthenon. Horses were great status symbols and usually associated with aristocratic citizens, or when trying to emphasise status such as for Heroes. To depict contemporary mortals, whether the Parthenon was a temple or not, was unprecedented in an age where portraits were rare and a great honour.

I see great difficulties in identifying the procession on the frieze as a purely contemporary depiction of the Panathenaic procession, since there seem to be large discrepancies between what is depicted and what we know formed part of that procession. The idea that the frieze instead depicted the Marathon Panathenaia is highly appealing, and in my opinion one of the most convincing interpretations put forward so far. Detractors of this theory point out that the Greeks at Marathon fought on foot, while the figures in the frieze are mostly on horseback or in chariots. Although ordinary Athenian soldiers did fight on foot, those that died had of course by then become Heroes, and so it is appropriate that they would have been represented riding horses, as befitted their new status. Placing them on horseback lifted them above ordinary mortal Athenians, and honoured them.

To see the frieze as representing a Panathenaic procession from the time of Pericles is problematic. Most Athenians either took part in the Panathenaia, or watched it, so they would have been aware that their great procession differed from the procession carved in the frieze. The figures in the frieze are of course highly idealised, although almost all images of humans were idealised at the time. This would thus be a self-portrait of the Athenians, of their Heroes, and of their gods.

Although contemporary events had never been represented in the sculptural decoration of a temple, one can point out that the Parthenon was not a temple proper, but rather a giant votive to Athena, which glorified the Athenians themselves, and contemporary events were regularly and routinely represented in votive reliefs. In any case there are so many features of the Parthenon that are unprecedented and unique, that one more of these should not cause alarm. Just as the boundary between history and myth was blurred to the Greeks, so one could argue that the difference between what was represented and what took place in the procession could also be nebulous.

Since the French Revolution in 1789, and through communist

propaganda in the twentieth century, we have become used to the notion of an idealised representation of the 'ordinary man'. Although the Greeks favoured personifications as concepts, ideas or emotions, they generally did not have a concept of an idealised mortal. Today we have the concept of the Unknown Soldier to represent the dead in a war, but the Athenians knew all those who had died in any particular battle, since Athens was a very small state. To read the frieze as a generic procession of idealised Athenians is almost impossible to reconcile with what we know of their art, and would have been even more lacking in precedent than the depiction of a contemporary or near-contemporary event.

The Byzantine windows broke the frieze in several places. One window removed block 22 along the south side, removing several of the riders from the procession. Block 30 originally had a chariot group, but again was lost to create a window. Another window removed block 38, where there had once been musicians. Many of the central blocks are also lost since these were destroyed during the explosion in 1687, and so blanks must be filled in using a combination of seventeenth-century drawings and conjecture.

Carving all the exterior metopes of such a large temple-like building was an extremely extravagant gesture. In the past small temples and shrines, such as the treasuries of Delphi, had sometimes had all of those panels decorated with relief sculpture, but monumental buildings, such as the Parthenon, had never been decorated so elaborately. Doric temples in the Peloponnese had had figured metopes, but those were always restricted to the interiors of the temples, across the two porches within the colonnade, and so were far fewer in number. The original design of the Parthenon may well have had metopes in that same location, crowning the wall around the inner chamber.

At some point, however, Pheidias must have decided to replace those metopes with a continuous Ionic frieze. This meant that the temple's plan would also have had to be revised. In recent years we have discovered, thanks to the work of Greek archaeologists such as Manolis Korres, that the frieze not only ran around the exterior of the cella, but also around the interior of the two porches at either

end of it. Actually, evidence has only been found for the frieze continuing within the pronaos, but given the ancient love of symmetry
shown by the designers of the temple, and the lavish decoration of
it, it is likely to have been planned for the other porch as well.

From this we can deduce that the architecture was of secondary
importance to the architectural sculpture, and even more so to the
great statue of Athena Parthenos within the building. Pheidias is only
known for certain to have created the statue inside, but from later
sources we know that he was in charge of the project, and so it is safe
to assume that he designed the architectural sculpture, although its
execution was left to lesser sculptors and to masons. A hierarchy of
importance among these is difficult to ascertain. We know that on
prestigious projects, such as the Parthenon, and later the creation of
the temple of Asclepius at Epidaurus, the pay was a token one drachma
a day. Although some try to use this drachma to work out the wages
of skilled labourers and workmen, the figure remains static over several
centuries and so probably had a symbolic financial value.

At Epidaurus the architectural sculptors, some of whom subsequently became famous, are also known to have created the model
for architectural elements such as lion-headed waterspouts.
Elsewhere, simple designs in architectural sculpture, friezes that were
often no more than ornamental bands, were often carved by the
same masons that carved the architectural elements. The evidence
is confusing, and one can deduce little concrete from it; sometimes
architects designed ornament, and at other times those who normally
worked in ornamentation also carved sculpture.

It is highly unlikely that Pheidias carved any of the Parthenon
himself; it would have been delegated to lesser sculptors, and it is
in any case difficult to find a point within his career when he would
have had the time to do so. He was busy creating and overseeing
the construction of the Athena Parthenos until 438 BC, when it was
installed in the Parthenon. After 438 he was no longer in Athens;
he had gone to Olympia, where he would create the colossal gold
and ivory cult statue of a seated Zeus for the temple there, a statue
which would become a Wonder of the Ancient World.

The set-up of ancient sculpture workshops, which centred on a
master, can be compared to those of the Renaissance in Italy. We

rarely know who the sculptors that formed part of one of these work-shops were, unless they subsequently became famous in their own right. Agoracritus and Alcamenes, later famous Athenian sculptors, are known to have been Pheidias' pupils, and are usually assumed to have done much of the work on the pedimental sculptures and on the frieze. The metopes are much poorer in style; although the technique used in the high relief is admirable, they are generally assigned to masons. Another assistant of Pheidias we know of is Menon, because of his later treacherous behaviour. The only exception to this is a minor sculptor who worked for Scopas at Tegea; we know of him because he died an unusual death, rather than for his skill as a sculptor. In recent years, as the Parthenon has been dismantled to remove the remaining sculpture, and in preparation for reconstruction of the building, one block has been found with a name painted in red; this signature, of Xanthias the Thracian, would not have been visible in antiquity. He may well have been involved in the carving of the metopes, or been one of the masons who worked on the architecture.

The exact nature of Pheidias' role in the overall design of the Parthenon can never be certain, but it is likely that he supervised the architecture that would frame his colossal Athena Parthenos, and that he designed much of the architectural sculpture, presumably making at least drawings of the scenes he envisaged as decorating the Parthenon, possibly even making small terracotta maquettes of the pedimental sculptures, a practice that seems to be attested at other sites.

Within the Parthenon sculpture one can see many forms of hierarchy. The Athenians themselves, whether contemporary or of the recent past, are carved on the frieze in low relief. The more heroic and more ancient Athenians are carved in high relief in the metopes. The gods, however – and many Greeks in the period before the Parthenon was built saw the gods as partly inhabiting sculpture carved to represent them – are depicted larger than life-size, and carved fully in the round. The frieze was partly hidden and so less visible; this made it the appropriate place where mere man should be depicted. The Gods in the pediment are the most visible, and the biggest, figures, showing that there was a hierarchy both of scale, of relief and of visibility.

The Greeks who built the Parthenon lived two and a half thousand years ago, and although many of their texts and histories survive, it is almost impossible to put ourselves back into their shoes, or sandals, and to be able to understand how they themselves interpreted the Parthenon sculptures, because they are extremely remote from us. Therefore it is difficult for us to interpret the sculptures, and to be certain exactly what was represented, and what meaning was intended.

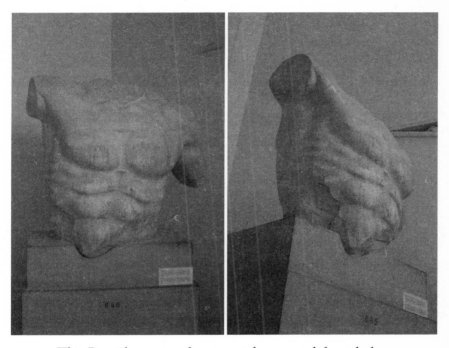

The Poseidon torso from straight on and from below

The two photographs above show the torso of Poseidon from the west pediment. On the left he is seen front on, as arranged in the display in Athens, and photographed at eye level. Heavily muscled, he looks like a male stripper, but the pose seems banal and of little interest. But since the statue originally stood fourteen metres off the ground and at an angle within the gable, as seen in the photograph on the right, this added interest and emphasised his pose, making it far more dramatic. I also crouched down to take the photograph, showing how lowering the viewing angle by even a metre changes the whole mood of the sculpture.

When we see the sculptures in a museum today, whether in London or in Athens, it is a distorted vision of them that we gain. The pedimental sculptures were of course designed to be far off the ground, so when we view them close up, we can note many details that Greeks viewers would have been unaware of. These details are even more noticeable on the frieze, which was carved with great delicacy and includes such minute details as fingernails, and the small lines everyone has over their knuckles, as well as the veins under the horses' bellies and other minutiae. Since we have established that the frieze was barely visible on the building, and that paint was used to highlight the figures, these details would not have been visible to the Athenians. They seem almost to be a waste of carving, in our modern world vision, where we assume that what cannot be seen cannot be appreciated.

To the designers of the Parthenon they were probably creating these details to show that they could, as much as anything else. Also, the sculptures were designed to be viewed by the gods, who would be able to see and appreciate those details. In this sense one can argue that the Parthenon frieze was not a success. I wrote my Ph.D. thesis on the temples and monuments built in the following centuries, studying how they were decorated, and how they were influenced by Periclean buildings. No subsequent temple or monument had such detailed architectural sculpture, almost as if later generations had realised that the effort had been largely futile.

Although we have noted the many refinements that were incorporated within the architecture, we often forget that similar refinements were incorporated within the sculptures. These optical illusions mean that the sculptures sometimes appear distorted when seen at eye level in a museum, but that they would have appeared more 'correct' when seen from far below. In many ways these distortions were more useful within the sculpture than the architecture.

A good example is on the frieze of the Parthenon. When one

looks at the many rows of riders, proportionally the riders themselves look almost too large for their horses. Although ancient horses were slightly shorter than modern ones, part of the reason for this is so that the riders would look in proportion when seen from the ground twelve metres below.

Distortions are particularly notable in the metopes where limbs, in dramatic poses, are often 'corrected'. Interestingly, some metopes whose compositions are criticised as being 'stilted' or 'weak' when seen in a museum often look a lot better when seen from far below. A prime example of this is S26. It is sometimes criticised by art historians as being 'crude' in design, and having an inferior composition. Its neighbour S27 looks perfect when seen from straight in front, but would in fact have been less successful high on the building. Elsewhere within the battle, one can see that in S31 the head of the Lapith is too large, again for the same reason, but the great height at which it would have been placed on the building would have compensated for this.

Going back to the frieze, we can see that the figures closer to us are carved in high relief and those further from us in lower relief against the background. To emphasise the figures that were considered more important, we can note that they were carved not just in two dimensions but that the sculptors worked a little around them, almost as if in much-flattened three dimensions. This makes the figures look as if they are sinking into the horses, which are soft and cushioning them, and designed to make the figures stand out. Otherwise, the frieze mostly looks almost as if it has been drawn on to a long strip of paper, and then the figures 'fleshed out' so that they are lightly in relief.

The pedimental sculptures were finished and inserted within the gables of the Parthenon by 432 BC, according to the preserved building accounts. Although the blocks on which the frieze was carved must have been on the building before the roof and architectural elements above were added, and so at least a year or two before the building was complete in 438 BC, this does not mean that the frieze had also been fully carved by then. Several scholars suggest that the frieze was carved when the blocks were already *in situ*, that is in place. They point out that both the frieze and the pedimental sculptures are similar in style, and considerably more advanced than the sculptures on the metopes. The metopes and the frieze were twelve metres above ground level, and the pedimental sculptures even higher, making them difficult to view.

The various myths a city adopted to illustrate its history are vital in trying to identify the way in which they thought of themselves. Myths defined national identity. Even before the age of literacy the names of those heroes who featured in mythology lived on through their stories, passed from father to son through the generations. The sculptures on the temple at Tegea for example represent local myths. The scenes carved in the sculptures of the Parthenon make it clear that Athena was supremely important to the city. She is involved in almost every battle depicted in the Metopes. Her birth and the manner in which she won Athens are depicted in the pediments. The continuous frieze that ran around the temple does depict Athena, but its main emphasis was to represent the festival the Athenians held in her honour. Some scenes represented ancient kings, born from the earth, to emphasise that the Athenians were indigenous to Attica rather than conquerors. Elsewhere Theseus, another ancient Athenian king, was shown achieving great things, all of which would bring glory to his city.

The birth of Athena and the contest between her and Poseidon were central to the myth of Athens. Both episodes were depicted in the two gables of the Parthenon, and in statue groups elsewhere on the Acropolis. Athena was mostly depicted as a warrior in Athenian sculpture. It is rather surprising that in the Parthenon frieze she is represented more as a woman, immediately to the right of the central scene. The goddess wears a dress, a *peplos*, rather than full armour. The armour is still represented, allowing us to identify the figure of Athena; her goatskin cloak is draped over her lap, and she once held a spear added in bronze. She has however neither a helmet nor a shield. Athena is represented in one of her usual martial guises, but rather as a woman having a well-earned rest after all the victories she had helped the Athenians to win.

Athena as warrior was the predominant image of the goddess on the Acropolis. Pheidias was responsible for several of these images; the Athena Promachos, the Athena funded by the Athenian colony on Lemnos, and not least the Athena Parthenos. Reliefs and small bronzes also depicted Athena in the guise of a warrior. Several ancient writers praise the Athena Lemnia as the greatest sculpture created by Pheidias. The giant bronze Athena Promachos had, according to several sources, been funded by Persian goods seized after Marathon, showing that the importance of Marathon continued to be emphasised by the Athenians in the Roman period, when they still repeated this fact to Roman visitors such as Pausanias.

A Greek inscription preserved today allows us to know that the statue cost eighty-three talents and took nine years to make. The way in which Greek letters were carved changed continuously over the years, allowing us to date many inscriptions with great precision even if they do not include a date within their text. The shape of the letters on this inscription belongs to the early 450s BC, and so the statue must have been created in the decade before that, probably after the Peace of Kallias. Persian armour and spoils had been melted down and used to create instead a colossal statue to the Athenians' victory in the battle, standing in a prime position immediately opposite the gateway, and so the first image anyone climbing up on to the Acropolis would see.

The Palladion became the most famous statue type depicting Athena. There Pallas Athena was shown standing in full armour. The origin of the Palladion was a statue in Troy, taken after the fall of the city in the Bronze Age, first by the citizens of Argos, and later captured from them by the Athenians. This depiction of Athena as a warrior became popular in the Archaic period and continued well into the Classical one; the statue of Athena in the Parthenon was a variation of it. The Palladion itself was depicted twice in the north metopes on the Parthenon. In one scene Helen clings to the statue, seeking sanctuary, and protection from the wrath of her husband whom she had abandoned ten years before. Another scene shows the rape of Cassandra in front of the Palladion.

This statue type developed into a more active, less emphatic depiction of the goddess as warrior; the Athena Promachos. A colossal bronze statue of this type was created by Pheidias on the Acropolis, one of his first large commissions. The statue was famous not just for its size, but also because it reflected the sun, and sailors out at sea would know that it meant that they would soon be returning to Athens. The statue predated the initiation of the Periclean building programme, but was the first major commission for the Acropolis after it had been sacked by the Persians. The statue therefore acted as a trophy, to celebrate the Athenians defeat of their eastern neighbours. The piles of armour taken off the Persians were later stored in the Parthenon, but before it had been built may well have been stacked around the base of this statue.

The pediments are the triangular spaces within the ends of the gables, and into which statues were placed to create narrative scenes. They measured just under twenty-nine metres across, and 3.4 metres high; although this appears to be a large space, the shape of the gable, like a squashed triangle, meant that it was difficult to position figures within it. Earlier Greeks had chosen simple motifs to decorate pediments, such as the head of a gorgon in the centre, or two figures facing each other; mythological beasts, which could have snake tails that crawled behind them and filled the angles of the gable, were popular.

By the time of the Parthenon pediments, which were filled with larger than life-size figures, a solution to filling this awkward space with sculpture had been found. Standing and near-standing figures filled the centre. The figures become smaller in scale if they were less important as they moved towards the corners, to compensate for the diminishing height of the gable. They were followed by seated figures, and then reclining ones, figures lying down being the only thing that could be fitted into the wings of the gables. Battles, although not represented in the Parthenon pediments, were particularly appropriate for pediments because one could show dying soldiers and then dead ones, corpses, which were a convenient way of filling the space.

After Pericles

The Fourth Century and the Macedonians

In 393 BC, after the Peloponnesian Wars, Konon rebuilt Athens' Long Walls which linked the city to her Piraeus port. That the rebuilding of these walls was paid for with Persian funds seems ironic, since the Persians had funded the Spartans during the wars, and it was those Spartans that had destroyed them. Despite Athens' defeat, the city survived as a remarkably unstable democracy engaged in constant warfare until 338 BC. In 378 a Second Athenian Confederacy was formed, exactly a century after the first one, and included cities such as Byzantium and islands like Rhodes among its members. The economy was not as strong as it had been in the fifth century, but the city remained prosperous.

The treasurers of Athena took annual inventories of her riches in the Parthenon, which they had engraved on a marble stele placed in public view on the Acropolis for anyone who wished to read it. Each year her treasures increased, as did the number of statues dotted around the Acropolis, joining Kresilas' portrait of Pericles and the many marvels carved by Pheidias on top of the sacred rock. Although there had been many High Classical sculptures on the Acropolis, even more joined them in the fourth century, almost always dedicated by Athenian citizens. Most were private dedications, such as the statue of Pericles, but some were state-funded, such as the bronze of Konon on a semicircular base. The bases of some of these, such as the fourth-century monument of Cephisodotus, were later reused in the Byzantine Parthenon when the building was turned into a church.

Very few subsequent writers praised the Parthenon. Given its modern importance we often assume that it was also important to the ancients, but it was almost entirely ignored by the surviving ancient sources. Many writers praise the Propylaea which led to the Acropolis, but none the Parthenon which crowned it. Although we know that Callimachus wrote a book about the architecture, and that there was a work on the Acropolis as a whole, these have vanished. No ancient sources even describe it as a temple, let alone as a sight worth seeing; no writer has left us a description of the Parthenon's beautiful sculptures, or even an account of what they depicted. Although copying classical sculpture was popular in the Hellenistic and Roman periods, only two certain copies of the Parthenon sculptures from the Hellenistic period survive: a painting of the metopes and small carved copies of the pedimental figures. No certain copies from the Roman period are known.

Only one major building was set up on the Acropolis in the fourth century. The bronze storehouse (*chalkotheke*) was built to the west of the Parthenon, between it and the sanctuary of Artemis Brauronia. It served as an arsenal, a store for armour and for weapons made of bronze. To the north of the Parthenon the last remains of the old temple were dismantled; the temple had blocked the view of the Erechtheion and the Maiden Porch, but now the space between the two Periclean structures was opened up.

In the Parthenon, Persian booty was stolen and the wings of the Athena Parthenos' Nike statue were damaged by her caretakers. Although the Parthenos was not a cult statue, as a dedication to the goddess it was still sacred. Even worse, an inscription reports that the treasurers of Athena lit a fire in the opisthodomos to cover up their thieving of her treasures. Despite this, there were many offerings listed in the inventories of the treasury, which continued to grow richer each year despite the odd loss.

Although many may well have admired the Periclean buildings, what they praised most often was the magnificent entrance to the Acropolis. When Demosthenes delivered a speech in 352 BC mentioning the great buildings of fifth-century Athens, he mentioned the Propylaea not the Parthenon, and this format was followed by many of his contemporaries. Aeschines used a similar technique, asking his fellow citizens to look up at the Propylaea and Acropolis, and to remember the Persian Wars and the Athenians' victories over them. The symbolism of the Acropolis and the Parthenon as monuments to victory over the Persians remained strong throughout antiquity, and the concept of a Periclean golden age had already been developed by the fourth century; this covered not just the buildings, but also the plays of the fifth century, which were revived in the 330s.

Praise of the Periclean building programme had not, however, been unanimous. To Plato, Athens was barbarian in its ostentatious monuments, and he modelled the buildings of his Atlantis on Pericles' Acropolis. This philosopher also disapproved of the telling of myths, because they were untrue, so would not have thought much of the sculptural decoration of the Parthenon either.

Philip II (359–336 BC), better known today as the father of Alexander the Great, was ruler of Macedonia, a northern kingdom on the fringes of Greece seen as barbarian by the Athenians. Unlike the Persians, this 'barbarian' defeated the more civilised Greeks at Chaeronea in 338, and imposed a peace on them, sending the eighteen-year-old Alexander to Athens to deal with that city. Greece was now Philip's and historically this was the first time the cities of Greece had been unified, although this unification was imposed by force of arms. Philip enforced membership of a new League of Corinth. This Greek unity would not outlast Alexander's death, but Athens would never again be a major power, and it was to take its last bows on the world stage under Alexander's successors.

Under Lycurgus Athens enjoyed a brief silver age, although it could not rival Pericles' golden age. As a priest of Poseidon and Erechtheus, Lycurgus would have spent a lot of time in the Erechtheion, and been familiar with the Acropolis. As the man in charge of Athens' finances, Lycurgus was in control of the state building programme from 338 to 326 BC, during the time of Philip

II and Alexander's political dominance over Greece. Once the Greeks had been defeated by Philip, all the monies that had been tied up in the war were now free for the redevelopment of the city. Lycurgus first repaired the Long Walls and made sure the city's defences were in perfect condition, amassing a stock of weapons on the Acropolis and many ships in the Piraeus.

Once the military considerations had been dealt with, he improved the area around the Acropolis. Public buildings earlier in the century had been far from monumental; he remedied this by constructing a wall to the south of the Acropolis, which embraced the reorganised sanctuary of Asclepius, and within this building the monumental theatre. Pericles had built on top of the Acropolis and Lycurgus built around it, using a mixture of public and private funds, and turning the lower city into an appropriate setting for the Periclean jewels.

In the Agora he built the temple of Apollo Patroos, and constructed porticos all over Athens in many of which philosophers would teach, as well as refurbishing the Lyceum, which was Aristotle's school. Lycurgus also built at Eleusis and undertook much work at Piraeus. On the Acropolis he built up a stockpile of shields and weapons in the bronze storehouse. Lycurgus added new vessels to the treasure of Athens, as well as replacing those which had been melted down, and by doing so he put Athens' bank account in order, for the treasure of Athena was of course the city's gold reserve.

We know that the first stone theatre in Athens was built during this period, and that Lycurgus' building programme was second only to Pericles' in terms of importance for Athens. We know from archaeological evidence that repairs were made to the architecture of the Parthenon around this time, and that some of its sculptures show signs of repairs that also stylistically date from this same period. The Athena from the west pediment in particular has several features that do not appear to be fifth century, and so are dated to repairs made in the fourth century. Before Lycurgus, Athens was devoting most of her resources to war rather than to art or architecture, and after him the state was in almost constant turmoil. Therefore, the dozen years in which this statesman was in charge are the most likely ones for the first major restoration of the Parthenon.

The sculptures of the west pediment of the Parthenon show signs of fourth-century repairs, presumably after they had been damaged during an earthquake. The damage is unlikely to have been as a result of exposure to wind and rain; the elements can cause a great deal of damage, but not so quickly. The only explanation is that one of the earthquakes that regularly hit Athens struck the Parthenon, the central figures shook and fell out of the gable; this is certain for the west pediment, but the figures from the east are lost. The four-teen-metre fall down to the ground damaged the figures and so their surfaces had to be slightly recarved to mask and repair the damage. The figure which was most damaged and so had to be largely recarved is the Athena; she has a number of features, such as press-folds, which are not found in fifth-century sculpture.

Under Lycurgus the theatre of Dionysus was rebuilt as the first permanent stone theatre, on the south slope, next to the Odeion of Pericles; the assembly often met there rather than on the Pnyx as the theatre's seats made it more comfortable. When speakers addressed the citizens of Athens, they could look up to the top of the Parthenon on the Acropolis behind their audience. Aristophanes also used the Acropolis as a setting for many of his comedies, and in others referred to events on it, which would again have been behind the theatregoers.

The new theatre, where the classic fifth-century plays of Sophocles and Aeschylus were revived, revitalised the festival of Dionysus. This in turn led to a brief period in which a series of small but beautiful monuments were erected in the area to commemorate victories in the festival. These are called choragic monuments, so named because they were erected by the patron who had funded the winning chorus (the *choregos*). They were a specific type of monument only seen in the later fourth century, and only in Athens, but several would play a role in the later history of the city.

To the west of the theatre stood the Nikias Monument, which was built in 320/19 BC. Its form was that of a small Doric temple, and it imitated the design of the central section of the Propylaea. This architectural similarity was fortunate, for in the late third century AD its frieze would be used in the construction of an additional gate to the Acropolis, directly below the Propylaea. A certain

Thrasyllos, not content with a mere monument, turned a cave on the Acropolis, directly above the theatre of Dionysus, into his monument. A millennium later this would become a Christian church.

Only one choragic monument still stands in Athens today, in a small square to the back of the theatre, at the foot of the east end of the Acropolis. Every visitor to Athens should build time into their itinerary to sit at the café next to it for a few minutes, for not only is it the first example of the use of the Corinthian order on the exterior of a building, but it sums up so much of Greek history. This monument is the Lysicrates Monument, named after the festival winner in 335/4 BC, one of the first of the newly revitalised festivals.

The Lysicrates Monument at the foot of the Acropolis

A later Archbishop of Athens, Michael Choniates, thought it was the Lantern of Demosthenes, the famous Greek philosopher, and it was still referred to as this when the Capuchin monks bought it in 1699. When Byron visited Athens in the early nineteenth century, he was *persona non grata* with the British after behaviour that had forced him into exile, and so had to stay with the Capuchins. By then the Lysicrates Monument was a library and, small as it is, he wrote many of his poems inside this cylindrical monument.

After Philip's death Thebes revolted. It was razed to the ground as punishment by his son Alexander. Athens was wiser, and although under Alexander the city had been a centre of anti-Macedonian resistance, it did not revolt and so survived. After defeating the Persians at Granikos (334 BC) Alexander dedicated three hundred suits of Persian armour inside the Parthenon, with an inscription commemorating his dedication. He also attached fourteen gilt bronze shields to the east façade, immediately under the metopes depicting the gigantomachy. No other Greek had conquered so much land, nor gone so far east, so Alexander's defeat of the Persians must have seemed as amazing to the Athenians as their gods' defeat of the giants. The shields were soon lost, melted down. All that remains of them are the cuttings for pegs that held them in place, perfectly aligned under each of the metopes.

Alexander's wife, Roxanne, is listed in the Parthenon inventories as having dedicated a gold necklace and a drinking horn to Athena, which were kept in the Parthenon. In 330 BC Alexander captured Susa, the capital of the Persian Empire. There he found bronze statues by Antenor of Harmodius and Aristogeiton, the two men who had slain the sixth-century Peisistratid tyrants of Athens. The sculptures had been taken by the Persians after the 480 sack of the Acropolis, and Alexander returned them there a century and a half later. The Parthenon and the Acropolis as a whole commemorated the Athenians' defeat of the Persians, and by enriching it in this way Alexander made it a symbol of his own, far more thorough victory over the Persians. He was taking on the mythical heroes and the gods, almost exceeding their exploits, by fighting strange foes and then marching on to the ends of the Earth;

East front of the Parthenon with dowel holes to
hold Alexander's shields

Alexander was a new Theseus, and so it was fitting that he honoured
Theseus' city.

There was at least one portrait of Alexander on the Acropolis,
and his reign marks the time in which the patrons' dedicated sculptures on the Acropolis changed from entirely Athenian citizens to
include foreigner kings. The steps and terrace of the Parthenon were
prime spots (the *crepis*), and these become almost a monumental
sculpture base. The portrait of the general Iphicrates, later described
by Pausanias in the Roman period, was probably in the colonnade.
Portrait statues were the popular form of sculpture on the Acropolis,
closely followed by mythological groups and gods and goddesses. On
the south slope of the Acropolis, beneath the west end of the
Parthenon, there was a foundry where bronzes were cast for dedication on the Acropolis. With each year the rock must have become
more crowded, but an inscription from the time of Lycurgus shows
that recycling was employed, and broken or damaged bronzes melted

down after the names of those who had dedicated them had been carefully noted down. Although Alexander had been allowed to add shields to the east façade of the Parthenon, no others had been allowed to alter the exterior, nor to build monuments that blocked the view of it, so physically the Parthenon and its sculptures looked almost the same as they had when Pericles died in 429 BC.

After Alexander's death in 323 BC there was an uprising in Athens against the Macedonians, which was promptly crushed by Cassander. This general installed a philosopher, Demetrius of Phaleron, as a puppet ruler. Demetrius criticised Pericles for the sums he had spent on the Propylaea a century before, rather hypocritical for a man who at the same time was having 360 statues of himself erected around the city, including one on the Acropolis itself. After Demetrius' fall these bronzes were melted down, and some deliberately turned into chamber pots, such was the hatred of the Athenians for him. Demetrius had instituted sumptuary laws, which banned private monuments, both funerary and those recording accomplishments such as the choragic ones. Athenians could no longer decorate their tombs with sculpture, and they were extremely unhappy at this constriction on their ability to glorify their ancestors. His least popular measure, however, was a decree giving central control of the philosophical schools to the government, which soon had to be repealed as many philosophers chose exile instead.

Another Demetrius, nicknamed Poliorketes (besieger of cities), 'liberated' the city in 307 BC and was accorded divine honours by the Athenians. The next year the Long Walls were once again repaired by this Macedonian follower of Alexander. In thanks, images of Demetrius and his father Antigonus were woven into the Gigantomachy on Athena's *peplos* for the Panathenaic festival.

His popularity soon waned when his newly acquired divinity went to his head. During the winter of 304/3 this second Demetrius moved into the opisthodomus, the back room of the Parthenon, with his mistresses, and held orgies to which he invited Athenian matrons. The annual inventories of the Parthenon had listed furniture as well as gold and silver versions of household goods as having been dedicated over the years, and presumably Demetrius used these. Had the Parthenon been a temple he is unlikely to have committed such a sacrilege; because it was a treasury with a large stock of showy furniture, he was able to do so.

Although the Athenians had made Poliorketes a god, and the Greek gods were as carnal as any playboy today, sex in the Parthenon was a step too far for Athenian sensibilities. Several of the mistresses he housed on the Acropolis are named in the sources, including Lamia, fabled for her sighing, a flautist who had previously been mistress to Ptolemy of Egypt, and whom Demetrius had seized after his victory over the Egyptian king. Demetrius fell at her feet, and announced Lamia to be the incarnation of Aphrodite; he declared himself to be the younger brother of Athena, and so moved in with his 'big sister'.

In 301 BC there was a civil war and Cassander once again seized control of Athens; this time he installed Lachares, an Athenian demagogue, in power. Lachares is today only remembered for having stripped the Parthenon to pay his troops (296/5 BC); he melted down the gold drapery of the Athena Parthenos, the gold and silver treasures dedicated to her and stored in the Parthenon, and the gold Nikes replaced by Lycurgus, as well as stealing the shields that had been dedicated by Alexander.

Some question whether Lachares would have been able to steal the goddess's drapery, despite the numerous references to this act of vandalism in ancient literature. One has to hope that Pheidias' original moulds were stored somewhere on the Acropolis. The Parthenos' drapery was eventually restored, but the new drapery was probably of gilded copper rather than the solid gold it had once been. Alexander's shields were eventually replaced with smaller ones, which were attached to the architrave all around the building, forty-two in number. In effect, Lachares was the man who robbed the Bank of Athens.

Fortunately, the architectural sculpture that decorated the Parthenon was made of stone. It could neither be melted down nor sold off for cash, and so it survived Lachares' brief tenure in power. Athens and the Acropolis had suffered repeatedly at the hands of

Macedonian leaders and their puppets, and the glory of Periclean Athens must have seemed distant. They may well have looked up at the Parthenon and the exploits of Theseus depicted in its sculpture, and prayed that Athena would send them another hero to save them and to help them regain their independence. If so, they were to be bitterly disappointed, for Athens would never again be free as an independent state, and would have to wait a further twenty-one centuries to form part of an independent Greece.

Although today we consider it axiomatic for Greek temples to have sculpture in all their metopes, as on the Parthenon, this was exceptional rather than the rule. Small buildings, such as the treasuries at Delphi, were cheaper to erect and so could be filled with sculpture. On large buildings it was extremely rare. The only temple after those of Periclean Athens to have had all its exterior metopes filled with sculpture is the temple of Athena at Ilion, ancient Troy, a city in Asia Minor which also instituted a Panathenaic festival. Alexander passed through and gave money for the construction of the temple, but it was built by his general and successor Lysimachus (301–280 BC).

We are not certain if this temple's very fragmentary sculpture copied the Parthenon metopes scene for scene, but the same four battles were depicted on each side of the metopes. Rather ironically, one of these battles was the capture of Troy by the Greeks; by then the inhabitants of Ilion saw themselves as 'civilised' and Greek, so they identified with the Greek victors rather than the losers. Like the Parthenon, the façade of the temple of Athena at Ilion is dotted with small holes that once held a Roman inscription in bronze. These state that Augustus rebuilt the temple, probably just repairing it, to emphasise his descent via Julius Caesar from the Trojan prince Aeneas. Another battle depicted the defeat of the Amazons, and may well have reminded him of his own defeat of Cleopatra.

The artists and art historians of the Neo-Classical period embraced the false illusion that ancient sculpture and architecture was always gleaming white. Over the course of the nineteenth century, the evidence for polychromy mounted, and our impression of ancient art changed for ever as travellers and archaeologists noticed traces of paint on architectural elements and sculpture they unearthed. There is evidence for the original polychromy of earlier archaic architectural sculpture on the Acropolis, but for the Parthenon itself it was minimal. The Archaic temples on the Acropolis were razed by the Persians. When the Athenians returned, they buried the architectural remains of their sacred temples within the ground on top of the Acropolis, and so they are now preserved for us with much of the original paint. Below is a detail of a figure of Athena from one of these archaic gables in a small temple on the Acropolis, showing how elaborately the figure was painted and the detail that went into her costume. The *peplos* presented to Athena at the Panathenaia would have been similar, but even more elaborate.

An interesting recent discovery in Greece was of a Macedonian tomb excavated at Lefkadia, dating to *c.*300 BC. Macedonian tombs, from the period of Alexander the Great and his successors, were composed of one or more chambers with a stucco architectural façade. Once the body of the deceased was interred, it was immediately covered over by a mound, and so these architectural façades were often well preserved along with their decoration. As the façades were exposed to the elements for such a brief time, the paint is often remarkably well preserved. At Lefkadia all the elements are very brightly coloured, except for the metopes, which are in more subdued hues.

The eight metopes depict scenes from a Centauromachy, the battle of the Lapiths and Centaurs, and are also the only part of the decoration painted in *trompe l'œil* rather than modelled in stucco, with shadows painted in to make them resemble sculpture. The scenes depicted are identical to those depicted in some of the metopes on the Parthenon. One interpretation of the differences in colouring between the metopes and the rest of the façade on the Lefkadia tomb is that the builders of the tomb not only copied the designs of the Parthenon scenes, but also the contemporary state of their colouring, which by 300 BC, after more than a century of exposure to the elements, would have been rather faded. If this interpretation is correct, and it seems a logical one, then it constitutes our best evidence for the condition of the polychromy of the Parthenon in the early Hellenistic period.

The evidence for ancient paint on stone is scarce, as paint was the outermost surface, and so the most exposed to damage. If stone sculpture had to be periodically restored (the surface of the faces of the figures on the exterior of the Ara Pacis in Rome are the best evidence for recarving due to erosion from the elements), then common sense suggests that the paint covering the stone also had to be 'touched up'. Plutarch describes the surface of the sculptures as looking almost new in the second century AD, but we have proof that the paint had in fact faded considerably by around 300 BC. The only conclusion one can draw is that at least once in between the sculptures and architecture of the Parthenon were repainted.

Pergamene Patronage
and the Roman Empire

Although the Athenians had made Demetrius Poliorketes a king, at the beginning of the Hellenistic era Athens was still a city state. By the time of the Battle of Actium (31 BC), when Augustus became the first Roman emperor, it was just a provincial town within the huge Roman Empire, known for its philosophical schools and some old buildings. In 267 BC Athens chose to support the Ptolemies over the Macedonians, and this was just one of a long list of conflicts in which they chose the losing side. Although Roman tourists would visit Athens, and might admire the Parthenon and its sculptures, the building would become a monument to a former glory which Athens would never regain.

In the third century BC the Romans began to expand eastwards. In 216, during the Second Punic War (218–201), the Macedonians took the side of Hannibal and the Carthaginians, and so became the enemy of Rome. Fortunately, Athens became an ally of Rome, probably the only time in the Hellenistic period in which they chose the winning side. In the summer of 197 BC Flaminius' Roman army defeated the Macedonians under Philip in Thessaly, and so during the 196 Olympics the Greek cities, including Athens, were declared free from Macedonian rule. Rome finally wiped out the Macedonians, who had dominated Greece for two centuries, when Aemilius Paullus defeated Perseus, Philip's son, in 167 BC. Rome in turn gave Athens the island of Delos the following year, which helped the Athenians economically, and provided a base for them in the Aegean.

Pergamon was an ally of Rome, and so naturally a friend of Athens. In c.200 Attalus I, king of Pergamon, erected what became known as the Smaller Attalid Monument to the south-east of the Parthenon, between the building and the Acropolis wall. This was a monument with a dozen half-life-size bronzes depicting enemies of Athens and Pergamon lying dead and dying on the rock of the Acropolis. Only the defeated enemies were shown, unlike at the Parthenon, where the battles themselves were depicted, and some scenes showed Greeks losing. Giants defeated by the gods (depicted in the east metopes), the Amazons that had besieged the Acropolis (shown on the Parthenos' shield) and those defeated by Theseus (in the west metopes) were depicted on this new monument. Also shown were the Persians who had died during the Battle of Marathon (depicted on the frieze of the Nike temple), and the Gauls that the Pergamenes themselves had recently defeated. Mythical and historical Athenian history and the defeats of barbarians in the east were linked to contemporary events, the whole echoing many of the motifs of the Periclean buildings, and reinforcing the symbolism of the Acropolis as an emblem of Greek superiority over the East.

The west end of the Erechtheion had been badly damaged in a fire, and although traditionally the repairs were dated to Augustus' reign, new research has shown them to have been undertaken by the Attalid kings of Pergamon. Some Hellenistic repairs to the Parthenon have been noted, and since the Pergamene kings were such great patrons, it might be possible to link them to these repairs as well. Although the architecture of the Parthenon was tinkered with, and the gable frame that held the pedimental figures reinforced, none of the sculptures themselves have repairs that date to this period. The repairs thus appear to have been undertaken to prevent future damage, rather than after it had taken place.

In front of the Pinakotheke (picture gallery) in the north-west wing of the Propylaea, on a level with the Nike temple, a grey hymettan marble base was erected which held a statue of Eumenes II (197–159 BC). The monument was just outside the boundary of the Acropolis, but dominated the skyline from the administrative centre, the Agora. Anyone going about their business there could not have failed to see the monument, crowned by a statue of the king, and known he was an important man.

The base of Eumenes' statue dominates the view
of the entrance to the Acropolis

A few years later Eumenes' brother built another similar pillar, which this time stood in an even more prominent location, directly in front of the east façade of the Parthenon, blocking off the northern end of it. This held a chariot group of Attalus II (159–139 BC), on the same level as the metopes, and directly in front of the metope of Helios in his chariot; the group shielded the metope from the elements, so this one is better preserved than the other panels on the east. Helios, the sun, rose in the east, and the city state of Pergamon was in the east, so the symbolism of the location of the monument is not too obscure.

Attalus II erected a third such base in front of the stoa he built in the Agora, which commemorated his time as a student of philosophy in the city, and the Panathenaic Games in which he and his brothers had taken part. Eumenes II had also previously built a monumental stoa on the south slope of the Acropolis. As well as being great patrons in Athens, the Pergamene kings modelled their own acropolis on the Athenian one; they instituted a Panathenaic festival, and copied several sculptures from the Acropolis, such as the Athena Parthenos and the Athena Promachos.

Although Antiochus IV, the Seleucid Greek ruler of Syria, was an enemy of Rome, around this time he too was a benefactor of Athens, as he was of numerous other Greek cities. On the Acropolis he dedicated a giant aegis which hung just below the Pergamene Monument, above the theatre of Dionysus. The aegis was a symbol of Athena, and also the emblem of the Seleucids, the dynasty to which this king belonged. Like the Attalids at Pergamon, Antiochus had a copy of the Athena Parthenos made for Antioch, his capital. He also restarted work on the colossal temple of Olympian Zeus but, as those before him, found the task too immense to be able to complete it.

The philosophical schools flourished at this time, and philosophers were among the leading citizens. When a dispute between Athens and the neighbouring Oropos arose, the city sent a Platonic philosopher to Rome to fight her cause. The city had always had philosophers but did not become an important philosophical centre until after the Persian Wars. By the end of the Classical period it was the philosophical capital of the world, a position it maintained throughout Antiquity. In the fourth century BC the Academy was rebuilt, and extensive additions and renovations took place towards the end of the Hellenistic period. Aristotle's Lyceum, on the eastern side of what is today Syntagma Square, was refurbished by Lycurgus. Aristotle's pupil Theophrastus started a school next door. Other schools were based in stoas, after whom the Stoics were named, in private homes and increasingly in permanent establishments founded to the south of the Acropolis.

Athens was favoured by Rome, and so was spared tribute, unlike Corinth which was sacked and looted. But while Rome at that time was a republic, its empire's residents were not Roman citizens, and so had no right to vote; this right was not extended until the imperial period, by which time it was far less useful.

In the civil wars the city was less wise, repeatedly choosing the loser. Encouraged by a philosopher, she favoured Mithridates of Pontus over Sulla, so the Roman general besieged the Acropolis from July 87 to May 86 BC, a siege during which Athena's sacred lamp in the Erechtheion went out for the first time; the theatre and Asclepieion also sustained damage. The Athenians chose to destroy Pericles' Odeion rather than let its valuable timber fall into Sulla's hands. The Acropolis fell on the same day Sulla defeated Mithridates at Chaeronea, and he returned to sack the city, taking much of its art back with him to Rome, but sparing the Acropolis itself. Soon after though, Verres, a lieutenant of Dolabella and an avaricious art collector, looted gold from the Acropolis, according to Cicero, and art from the temple of Minerva, which in those days was the Erechtheion (Cicero, *Against Verres*, 2.1.44–5; 2.4.71). The Parthenon and her sculptures seem to have been spared; if they were damaged this was ignored by our sources, as was the building itself.

Next, Pompey came through Athens, giving the city fifty talents towards the restoration of buildings. Julius Caesar gave matching funds a few years later, which went towards building a Roman agora to the north of the Acropolis. Despite this, Athens chose to support Pompey in their civil war, although Julius Caesar did not hold it against the city when he won. His heirs were less happy when the city provided shelter for, and erected monuments to, his murderers, Brutus and Cassius. Mark Antony and Octavian hunted these two down, and yet again Athens had chosen the wrong side. But Athens was a backwater by then, and all these wrong choices were mere dents on the world stage.

Antony divided the empire with Caesar's heir and adopted son Octavian; he took the east. Antony favoured Athens, and lived there for several years. Although today Antony would probably be described as an alcoholic, when one ruled half an empire one could call oneself whatever one liked, and he chose to call himself the New Dionysus, god of wine and debauchery. Although deification was the norm by then for rulers in the Greek world, in Rome it was still severely frowned upon; living mortals could aspire to be heroic, but they could not put themselves on a par with the gods. In Ephesus a temple was erected to Antony as Dionysus, but in Athens this self-created living god chose instead to marry Athena in a lavish ceremony; he received a wedding gift of a thousand talents from the city. The celebrations took place on the Acropolis – the marriage itself probably in the Parthenon – and everywhere in the city wine was available. Antony also claimed descent from Heracles, and since Heracles was depicted in the metopes of the Parthenon – and possibly even in one pediment – it seemed an appropriate setting for him to marry the goddess in a building decorated not only with earlier Athenians but also his own progenitor.

It was also in Athens that Antony ended his marriage to Octavian's sister; he did so not in favour of Athena, but rather cheated on the goddess and declared his alliance with Queen Cleopatra of Egypt. This led to war, which Antony lost. At Actium (31 BC) his and Cleopatra's combined forces were defeated, and the two chose suicide. A source claims that a statue of Antony, which had stood on the south wall of the Acropolis, fell into the theatre of Dionysus the night before the battle; this apocryphal story was recorded as an omen, though the statue is likely to have been pushed off the Acropolis after his defeat, it being no longer politic to honour the Roman loser in this civil war. Actium officially marks the end of the Hellenistic period, and the beginning of the Roman imperial era. Unfortunately, Athens had favoured Antony, once again choosing the losing side.

Octavian visited Athens soon after the battle, but swiftly moved on to Aegina. He returned during the winter of 22/21 BC, by which time he had been given the name Augustus by the senate, and was de facto the first Roman emperor. His final brief visit was in 19 BC.

We do not know whether or not Augustus visited the Parthenon, but the Acropolis was one of the 'sights' of Athens, so it is likely that he did. What we do know is that he tended to favour gods other than Athena. After his victory at Actium his propaganda depicted Antony as his 'ancestor' Heracles, with the Hero seduced by the Lydian queen Omphale into giving up his weapons and wearing women's clothes. Omphale was of course Cleopatra, a dangerous woman who had tried to take on for herself the role of a warrior and a man.

The Amazons fighting in the Parthenon metopes must have symbolised to Augustus the recent danger he had defeated, and again the Egyptian queen was represented as a dangerous Amazon in Augustan propaganda – female power was to be condemned rather than encouraged. Parallels could also be drawn with the prehistoric attempt by the Amazons to besiege the Acropolis, depicted on the shield of the Athena Parthenos in the Parthenon. Then the Athenians had valiantly fought off these female usurpers. To Augustus it must have seemed ironic that not only did Athens not try to fight off Cleopatra, a contemporary Amazon, but had even sided with her against him.

Augustus did not favour Athens, although his greatest general and son-in-law Agrippa seems to have been a patron of the city. The monument of Eumenes II in front of the Propylaea had been rededicated to Antony a few years before, but now was again quickly changed to hold a portrait statue of Agrippa. Attalus' base in front of the Parthenon was equally quickly rededicated to Augustus after his victory at Actium. There were numerous statues of Augustus on the Acropolis, and as his reign progressed, his family were added, including each new heir he named and then outlived – Marcellus, Gaius and Lucius – until finally Tiberius, who succeeded him as emperor. Ever economical, the Athenians repeatedly recycled one statue of Augustus in the city, changing the head and inscription, so that it in turn became Tiberius, Nero, Vespasian and finally Titus, the Caesar who sacked the Temple in Jerusalem.

Many gods, at this point, became known by their Roman names in Latin inscriptions, so Athena became Minerva and Zeus became Jupiter. Although this was in part simply the use of a different name in a different language, there was also initially some differentiation between Roman gods and their Greek counterparts since the former were derived from Italian and Etruscan traditions. In time, with the introduction of exotic Eastern cults, such as those of Isis and of Christ, and then the assimilation of local characteristics of regional cults of goddesses such as Athena, there were fewer anomalies between Roman and Greek gods. Superficially, it is easier to say that Minerva and Athena were the 'same' goddess, while simultaneously noting that Athena herself varied greatly from cult to cult; since there was such a great divergence between the Athena of Athens and the Athena of Thebes, one would be foolish to concentrate too much on the differences.

Agrippa funded an Odeon in the Agora, and possibly repairs on the Acropolis, including the refurbishment of the base of Pheidias' Athena Promachos. In front of the Parthenon, about twenty metres in front of the east façade, a small circular temple dedicated to Rome and Augustus was erected. This seems to have been built by the Athenians themselves, to coincide with the visit in the summer of 19 BC, and to ingratiate themselves with Augustus. Officially, it celebrated his victory over the Parthians in 20 BC, the Parthians being the successors of the Persians as the enemy in the East. A whole series of Periclean, Pergamene and now Roman monuments all commemorated victories over the 'barbarians' and the East. The temple's elements echoed those of the Erechtheion, and it was deliberately built low so as not to block the light falling on the Athena Parthenos in the Parthenon.

Although Augustus probably did not repair the Erechtheion as was previously thought, the building was highly influential in terms of Augustan architecture. The attic of the temple of Mars Ultor in Augustus' Forum in Rome was articulated by reduced-scale Caryatids copied from the Erechtheion's Maiden Porch, and the façade of the octostyle temple with a low gable was closer to the proportions of the Parthenon than to the norm for Roman temples. Many other architectural elements of the forum were copied from the Erechtheion and from the Propylaea, and when the Forum was dedicated the ceremonies included a re-enactment of the Athenian naval victory over the Persians at Salamis. Augustus' Ara Pacis, an altar dedicated to Augustan peace, had a sculpted procession around the exterior, which was a contemporary Roman version of the procession around the Periclean building.

There were extensive repairs to the east end of the Parthenon, notably the gable that held sculpture depicting the birth of Athena. These, based on the style of the work, are dated to the first century AD but cannot be linked to any one emperor. The temple, which had suffered earthquake damage, was repaired, and the first-century cornice blocks under the gable attest this. If such work needed to be done to the structure of the pediments, I doubt that the sculptures within them fared better and it may well be as early as the Roman period that the central figures of the east pediment were damaged and lost. The exterior metopes of the Parthenon show two different sets of Roman repairs to the sculpture, the first of these likely to date to the Augustan period.

By Augustus' day Corinth was the administrative capital of Achaea, as the Romans called Greece, the city having been refounded as a Roman colony by Julius Caesar. Athens itself was a giant museum of classical sculpture and architecture, and a centre of learning due to the philosophical schools, whose days of political importance were firmly in the past. The city was an ancient Oxford, beautiful and learned, but playing no role on the world stage. Horace described it as 'empty Athens', and Ovid claimed only the name was left. Athens was firmly on the periphery of the Roman world, her importance by then based less on the contemporary city than on her past glories, such as the unexpected victory at Marathon, an event mentioned repeatedly from Hellenistic to Byzantine times by visitors.

Athens did, however, remain one of the cultural capitals of the Roman Empire, and was visited by those who could afford to travel. They came to see the Classical buildings on an Antique version of the Grand Tour, and to study with the philosophers. The city now became a tourist attraction, visited by those who admired Greek culture.

The occasional copying of sculpture from the Periclean Acropolis had always taken place, but by the first century BC it had become a large trade, with workshops dedicated to copying such works as the Nike temple parapets and frieze. Numerous small-scale copies of the Athena Parthenos of the Roman period have come down to us, and would have been bought by visitors in a variety of sizes just as visitors to Paris today can bring back miniature models of the Eiffel Tower. A ship sank just outside the Piraeus in the second century AD; as well as carrying Greek originals on their way to Rome, it had panels with scenes of the Amazonomachy from the statue's shield. Salvaged in the last century, these are now in Piraeus Museum.

The Hellenistic Lefkadia tomb is, however, the only example of copies of the Parthenon metopes. The pediments were copied on a small shrine at Eleusis in the first century BC, and these figures, a mere hand-span high, are today in the National Museum in Athens. Given the importance we now ascribe to the sculptures, and the many arguments over ownership of the Elgin Marbles, it is surprising how little the Parthenon sculptures were reproduced. Copies were made commercially, bought and sold, so they were the ultimate financial indicator of value and desirability of art. Pheidias' statue of the Athena Parthenos was thus valuable to Roman collectors and connoisseurs, but the sculptures on the Parthenon were not.

The Romans were avid collectors of Greek art, shipping paintings and statues back to Rome to fill their homes. Greek art was the ultimate status symbol, and temples were not spared. Not only were portable statues taken, but there are several examples of temples whose pedimental sculptures were removed, and reused to fill the gables of Roman temples.

Caligula (AD 37–41) took seven statues from the Acropolis, but these were returned by Claudius (AD 41–54), who was a great philhellene (*IG*, II², 5179). His contribution to the Acropolis was replacing the ramp leading up to the Propylaea with a monumental marble staircase; this was on the axis of the doorway, and Roman in style. He added a similar staircase to the Hephaisteion. Nero's agents also took a few statues from the Acropolis, which was by then a veritable forest of sculpture, but when the emperor visited Greece he would not set foot in Athens, and so did not visit the Acropolis. Despite this, the Athenians added an inscription to the east façade of the Parthenon in AD 61/2, celebrating Nero. The letters were in bronze rather than carved on to the marble. The inscription was removed after Nero's fall in AD 64, but the pins that held these letters in place are preserved in the stone, and so the wording can still be deciphered. The inscription, twenty-five metres long and slightly off-centre as the north end of the façade was covered by Attalus' monument, read:

> The Council of the Areopagus, the Council of the Six Hundred, and the Athenian people [honour] the Greatest Emperor Nero Caesar Claudius Augustus Germanicus, son of a God, when Tiberius Claudius Nero, son of Philinos, was Hoplite-General for the eighth time, as well as Epimelete and Nomothete, and the priestess [of Athena] was Paulina, daughter of Kapito.

$$IG, II^2, 3277$$

The rows of small nail holes which held Nero's bronze inscription in place are clearly visible under the mutules of the triglyphs, between the larger holes which held Alexander's shields.

Nero, who famously wanted a statue of himself in the Holy of Holies of the Temple in Jerusalem, such was his megalomania, might well have been depicted in the Parthenon. Nero's armies were fighting the Parthians and Armenians in the East at the time, and victory was expected, so this inscription once again reinforces the Parthenon as a symbol of victory over Eastern enemies.

Augustus had added an inscription to the façade of the temple of Athena at Ilion, a temple which imitated the Parthenon. The inscription implied that he had built it, although he had only repaired it, and the lack of such an inscription may be read as a sign that the repairs to the Parthenon do not date to the reign of Augustus. These inscriptions, commemorating individuals who funded buildings, were a fourth-century innovation and the first known examples are by Mausolus at Labraunda in Turkey. Alexander swiftly adopted this concept, and offered to fund the completion of the colossal temple of Artemis at Ephesus if his name could be added to the façade. The Ephesians declined, but the good people of Priene were happy to take his money, and to inscribe their own temple of Athena with his name.

Plutarch writing c.AD 100 described the Parthenon as still looking fresh. This reference is often cited today by restitutionists, who want to claim that the Parthenon was still in perfect condition well into the Roman period, and to accuse the British Museum of having stripped off the original fifth-century paint from the Elgin Marbles. Plutarch can also be interpreted as meaning the complete opposite, and since the Macedonian tomb at Lefkadia shows that the paint on the metopes had faded considerably by 300 BC, it is more likely that he is referring to the many restorations of the Parthenon that kept it in good condition. Traces of paint on the sculptures show that the background of the Parthenon frieze was blue, and that the metopal panels were red. Elsewhere Plutarch noted that Athens' buildings were the only sign of her former greatness.

Hadrian was another philhellene, who formed the Panhellenion in AD 131/2, a league of Greek states of which Athens was the head, as well as setting up organisations to revive the ancient cults. His bronze portrait statue inside the Parthenon, next to Athena, was seen a few years later by Pausanias, and some scholars believe that he might have repaired the statue, but there is no evidence for this. There are repairs to the metopes on the exterior of the Parthenon that stylistically can be dated to Hadrian or one of the Antonine successors.

Pausanias wrote his ten-volume guide to the splendours of Greece c.AD 160–80, and this is the only ancient source that mentions the sculptures of the Parthenon. He does not describe them, but only names the themes of the pediments; he does not mention the frieze or the metopes. This description provides us with the iconography of the pediments; since so many sculptures are lost, without it we might be at a loss to know which scenes were depicted. Pausanias was rather circumspect about the interior of the Parthenon, given how excited he could become about the highly trivial elsewhere. From Pausanias' guidebook we know that in the mid-second century a statue of Hadrian stood near the Athena Parthenos in the cella, a statue to which he devoted much of his description, and that there were also painted portraits of Themistocles and Heliodorus inside. Since the exterior was refurbished several times, we can assume the same was necessary for the interior.

In the mid-second century Agrippa's odeon had to be rebuilt, and the new builders added Tritons and giants to the façade, heavily influenced by the figures in the Parthenon metopes depicting the battle between the gods and the giants. This new odeon was used by a philosophical school, as was the building that in turn superseded it in the early Byzantine period.

Further repairs to the Parthenon may well date from the reign of Septimius Severus (193–203), since we know that he funded extensive rebuilding of the Erechtheion. It was then rededicated jointly to Athena and to his wife Julia Domna (d. 211), and a portrait of the empress placed inside the temple of Athena. Portraits of rulers had begun on the Acropolis with Alexander, increased during the Hellenistic period and become the norm in Roman times. The emperor was often shown as part of a family group with his wife and heirs, and sculptures of Septimius, Julia and their children in the company of gods and heroes seem to have stood in the peristyle of the Parthenon by the end of the second century.

In AD 267 the Heruli ravaged Greece and sacked the city of Athens. Barbarians at the gate were not a new phenomenon. In AD 170, during the reign of Marcus Aurelius, the Kostoboks had attacked Eleusis, although they spared Athens, and in the mid-third century the Goths briefly took Athens from Valerian. After the Herulian sack of the lower city, new walls were built using the monuments the raiders had torn down. These walls formed a rough square to the north of the Acropolis, and enclosed a small strip to the south of the Acropolis; the city shrank to within these walls. The so-called Beule Gate was added as a supplementary gate immediately below the Propylaea to make the Acropolis' defences stronger. This new gate was built reusing the façade of the early Hellenistic Nikias Monument, whose façade had imitated the Propylaea, and which made it ideal to preserve the architectural harmony between the two gates. This marked a turning point in the nature of the Acropolis. Although the Athenians had locked themselves within it at regular intervals during their history, the sacred nature of the mound had come first since the Peisistratids, but now it became a fortress once again, as it had been in Mycenaean and prehistoric times. The agora itself was abandoned until *c.* AD 400.

The structure of the Parthenon makes it clear that there was a major repair in late antiquity, but though a large undertaking, it is not recorded in any written sources. The marble of the Parthenon has large fissures and fractures that could only have been created by an immense fire that lasted days. The roof must have fallen in, burning at a high temperature, which in turn cracked the beams of the colonnade and affected the outer columns. The interior colonnade collapsed under the weight of the roof, and the statue of Athena almost certainly perished in the inferno since it would have been almost impossible to have removed Pheidias' masterpiece quickly. The floor inside the Parthenon still has cuttings for the interior colonnade which was rebuilt in the late Roman period after the fire. We can also tell that the base of the new Athena statue – the one which the Christians later removed – was considerably smaller than the base of Pheidias' statue.

The new statue (Athena Parthenos III) was now a cult statue in the proper sense, but it was far more modest than Pheidias' goddess, and may well have been a classical statue reused rather than a new creation. At some point, late in the Roman period, the cult of Athena moved from the Erechtheion to the Parthenon, making it for the first time a proper temple. The ancient wooden Erechtheion statue had by then more or less disintegrated, and the Parthenon in any case probably better suited the Romans' idea of what a temple should be like. The Erechtheion also seems to have been badly damaged at around the same time.

Elements of the original fifth-century BC colonnade of the Parthenon have been found built into the foundation walls of a fifth-century AD stoa in the agora. This gives us a date before which the Parthenon must have been destroyed by fire. The colonnade had to be removed after the temple had suffered extensive damage, caused either by accident, perhaps the result of an earthquake, or by an invading army. The date of the fire and subsequent repairs has been debated for years, and was often romantically ascribed to Julian, the last pagan emperor, in the 360s. Now thanks to the work of Manolis Korres, who for many years has been in charge of the Parthenon and has done invaluable research on the monument, we can now pinpoint the repairs to the Late Roman period, and the decades on either side of AD 300. An inscription probably dating to the third century (although the fourth century cannot be ruled out) was incorporated into the Late Roman rebuilding, providing a date before which the Parthenon could not have been rebuilt. The Heruli cannot be blamed for the destruction of the Parthenon, unless it was left as a ruin for several decades while precedence was given to reconstructing other buildings.

The interior as rebuilt is described by an anonymous writer at the time of the Ottoman capture of the city. Known as the Vienna Anonymous after the library in which his guide to the city is kept, he described the interior colonnade as having a double row of columns with Doric capitals on the lower level, and capitals carved like palms on the upper level. Palm capitals are rare in Greek architecture and mostly used by the Pergamene kings. These kings built several stoas in Athens, two of which survive. The stoa of Attalus was in the agora to the north of the Acropolis, and had capitals on the interior carved like palms, an example of which is illustrated below. His brother Eumenes had built a similar stoa to the south of the Acropolis.

Capital from Stoa of Attalus, of the type used within the rebuilt Parthenon

The later columns used in the rebuilding of the interior colonnade of the Parthenon have been found by archaeologists. They were slimmer and shorter than their predecessors, so the full entablature had to be used, and there may well have been arches between the upper columns and the roof to bridge the gap. New columns were not made, probably because of lack of funds, but rather the elements of a pair of long Hellenistic porticos believed to have been in the Roman agora were used. Because we know from the description that those two stoas had had palm capitals which were reused inside the Parthenon, we can be certain that they were built by a king of Pergamon.

Columns (left) and a capital and entablature (right) on the
Acropolis, from the rebuilt interior of the Parthenon

The two buildings were probably destroyed during the Herulian
sacking of the city, and it was more economical to recycle them.
Elements of these columns survived the numerous subsequent events
in the building's history, and so are preserved. The porticos must
also have been very long, for columns from the same source were
also used to repair a portico in the sanctuary of Dionysus on the
south slope. From the architectural details, we can tell that the
porticos they originally came from were designed by a Pergamene
architect. The Pergamene kings did much to beautify the city, and
erected many monuments on the Acropolis, so it is fitting that over
four centuries after their death their gift was able to rebuild the
Parthenon. While reusing the Pergamene porticos was an economy,
the temple was severely damaged and roofless, its interior gutted, so
the refurbishment was still a monumental undertaking.

The biggest difference between this Parthenon and the original,
to the Athenian of the day, would have been the roof. The old roof
of the Parthenon had consisted of marble tiles on thick wooden
beams, and covered the entire building. The new roof, using marble

beams of cut-down columns from the same porticos as the colonnades, was more modest and covered in clay tiles. Wooden beams
large enough to span a roof were prohibitively expensive, so this too
was an economy. The new roof did not cover the whole building,
and was made of two sections, of differing pitches. One higher
pitched section covered the old cella, but not the east porch or the
peristyle around it. Another section covered the west porch. The
colonnade around the Parthenon was no longer sheltered by a roof,
and so for the first time the Parthenon frieze was exposed to the
elements. It was better preserved than the other sculptures, and had
never been in need of repairs, but it too began to be battered by
wind and rain in winter, baked by the hot sun in summer which
made the marble expand and then contract again at night.

The architrave blocks of the opisthodomus in the west, later built
into a tower, were badly fire-damaged and had to be repaired. The
capitals of the pronaos and opisthodomus had cracked, and were
repaired with mortar, as were the interior antae capitals. Plastering
over cracks was cheaper than carving new architectural elements,
so small cracks in the marble were plastered over, while large ones
were covered by the addition of a thin marble veneer nailed to the
surface. The west door was recreated using a patchwork of almost a
hundred assorted classical, Hellenistic and Roman marble blocks,
covered in inscriptions and from monuments that had previously
dotted the summit of the Acropolis. The lintel over the west door
had cracked in the fire, and was replaced with a recut Hellenistic
column shaft. Its equivalent to the east is no longer preserved, but
one can assume a similar arrangement.

The architrave blocks from the Pergamene porticos were used for
the thresholds and posts of the Parthenon's east door, and for other
repairs to the temple. The east door was also repaired with marble
blocks from other Greek and Roman monuments. The lower south
door jamb is preserved, with the reverse of an inscribed stele carved
to continue the lines of the original door. The door was later widened
to create an apse, but this section of the door was not cut back since
it later fell below the level of the raised Byzantine apse. This shows
definitively that these repairs must predate the conversion of the
Parthenon into a church. The stele is mid-fifth century BC, and

details the building accounts for the construction of the Parthenon, thereby preserving them for us to study today. The threshold through this new doorway became extremely worn, and is now under the later church's raised floor. This shows that the interior of the Parthenon was rebuilt long before it was transformed into a church, and there must be a time lag of a couple of centuries between its rebuilding and its subsequent abandonment to show so much wear in the stone from Athenians just walking in and out of the door.

Many lists of ancient wonders exist, the most famous and most often cited going towards the creation of a canon: the Seven Wonders of the Ancient World. These lists were compiled mostly in antiquity, in the period covered by this chapter. They exclude anything in Athens, which was by then a minor town, and none of the lists ever cites the Parthenon and its sculpture as one of the great wonders of Antiquity, nor praises them as a sight to be seen. The Altar of Zeus at Pergamon, now in Berlin, is also today considered a great masterpiece, but it too was excluded from the lists of wonders. If the Parthenon sculptures were considered by the ancients so little worthy of praise, we can only weep at what superior works we have now lost.

The Coming of the Christians

The reign of Constantine (306–37) marked several important changes in the Roman Empire. Most important was that the capital moved from Rome to a new city in the East, shifting the centre of power to Byzantium as the New Rome, and to Asia Minor. The second was that Christianity was officially recognised, and then became the state religion. This event was sparked by Constantine's defeat of Maxentius at the Battle of the Milvian Bridge (312) in Rome. Just before the battle he had a vision of the cross, painted Christian symbols on his shields, and attributed his victory to the help of Christ. Although Christians had been persecuted and martyred only a few years before under Diocletian, in 313 the Edict of Milan called for toleration and allowed Christianity to be practised. Constantine erected a colossal five-aisled basilica to St Peter in Rome, a church which survived until the Renaissance when it was rebuilt as the cathedral we know today.

The Christianisation of Athens was a very slow process. St Paul had preached to the Areopagites in AD 53 on the Pnyx, a hill facing the Acropolis. He made a few conversions, including Dionysus, a member of the Areopagus Council, but these were quite modest in number compared to his successes elsewhere (Acts 17:34). Athens sent a representative to the Council of Nicaea in 325, but Christianity was still weak there, as it was in the rest of Greece; the region had only three bishops, and only one church, at Epidaurus, can be dated to the fourth century. Constantine's heirs, Constantius II and Constans I, issued an edict closing the temples, but this was almost universally ignored (c.350).

Julian, a prince of the Christian imperial family, spent two months in Athens, studying at the foot of the Acropolis with Libanius, a pagan philosopher. Among his fellow pupils were two Christians, Basil and Gregory of Nazianzus. Basil, who is known today as Basil the Great and was canonised, particularly admired the fusion of Christianity and the pagan philosophical tradition. The odd teacher and a few of the pupils were Christian, but the overwhelming majority were pagan. Julian later became emperor (361–3), and tried to revive the pagan cults during his brief reign. Given this emperor's love of Athens, much is enthusiastically ascribed to his reign, and many have tried to ascribe the late renovation of the Parthenon to him; although some say he 'reopened' the temples in Athens, in truth they had never ceased operating. Alison Franz, a great authority on the Late Antique city, argued persuasively that this patronage of Athens was unlikely. Constantinople as his capital, and the war he was fighting on the Persian front, took up most of Julian's attention during his reign, and he was never able to revisit the Athens of his student days.

Although the Parthenon remained pagan, in a largely pagan city, there had been a number of changes to the Periclean concept of the building. At some point in Late Antiquity the Erechtheion ceased to be the temple of Athena, and the cult was moved to the Parthenon. The old wooden Mycenaean cult statue of Athena probably finally disintegrated, and the Erechtheion was damaged by fire. For the first time the Athenians walked up to the Parthenon, still adorned with its original sculptures, and saw it as a temple of Athena. Then, after Valentinian's death in 375, having seen the hero in a dream, a Nestorius set up a statue of Achilles in the shadow of the great Athena Parthenos, and instituted a small cult. This is our last text showing the Parthenos statue as in situ, and by then paganism was being outlawed by a series of imperial decrees issued by the new Christian Roman emperors.

In 393 Gratian and Theodosius I issued another edict allowing certain temples to remain open, as long as no sacrifices took place in them, and if the statues inside them were being viewed for artistic rather than cultic reasons. The Olympic Games were disbanded the same year; pagan worship was banned both in public and privately at home. The situation had been reversed, and the Christians had come out of the catacombs and forced the pagans into hiding. Although the many laws issued are confusing, at times condemning paganism, at others safeguarding temples, we do know that the famous Serapeion at Alexandria was destroyed towards the end of Theodosius' reign. He still allowed some of his leading officials to be pagan, even after he had crushed the pro-pagan usurper Eugenius (in 394); public order and political stability took precedence over religious beliefs. In a city that was overwhelmingly pagan such as Athens, it was better to turn a blind eye, and let the Parthenon remain open. Closing it, or desecrating the sculptures that decorated its exterior, would have caused riots.

Even in Rome and Constantinople, the two centres of Christian devotion, many pagans remained for a further century, and the further one went from the Old and the New Rome, the more pagans one was likely to find. Some of the senators in Constantinople were 'Hellenic' under Theodosius, meaning that they were still pagan both in terms of religion and, even more importantly, in terms of culture. In Athens Christianity does not appear to have gained any great foothold yet, and the Parthenon remained pagan, its sculptures still intact and clearly illustrating pagan myths and the city's pagan heritage. Athenians still believed in and venerated the gods depicted in the pediments and on the frieze. In Constantinople too, the rituals and rhetoric around the Christian emperor remained largely pagan, so the base of his equestrian statue in his new forum described Theodosius as 'Rising from the East, in a blaze of light, like a second Helios'.

Helios, of course, was the pagan sun god, depicted both in the east pediment of the Parthenon and in the metopes. Although Christianity was encouraged, and part of the imperial rhetoric, the reality was more often one of reconciliation with pagans and heretics, for the sake of the empire. So in 382 a temple on the Euphrates, a border region where many of the troops were pagan, was allowed to reopen. One emperor had closed it, another reopened it, because, as under the Ottoman Empire, the emperor's word was the law. A few years later, in 387, he even appointed a pagan, Eutropius, as his co-consul.

Important temples like the Parthenon were allowed to continue operating as long as they did not sacrifice animals; the cows being led to their slaughter in the Parthenon frieze thus no longer reflected the reality of pagan religious practice in the Christian period. They were spared from destruction by the policy of tolerance, this element of the pagan nature of the frieze being no longer the norm, so that the procession became one of Athenians, but not Athenians sacrificing to Athena.

After Theodosius I died in 395, his empire was split into the East and the West Byzantine Empires, ruled by his two sons as two separate empires. Athens and Greece fell under the control initially of the Western Empire, then under that of the East based in Constantinople. The following year Alaric, who had been a general under Theodosius, and his Arian Visigoths ravaged Greece on their way to sacking Rome. Buildings that had survived the Heruli invasion now fell to his forces. The Gothic destruction of Athens has been greatly underplayed. Alaric was unable to seize the Acropolis, but the archaeological record shows a devastating destruction layer all around the hill and throughout the lower city.

In the first years of the fifth century there was much rebuilding in Athens following the Gothic destruction, but despite the fact that by 400 Christianity was the legal religion of the empire, most of the buildings were pagan in nature. As the century progressed there was a fine line between Christianity and pagans which increasingly became blurred: conversion to Christianity was necessary to further one's career, so some, such as the Athenian magistrate Theagenes, did so. A Herculius, at least nominally a Christian, was the prefect of Illyricum (Greece) at the time (408–12). Although the capital was Thessalonica, he chose to spend much of his time in Athens where he was on good terms with the philosophers (two of whom dedicated statues to him) and was tolerant of paganism.

A Neoplatonic Academy had been founded in fifth-century Athens by Plato. Originally to the north of the city, it was later housed on the south slope of the Acropolis. One of his successors, a Neoplatonic philosopher, Iamblichos, had helped Athens build new walls and a tower, for which he was honoured by the city. A Plutarch paid for the Panathenaic ship three times, the last time probably in 410/11, so the festival was still regularly celebrated in the early fifth century, although it appears to have wound down by the middle of the century. This Plutarch also set up a statue of Herculius in front of the Library of Hadrian, and another philosopher, Apronianus, erected a statue of the prefect on the Acropolis, next to the Athena Promachos, which was still standing at that time.

The Academy was rebuilt, as was much of the lower city. The agora, which had been empty since the Heruli, acquired some monumental structures which included a giant philosophical school in the centre of the agora. Very little of this new building was Christian, because the Christians at that point were still mostly the lower class in a city where the pagan philosophers made up the elite and ruling class. Phaedrus, an archon, paid for a new stage at the theatre of Dionysus, where plays were put on as part of the festival of Dionysus, showing that it was still used. The city of Athens was still small, and lay within the post-Herulian Walls.

In 435 the Byzantine Greek emperor Theodosius II (408–50) issued an edict ordering that all pagan temples be destroyed, and that a cross be erected over the ruins to exorcise the site. While some scholars have interpreted the law as allowing conversion, it was quite clear when it ordered the razing of the temples. The archaeological record is equally clear in showing that the edict was often disregarded. The problem with the order was that it had to be enforced by magistrates, who in Athens were still pagan, and so ignored it. Other edicts were also issued allowing some toleration to pagans, and so the Parthenon and its sculptures survived yet again. Throughout the empire there were around a hundred temples that survived, and were eventually turned into churches. The city with the highest concentration of surviving temple-churches was Athens, a city in which paganism persisted longer, encouraged by the teachings of the philosophical schools.

Theodosius was all too aware of the prestige of Athens and its schools, and in 425 founded a university in Constantinople designed to try to rival them. One tutor of the latter included a Helladius who, as a priest of Zeus in Alexandria, had previously killed Christians; now he dedicated himself to teaching. Under imperial control, all thirty-one teachers were meant to be Christian, but pagans had to be hired to maintain a high level of experience. Although it did provide competition for Athens' schools, these continued to flourish. It was at this time also that Greek became one of the legally accepted languages of the empire along with Latin. This marked the shift from a Roman Empire to a separate Byzantine Empire in the East, as opposed to the Roman Empire in the West. Even at the end of the second Theodosius' reign, the Isaurian troops were still mostly pagan. Acutely aware that they had the power, he is unlikely to have antagonised them.

Athens was by then a minor provincial city, but Theodosius II was well aware of its existence. In June 421 he had married an 'Athenian' called Athenais, whose father Leontis had been a Sophist philosopher teaching in the city. Although she lived in Athens, Athenais and her father were originally from Antioch; as she made clear in a speech to the people of Antioch: 'I am of your line and blood.' She would be a great patron of the city as empress, which confirms this. The description of her as 'Athenian' in the sources relates to her classical pagan culture and sympathies, rather than to the geography of her family. Her family was a prominent one and had connections with leading pagans at court. Her brother Gesius had been prefect of Illyricum and so in charge both of Athens and, as a pagan, presumably also of her temples. On marriage Athenais converted to Christianity, and changed her name to Eudoxia. The emperor had two empresses: his sister Pulcheria, granted her title through blood and because of her virtue, and his wife Eudoxia, through her marriage and fertility.

Until this time the cult of Mary had not been an important one in Christianity. Now it was promoted by Pulcheria, who had dedicated her virginity to God, and saw Mary as a model for female virtue, and through her the possibility of female power. She promoted Mary as a direct response to the teachings of Nestorius, a Patriarch of Constantinople, who had initially been supported by Theodosius and Eudoxia, but was eventually deposed as a heretic. The virgin Empress Pulcheria became associated with Mary, and pushed to have the mother of Christ recognised as *Theotokos*, the mother of Christ the Divine, as well as Christ the mortal, at the Council of Ephesus in 431. Christ was both human and divine, but previously Mary had only been recognised as the mother of the human aspect of him, and so less worthy of veneration and of great basilicas. Pulcheria came to be addressed as 'the Handmaiden of God', just like Mary before her. She built the first churches to Mary in Constantinople, and the dedication of the Parthenon as a church of Mary therefore cannot predate her time. The worship of the virgin Artemis at Ephesus was transferred to the Virgin Mary, and soon Athena too would fall in Athens. For now though paganism was strong enough in the city to keep the Parthenon open.

Although earlier scholars like to see the Parthenon as having been rededicated as a church around this time, and associate it with Athenais-Eudoxia, this is not possible. The empress-wife had had a conversion of convenience only, and was neither a great promoter of Christianity in Athens, nor a follower of this new cult of Mary. If anything, Eudoxia and her family encouraged paganism and promoted pagan Athens, and she may well have provided funds for pagan buildings to be refurbished in her adopted home. She is called 'the Athenian' because she was pro-pagan, and Athens was intrinsically linked to paganism. Constantly battling with Pulcheria for toleration, Eudoxia and her family might have thought this sweet revenge. Pulcheria's devotion built churches to Mary; Eudoxia refurbished temples in Athens dedicated to the pagan gods.

One of the earliest churches in Athens, the basilica on the Ilissos, later used by the Florentine rulers of Athens as the church for their suburban retreat, is apocryphally attributed to Eudoxia. Converted from a pagan temple, this is possibly the first example of such a transfer of use in Athens, but it was in a suburb. *Spolia*, the term used for dismembered elements of buildings, of the period is preserved in later walls, and from literary evidence we know that there were over a dozen churches scattered around Athens in the fifth and sixth centuries.

At the end of November 2004 I visited the Acropolis Museum in Athens, and re-examined some of the frieze blocks. I noticed a few details that were 'wrong', details that looked incongruous for fifth-century BC sculpture. Then I looked at them again, and consulted Michael Daley. We realised that the frieze had been retouched, and lightly recarved at some point. Although we know that the exterior sculptures of the Parthenon had been restored a few times in antiquity, no one had yet suggested this for the frieze. Several of the details looked Byzantine, even medieval, and certainly not Classical Greek. The relief in places seemed too shallow, as if it had been cut back at a later date. Similar features can be noted on the Ara Pacis in Rome; built by Augustus, it had been restored by Constantine.

The frieze was located high up on a wall, sheltered from the elements by the roof of the Parthenon, unlike the sculptures outside, so it has long been assumed that it was not damaged by rain and wind over the centuries. What many scholars forget is that around AD 300 the Parthenon was ravaged by fire, the interior gutted and the roof burned down. The Parthenon was rebuilt using elements

Details of the east frieze which show later recutting

from earlier buildings, but funds did not stretch to a whole new roof, so only the inner room was covered. The frieze, just below the old roof, was now exposed to the elements for the first time, on the windswept Acropolis.

When the Parthenon was turned into a church, the sculpture on the outside representing pagan myths was deliberately defaced and destroyed. The central block of the frieze, where an offering was made to Athena, was removed, but otherwise not deliberately damaged. The frieze itself showed a procession of Athenians, which could easily have been reinterpreted by Byzantine Christians as a Christian religious procession, and so was spared.

So when was the frieze restored and slightly recut? Did soot need to be cleaned off it after the fire? Was it cleaned later when the Parthenon church was refurbished by its new archbishop in the twelfth century? One hand on the frieze would not look out of place in a medieval Florentine painting. It seems fitting that Nerio Acciajuoli, a Florentine, was the Lord of Athens. In 1394 he left funds to refurbish and beautify the Parthenon in his will. Nerio so loved the Parthenon that he asked to be buried in it, and it would seem fitting if he turned out to be in some way responsible for the Parthenon frieze, one of the sculptures from the Parthenon we most admire today.

Further research is needed, however, and only time will tell, but the style of the cutting seems early Byzantine in nature. Later Byzantine carving tends to be cruder, with heavy drapery and almost iconic people. It was not until the later medieval period in Italy that artists again began to study classical sculpture and to return to a lighter, more 'real' style of carving. I suspect that these recuttings of the Parthenon frieze can only be fitted into two periods: the period of Athenais-Eudoxia, and that of Nerio many centuries later. Although Nerio loved the Parthenon, his heirs had to fight to regain Athens, and may not have honoured his will, so the earlier phase is more likely.

The cult of Athena had been recently moved from the temple of Athena Polias in the Erechtheion to the Parthenon. The Parthenon was a 'proper' temple for the first time in its history, and a woman from Athens, named after the city, was in a position of power for the first time in many centuries. While her rival Pulcheria was promoting Mary and building churches to her in Constantinople, it seems possible that some of the financial patronage Eudoxia lavished on Athens found its way to the Parthenon and was used for its restoration. Nominally forced to become a Christian on marriage, Eudoxia continued to delight in classical culture at court. Restoring the sculptures of the Parthenon, where the great myths and Greek gods were depicted, while her sister-in-law was busy promoting Christianity and emphasising her own virginity, may well have amused her. Built to honour a female goddess, by a city named after her, two women continued to play a role in the Parthenon's Byzantine history, and temporarily saved it from dilapidation or transformation into a church.

The philosophical and rhetoric schools remained open, drawing those eager to learn from the whole empire. A mid-fourth-century text refers to the Acropolis as still covered with ancient statues. The head of the Neoplatonic academy at the time was Proclus (412–485), and we know much about the Athens of his day as his biography is preserved. Just as Plato had recorded the teachings of his master Socrates, so the tradition continued of a student recording the wisdom and life of his predecessor, and Macrinus wrote a *Vita* of Proclus immediately after the latter's death. From this life we know that Proclus, as head of the academy from *c*.437, lived on the south slope of the Acropolis, to the south of the theatre and the Asclepieion, where earlier Platonic philosophers had lived before him. His academy was adjacent, and other texts show that the sophists had a school in the same area, as did several other philosophers. A few have been tentatively identified, but some appear to be under the site of the New Acropolis Museum, and so will be destroyed. In the second half of the fifth century there appear to have been no new pagan structures, the existing ones being instead refurbished, but also as yet no Christian structures in the centre of Athens. Athens was still a great pagan cultural centre, even if now only a shadow of her former glory.

From Proclus' *Vita* we know that the statue of Athena Parthenos was removed from the Parthenon *c*.460; he dreamed that the goddess came to him seeking shelter, after the Christians had removed her statue. The statue was not Pheidias' chryselephantine marvel but the Parthenos III, a much later replacement. The figure does not seem to have been a great work of art, so was probably merely removed rather than shipped to Constantinople. The building was deconsecrated, and Proclus was barred from entering shortly before his death. Deconsecration was not immediately followed by conversion into a church, and there was a time lapse between the two, so the Parthenon was probably abandoned for a while, spiritually no longer the home of Athena, but not yet that of Christ. After independence Greek archaeologists stripped away anything in Athens that post-dated antiquity from the temples and classical ruins, making it hard to piece together the period. It was normal also to pull down part of the temple, usually just a few blocks, when it was closed. The Parthenon seems to have remained architecturally intact for centuries, so it may well be that only the sculptures were damaged at the time. The Parthenon sculptures were pagan in theme, the reason the building was closed, and so are likely to have been a target for the Christian authorities.

Pheidias' Athena Promachos was seen by St Jerome on the Acropolis in 372, and was still in place in 410, but was taken to Constantinople in the 460s, where it decorated the Forum of Constantine. Long after the statue had left Athens, it remained an Athenian icon, and lamps of c.600 have been found depicting it. It was destroyed by a mob in 1203, just before the sack of Constantinople; the people were convinced that the statue was sending coded messages to assist the Crusaders outside the walls. This event was recorded by the Historian Niketas Choniates, whose brother was then Archbishop of Athens.

Despite the loss of the Athena Parthenos and the closure of the Parthenon, Athens' prosperity lasted into the sixth century. Its economy was built to a great extent on the schools and the pupils they attracted from around the empire; these survived even the Vandals, who in 466/7 stopped at Athens on their way to Rome. By 500 the majority of Athenians were nominally Christian, but no temples had yet been converted into churches. Then in 529 Justinian (527–65) issued a decree ordering that pagans were no longer allowed to teach, effectively meaning that the schools of Athens had to close.

In the same year heretics and pagans were again excluded from holding office within the empire, and from joining the military. Justinian's decree was enforced, and the schools were disbanded; this is confirmed by the archaeological record which shows that many buildings associated with philosophy were abandoned c.530. After a thousand years, during which they had flourished, this was the final clash between the culture of ancient Athens and the new world order, and the pagans lost.

After the closure of the schools, Athens' economy collapsed, since these had been the chief source of revenue for the city. Damascius, the last head of the Neoplatonic Academy, along with a number of the city's leading philosophers, chose to go into exile rather than stay in Athens. He went to Persia, the land that for a millennium the Athenians had characterised as barbarian, but which now welcomed this Greek philosopher and his teachings. Many other teachers also fled to Persia, the reason so much classical learning has been preserved in Arabic translations.

Evidence suggests that a few men at the Academy discreetly continued teaching for a couple of decades after the edict. Some Christian philosophers emerged as teachers, but the glory of pagan Athens as a cultural centre was over. Many of the pagan sanctuaries fell into decay, and an earthquake destroyed some more. In the sixth century, basilicas were built over the Asclepieion and the theatre of Dionysus on the south slope of the Acropolis. Shrines to Cosmas and Damien, saints associated with healing, replaced Asclepius to care for the Athenian sick. Justinian rebuilt the city walls and the Acropolis ramparts which had fallen into disrepair, but otherwise largely ignored Athens, not even the capital of Byzantine Greece. In the 580s the Slavs began to descend into Greece, passing through Thermopylae, where Leonidas and his men had once valiantly held off the Persian advance. They continued south, crossed into the Peloponnese and settled there. The inhabitants of many cities fled into the mountains to found new communities. The Spartans of the day moved to Mistras, and there founded a town that would become one of the capitals of the Byzantine Empire. Athens at least still existed; the once mighty city of Sparta no longer did.

* * *

The date remains open, but the Parthenon was probably converted into a church during the second half of the sixth century, or the early seventh century. It is covered with graffiti of the Christian period, but the first of these which is datable is from 694, which provides a *terminus ante quem* before which we assume it probably became a church. The last time it served as a temple is just before the death of Proclus, which provides a *terminus post quem*. Between these dates two centuries elapsed, at some point during which the Parthenon became a church dedicated to the Virgin.

The smaller, less important Erechtheion was converted into a church in the seventh century, as was the Hephaisteion. The Hephaisteion was similar to the Parthenon, a fifth-century BC Doric temple with unusual features such as a continuous Ionic frieze, and its orientation had to be reversed to face east before it became a church of St George, as churches needed to face east towards Jerusalem. (St Peter's in Rome, both as the original Constantinian basilica and the Renaissance cathedral, is one of the few exceptions to this rule, and is reverse-orientated due to a combination of the terrain it was built on and the desire of the builders for it to face the city of Rome.) Its Byzantine phase is better documented than that of the Parthenon, so we know that the conversion reused some earlier Byzantine architectural fragments. The seventh century also marked the first temple to be converted into a church in Rome; in 609 the Pantheon became a church, St Mary of the Martyrs.

The Parthenon as a church was dedicated to Mary, the Panagia Atheniotissa, and its orientation also had to be changed. The entrance was thus to the west, and this doorway had an inner frame of old marble blocks inserted into the existing one to make it smaller. Two more small doorways were cut, framing it, and patterns of wear show that the southern door on the west side was the most used entrance.

Low walls were built between the Doric columns of the peristyle to create a semi-enclosed walkway, though these were closed in and added to over the years. Some may have become small chapels. The opisthodomus became a narthex, and the wall between it and the main chamber of the Parthenon was pierced by three doors to allow access, so that the congregation would flow freely from west to east.

Small doorways were also pierced into the north and south walls of the narthex to provide additional access to it, and a section was walled off to demarcate a small baptistery.

Constantine's St Peter's had had five aisles, but most Christian basilicas, like modern churches, were built with only three. The Parthenon's interior colonnade easily accommodated this, since the cella was unusually wide. The colonnade of the cella was thus so useful in the creation of three naves, that some early modern archaeologists had assumed that it was an early Christian addition rather than a Late Roman one. The thinner columns of the replacement colonnade allowed easier viewing, which was key in a church. The only alteration made to the colonnade was the removal of the middle lower column on the west side; it faced the new entrance to the chamber and blocked access, so it was replaced by an arch.

In Byzantine churches, just as in mosques and some synagogues today, men and women were separated in the congregation. This women's section, the *gynaikeia*, was technically within the sanctuary of the church, from which women were excluded. A similar separation of the sexes was the norm in Byzantine homes. Because the colonnade inside the Parthenon was divided horizontally into two levels, it has always been assumed that a gallery was built, and that the women worshipped there. Although an appealing idea, no travellers describe this gallery – the fact that the capitals of the upper level could be seen by visitors even argues against it – and the crucial evidence for a lack of a gallery is that there are no keys (the cuttings to hold the beams in place) on the walls of the Acropolis. So, although a gallery seems the most sensible way of separating the sexes, it is likely that in the Byzantine Parthenon this was done by screening off an aisle.

The congregation and the clergy were also kept apart, so for liturgical reasons an iconostasis, a high wall that separated the congregation from the altar, was erected inside. The east doorway was enlarged to fit a semicircular apse created out of elements of a reused circular ancient monument. This apse was quite modest, and physically fitted within the peristyle; it was constructed using blocks from the round temple of Roma and Augustus, these blocks serving as the *synthronon*, the steps in the apse on which clergy sat during services. Windows provided light, the openings filled with thin translucent panes of marble, since glass was prohibitively expensive. The floor of the apse and the area behind the iconostasis was raised above the level of the ancient floor, and beneath this is preserved the evidence for the late Roman rebuilding. The iconostasis was described later as an elaborate columned wall, with jasper shafts.

In the centre of the apse stood the episcopal throne, a reused marble seat from the theatre of Dionysus, in which pagan priests and magistrates had sat when the theatre was still in use; the throne was in the same location in the later Byzantine church, and was seen by seventeenth-century travellers. It continued to be used by the Franks and then the Ottomans, and was found in the nineteenth century in the apse. An ever-burning light stood over a saint's tomb, and in c.660 an icon of the Virgin and Child supposedly painted by St Luke the Evangelist was brought from Thebes to join the other relics in the church.

The first Parthenon church was rebuilt so many times, our only clues can be parallels to contemporary churches and the few traces of structural changes left on the pavement of the temple. The structure travellers describe is a later rebuilding, because in the nineteenth century, after independence, all post-Classical remains were stripped off the Acropolis by Greek archaeologists working for the new Bavarian kings of Greece who did not want their great site to be sullied by anything that post-dated Pericles.

Ironically, one metope, the last metope on the western end of the north side, was spared by the Christians because they thought that it represented the Annunciation, where the Angel came to Mary to announce that she was carrying a son. The metope had been carved over four centuries and showed a scene from the fall of Troy, but this new interpretation saved it for us. The two standing figures are still, to this day, in much better condition than the figures in the scenes to the left of them, or the figures and horses in the Amazonomachy metopes immediately to the right of them. Thus one of the best preserved metopes survived accidentally, because the figures were surprisingly similar to a Christian motif; sculptural salvation through reinterpretation.

The Parthenon, the Erechtheion, and the Hephaisteion all

The metope on the left was believed to depict
the Annunciation and so spared

became basilicas. Even the Thrasyllos Monument above the theatre
was converted into a church. All pagan temples were abandoned,
though some families might have discreetly worshipped at home, in
secret, just as Catholicism went into the closet in Tudor England.
Athens was a famous city so kept its name, unlike other towns that
were reassigned Christian names, but Athena no longer ruled on the
Acropolis. She had been replaced by another virgin: Mary, Mother
of God.

Byzantine Athens
(529–1204)

In 582/3 the Slavs sacked the lower city, an event attested in the archaeological record by a destruction layer excavated all around the Acropolis. The Slavs seem not to have gained access to the Acropolis itself, but they sacked the agora, which was not resettled until the eleventh century. In the Byzantine period Athens was not only a provincial city, but one to which most officials would not want to be sent, as this often signified exile and disgrace. The only positive aspect of being posted to Athens for an official was that it was far enough away from the capital for him to feel free to embezzle liberally, the increased purse making up for the bruised ego.

Even long after the Slavs had left Athens there was panic, and many coin hoards were buried during the reign of Heraclius (610–41), the Byzantine emperor who was the contemporary of Mohammed. The Slavs continued to hold much of the interior of Greece when Constans II (641–68) wintered in the city in 662/3. According to the excavators, coins of Constans were found in the 'palace', probably a refurbished Late-Antique philosopher's home, on the south slope of the Acropolis, which will lie under the New Acropolis Museum. We know that the emperor stopped in Athens on his way to Sicily, where he died, but nothing else of this trip is recorded. Presumably he stopped to worship in the Parthenon since this was the most important church in Athens. The city was clearly rich enough to house him, his vast entourage and his army, but the period remains a 'Dark Age' in Athenian history as we have so little information about the city at that time. This in turn makes it particularly sad that one of the few sites associated with this time is now being destroyed by the Greek Ministry of Culture.

Soon after Constans' visit we find the first link between England and Athens. Theodore of Tarsus studied in Athens, where some Christian philosophical schools had been revived. Soon after, he was sent to England as Archbishop of Canterbury (669–90). Another seventh-century saint, Gislenus, studied in Athens. A few of Theodore's contemporaries in England also claimed to have been 'finished' in Athens, although whether this was true or merely an attempt to claim some of the city's ancient philosophical prestige is not known. Technically at the time the see of Athens was under the control of the Pope as Bishop of Rome. In 732 Leo III, during a dispute over iconoclasm, transferred it to the Patriarch in Constantinople. Since Leo had armies and the Pope did not, he could not do anything about the loss of this minor city and its Parthenon church.

Athens in the eighth century was still of some importance for her port, the Piraeus, since Byzantine military control at the time was exercised from the sea, rather than risking dangerous crossings overland. Thebes, with its flourishing silk manufacturers, had been the seat of the military governor of the Byzantine province of Hellas until the eighth century, the century in which Athens provided another empress of Byzantium. She was the first Byzantine empress the Sarantapechos family produced; her niece Theophano would be the second. The circumstances in which Irene became empress are shrouded in mystery – she may well have been chosen in a 'Bride Show', a sort of Byzantine beauty pageant in which well-born girls were brought out of their homes for the first time, and exhibited to courtiers who chose a wife for the emperor from them. It is more likely, though, that her family had power in Greece, a region where the emperor was trying to consolidate his control. He certainly seems to have had a policy both of appeasing Greece and of building closer links to the region, and a marriage would have helped cement these.

Unlike the earlier Empress Athenais-Eudoxia, Irene was genuinely a devout Christian, and would later be canonised. Irene married Constantine V's son Leo IV the Khazar, and bore him a son. When Constantine and then Leo died (in 775 and 780 respectively), she seized the imperial throne for herself, and exiled her brothers-in-law, who were rivals, to Athens.

Constantine V had favoured a religious policy of Iconoclasm, where images of saints and religious scenes were destroyed for being against the Commandments. This was not iconoclasm as in the Muslim world, where humans could not be depicted at all, but rather it was the forbidding of images of religious scenes for veneration. When this Constantine built and renovated churches, they were decorated with floral motifs, and also with animals and scenes such as chariot racing. The cross was also a popular motif, in place of the crucifixion, and one dating from the reign of Leo and Irene survives in Thessalonica. Irene, when she held sole power, revoked the policy, and allowed icons and religious images once again to be produced, and it was for this reason she was later canonised. The controversy continued for centuries though, with alternate emperors having differing views. Athenians, with their long history of beautiful sculptures and images, never took to Iconoclasm. When a later emperor, Leo V, once again favoured the destruction of images, the Athenians tried to launch an attack on Constantinople to depose him. Fortunately they realised the futility of the mission, and soon abandoned it.

Linked to Iconoclasm was the deliberate defacing of ancient sculpture, which was often then marked with inscribed crosses to exorcise its pagan associations. We cannot be sure when the Parthenon metopes were defaced, but those of the north, west and east sides were at some point, and this is usually ascribed to the Christians. Why the south metopes survived, nobody knows, although one north metope was not defaced and it is assumed that this is because it was given a Christian interpretation. Not all the destruction of the metopes can be assigned to the Byzantines, for in the Turkish period heads continued to be chopped off for sale to tourists, and stray pieces were burned to create lime. The Parthenon was then famous for an icon of the Virgin, the Panagia Atheniotissa, which was widely copied in Greece, rather than for the sculpture that decorated it.

By this time the exterior of the Parthenon was covered in graffiti, commemorating deaths and hopes, mostly in Greek with some earlier Latin inscriptions. Columns had crosses carved on to them or attached in bronze, and a series of small buildings abutted the exterior colonnade, so the Parthenon was no longer set within its own space, but became part of the maze of structures on the Acropolis. Attached to the exterior of the columns were also icons which, as on the Hephaisteion, have left a series of sets of four cuttings for the brackets which once held them in place. These images are now missing, but after the defacement of the exterior sculptures of the Parthenon they would have been one of the main forms of adornment of the building.

Since much of the graffiti records the clerics in charge of the

Peg marks left on the columns, showing where
Byzantine icons once decorated the exterior

Parthenon church, we know that around this time Athens was raised from a bishopric to an archbishopric. It would not be too great a leap to ascribe this elevation to Irene, ruler of Byzantium, caring for her home town. Certainly by 841 we know that Athens was an archbishopric, and the position was raised again by 981 to that of metropolitan bishops. The Greeks had suffered due to the Arab invasions, with some areas needing to be re-Hellenised and converted. Their churches had only recently been brought back into the fold, under the control of the Patriarch in Constantinople rather than the Pope, and so elevating the see of Athens would have been politically expedient. If it was not undertaken by Irene, then it may well have been the work of Constantine V, part of the same policy of appeasement that brought an Athenian bride to the throne.

By the late ninth century, then, Athens was an archbishopric, with ten bishops, and ranked twenty-eighth out of fifty-one in the Byzantine Empire. The pilgrimage of various Byzantine saints to the Parthenon church is recorded, including that of St Nikon in 970; the Byzantines had recently regained Crete from the Arabs, and Nikon had reconverted it to Christianity, as well as expelling the Jews from Greece. Athens was officially designated a *kastro*, meaning that it was a fortress that could be used for refuge. Byzantine Athens was heavily fortified, although the Acropolis was open to worshippers who wished to use the church. The walls on top of the Acropolis were kept repaired, and a middle Byzantine inscription tells us that a Leo had added a tower to the citadel. Its economy was improving, and the city was beginning to outgrow the Herulian walls, although it kept within the Themistoclean ones. Another Leo, governor of Hellas, died in Athens in 848, an event attested in graffiti on the Parthenon, and he may well have been buried in the church.

In 1017 Basil II (976–1025), soon renamed Basil the Bulgar-Slayer, defeated the Bulgarians after a war that had lasted thirty years. The following year he made a pilgrimage to Athens, where he celebrated his victory with a mass of thanksgiving in the Parthenon, dedicating this victory over the Bulgar infidels to Mary of Athens. Athens was poorer than Thebes, but its heritage was still remembered, and it was the more prestigious city. Basil gave the church gold and jewels that had been his booty from the sacked Bulgarian capital, and the gold dove that hung over the altar is also assumed to have been his gift. His gifts left the church in Athens well provided for, and the monastery at Daphne was founded at this time. He also, rather surprisingly, left funds on his departure for the repair of ancient temples, to preserve the beauty of the town. The second refurbishment of the Parthenon as a church cannot be directly linked to his visit, but began some decades later.

Anna, the Byzantine bride that Vladimir, I, Prince of Rus, had sought, made a considerable impact on his peoples, encouraging her husband's conversion of his lands to Christianity, and bringing some Byzantine sophistication to his court. Vladimir's own sons, Boris and Gleb, were murdered in 1015, providing the Russian Orthodox Church with their first martyrs, and thus their first saints. Another Byzantine princess, Theophano Skleraina, went to Italy as the bride of Otto II. The eleventh century thus brought about not only the embellishment of the Parthenon church by Basil, to commemorate his victories, but also marked the period when Byzantine culture spread in influence to the lands of the Balkans, and even far north towards the Baltic. The Byzantines, however, did not think of themselves as Greeks, but as the heirs to the Romans; messengers from the West bearing letters addressed to the 'Emperor of the Greeks' would not be granted audiences, Greek culture being seen as beneath them.

Athens was fortunate to have two educated men appointed as archbishops in the twelfth century. The first of these, Nicholas Agiotheodorites (1166–75), rebuilt the Parthenon church, turning it into a magnificent Byzantine structure. We know this from the physical remains of the building, as well as Euthemius Tornikes' funerary oration for Archbishop Nicholas, where it is stated that Nicholas had renovated St Mary of Athens, as well as building many churches. After his death the refurbishment and decorating continued under his successor. We know less about Nicholas than about the last Orthodox Archbishop of Athens, because the latter was a prolific writer, and many of his sermons and poems, often related to the glory of the ancient city, are preserved. Athens was undergoing a final flourishing of Byzantine culture, although one more suited in scale to a provincial city than a metropolis, and it is in this period that the last Byzantine church in the Parthenon was constructed.

Michael Choniates Akominatos was appointed as Nicholas' successor, although he may not have arrived in Athens until 1182. Michael's inauguration is the only ceremony in the Parthenon about which we have any details. Michael was highly educated, and a man steeped in Greek history; Athens was in theory the perfect post for him, combining his calling and the city's antiquity. Initially, he was clearly delighted but, used to the sophisticated court at Constantinople, he was quickly disappointed with the Athenians of the day who made up his congregation. In his first sermon he celebrated the ancient glory of Athens, the Greeks who had defeated the Persians at Marathon. Unfortunately, he spoke in the literary Greek of Constantinople, and most Athenians spoke only demotic Greek; they were literally speaking two different tongues.

Some years before, we know of a governor of the city, Michael Psellus (1015–1078), who held both Athens and the Greeks in contempt. Like Michael Choniates, he was steeped in ancient Athens, and for this the heroes of Marathon were on a par with Alexander the Great in their importance and the role they played in Greek history. The glory and greatness of Athens' victory at Marathon is a motif repeated throughout history, as was the importance of her philosophical schools.

Archbishop Michael's classical references fell mostly on deaf ears, but he continued to praise and to preach. He wrote poems on the glory of ancient Athens as well as sermons. He complained that the people were wretched and ignorant, but Byzantine Greece was sparsely populated, and the Franks would encourage Albanians to settle during the following centuries. Contemporary Athens was hell compared to the glory of Pericles' Athens for this civilised clergyman; it was poor and barbarous, with no appreciation of its past. Michael looked down on the Athenians in every sense: both physically down from his Acropolis palace, and metaphorically. He soon came to complain of food shortages in the city, and raiding by pirates along the coastline, but despite this he managed to complete the decoration of the interior of the Parthenon church. Unfortunately, although he praised the beauty and antiquity of his church regularly, he never described it.

The first description after Pausanias of the Parthenon dates to the end of the fourteenth century, but Michael's Parthenon continued in use through the Frankish period before being converted into an Ottoman mosque. It stood for centuries, and although each new phase brought successive adaptations, we can visualise his church from the numerous descriptions of travellers during the Ottoman period, and from the archaeological remains.

The apse was rebuilt on a larger scale, so that it extended to the outer colonnade, enveloping two of the Doric columns within its semi-hexagonal walls. Each of these walls had a large double-arched window filled with ornately pierced translucent marble, which many later visitors admired. The ceiling of the new apse was domed, and decorated with a beautiful mosaic of the Madonna holding Christ in her left hand, on a gold ground, and again described and admired by later travellers. To make way for the dome the central block of the east frieze with the *peplos* scene was removed, and the architrave from beneath it recut to create a sill for the central window. The cornice from the middle of the east pediment was taken down as part of this enlargement. The central figures in the pediment above – Zeus, Hephaestus and Athena – if they had survived as late as this, certainly vanished in the twelfth-century rebuilding.

The mosaic remained on view in the Ottoman mosque after the other Christian decoration had been covered over, because legends arose that if it were defaced then the plague would ravage the city. In the apse the bishop still sat on his throne, and just in front of him, hidden from the congregation, was the altar. This altar was covered by an elaborated *baldacchino*, not unlike the one in St Peter's, supported on porphyry columns, and from its dome hung a golden dove. The dove, a symbol of peace, is believed to have been dedicated by Basil after his victories, when by removing the Bulgar threat he brought his empire peace on one frontier. Evliya, the Turkish traveller who would later describe the Parthenon as the most beautiful mosque in the world, was sure that it must have been built by King Solomon. He described the capital of the *baldacchino* as Corinthian and noted that they were all different; this suggests that antique capitals were reused.

The other major structural change is that windows seem to have been added to light the nave. In drawings and from travellers' descriptions we know that there were at least three on each side. These windows were placed high on the wall, jutting into the roof line, and to accommodate them a whole block of the frieze had to be removed for each window, so the Parthenon lost even more of its Classical sculptural decoration. As well as the *peplos* block at the east, three frieze blocks showing the procession were removed on each side, making a total of seven blocks of the Parthenon frieze which were removed during this rebuilding. These windows made the church bright, as Michael was proud to boast, but must have been walled up later, when visitors described the mosque as dark and lit only by the windows in the apse.

The pulpit, or ambo, which had previously stood to the east of the old base of the Parthenos and in the centre of the nave, now moved closer to the apse and into the northern aisle, which was by then the norm in Byzantine churches. It was outside the chancel, among the congregation, and would later be used in the mosque as a mimbar, for readings from the Koran. This new ambo was raised on short columns, rather like the one still in the Byzantine church of S. Apollinare Nuovo in Ravenna.

The walls were covered in paintings, and two phases in the work are apparent. No overall decorative scheme was thought out, unlike for example the Sistine ceiling, so the composition of the design is unbalanced. The first phase might date to Nicholas' tenure, and the second is ascribed to Michael's. Many of the images were painted straight on to the marble using tempera, rather than executed in fresco. Because many of these were whitewashed by the Ottomans, Muslims being against the depiction of humans, some of the images survived into the modern era, when they were drawn and photographed; today they are almost invisible, with only shadows of the vibrant colouring they once had. In the apse the Apostles were represented. ·

The interior of the church had scenes of Christ's Passion as well as many saints. The most interesting frescos are those on the exterior of the opisthodomus wall, where the scenes are better preserved. One scene of the Virgin enthroned and flanked by angels covered over an earlier fresco of Christ; it is similar to an icon from Mount Sinai. On the tower wall, perpendicular to this, was a Last Judgement, and again these seem not to have been covered over in the Turkish period. Since the style of these is twelfth century, this is the best evidence for the date of the tower, which was built using architectural members from the Roman Philopappos Monument. A circular brick stairway inside the tower was lit by slits in the walls. The original height of the tower is unknown, but it certainly led up to a small structure of mysterious use behind the west pediment. Sometimes thought to be Frankish, bell towers were rare in Byzantine churches, but not unknown, and there was a ninth-century example in Constantinople.

We know that Byzantine Christians often slept in churches in the hope of being cured by relics, and they may well have slept in the Parthenon. Some were certainly buried in it, and a number of interments have been found. To the south of the Parthenon a series of burials have been excavated; they contained coins of three emperors – Justinian, Justin II and Tiberius II – so dating them to the period 527–582. Four more graves in the Parthenon itself, three in the narthex and one in the northwest corner of the peristyle, cannot be dated more accurately, but are certainly Byzantine.

Anyone visiting Athens should try to see the Panagia Gorgoepikoos, also known as the Little Metropolis. Standing in the shadow of the large modern cathedral, this twelfth-century gem, a small Byzantine church, was built using many classical marbles to decorate the exterior. It is sometimes attributed to Michael Choniates; the reuse was not only economical, but combined his Christianity with his love of antiquity.

In 1205 Michael Choniates handed over the Acropolis to the Crusaders. He died in exile in 1222, having only returned to Athens once, in secret, although he continued to correspond with friends in the city under Frankish occupation.

The Little Metropolis, Athens

Crusader Athens

Athens of The French:
Le Château de Sethines (1204–1311)

During the ninth century the Seljuk Turks moved west from Central Asia, their conquests increasingly nibbling away at the edges of the Byzantine Empire, and disrupted pilgrimages to the Holy Land. As a result Pope Urban preached what became known as the First Crusade; its aim was to regain the Holy Sepulchre. They were successful in 1099, holding the city for a century. But as the Latin kingdoms of the Holy Land rose, so the power of the Byzantine Empire slowly waned and a deep schism arose between the two Churches.

The Fourth Crusade in 1204 was a defining moment in Greek history, leading to the capture of Constantinople rather than Jerusalem. It was driven less by the spiritual purity of the First Crusade and more by a lust for lands and adventure. The leader of the Crusade convened in the summer of 1201 was Boniface of Monferrat. Boniface's army put Alexis IV on the Byzantine throne in 1203 as co-emperor with his father Isaac Angelus, but when a *coup d'état* replaced them with Alexis V in January 1204, Boniface led the army that seized and sacked Constantinople. The Crusaders had merely intended to execute a regime change, but lack of food and funds had forced their hand in the sacking of the city. Nevertheless, they decided to hang on to Constantinople and the Byzantine lands.

After the sack of Constantinople, Greece was subdivided by the Western Crusaders, creating a series of Frankish states that made up the Latin Empire of the East. The most important of these were the Latin empire of Constantinople, the Latin kingdom of Thessalonica, the principality of Achaea, and the duchy of Naxos. Thessalonica became the property of Boniface, as did Athens and Thebes, and he carved out for himself an empire in Greece to rival that of the new Latin emperor. The Greek Byzantine emperor held on to Nicaea, and eventually regained Byzantium itself in 1261.

With the Crusades, a new era and new conquerors came to Athens. The citadel surrendered to Boniface, Michael handed over the Acropolis, and the Franks installed themselves on it. Othon de La Roche, a Burgundian, was awarded Athens as a vassal to the king of Thessalonica. He made the Acropolis his home and castle, although technically Thebes was the capital. Initially, the Parthenon suffered after the Burgundian acquisition; the Metropolitan's library was broken up, and its plate melted down.

Othon fortified the walls along the top of the Acropolis, adding crenulations, and built a new wall at its base which followed the line of the Roman wall to the south. Large buttresses were added, particularly to the south and east sides, to strengthen the walls, which from some angles gives the Acropolis the look of a medieval castle. Later, Guy I (probably) strengthened the entrance to the castle by building a wall across the old Propylaea entry, and changed access to the citadel to a new gate beneath the Nike temple. A second new gate was built below the Propylaea, which gave access to the Clepsydra spring, a water supply which was vital in case of siege. The Burgundians as conquerors had to live in their castles, so that they would be safe, and from these they could dominate their regions. In Athens of course that meant the Acropolis.

More importantly, it was Othon who converted the Parthenon into a Catholic cathedral, where for the next two and a half centuries Frankish christenings, weddings and funerals were held. Gothic Burgundian sculptures now in the Byzantine museum in Athens show how fine their work was, of a quality comparable to Gothic sculpture

The buttresses at the east end of the Acropolis,
built by the Burgundian Lords of Athens

in France. Othon was soon visited in Athens by Henry of Hainault,
the second Latin emperor of Byzantium, who, like Basil before him,
came to celebrate his victory in the Parthenon. By then of course
the Parthenon was Notre Dame d'Athènes.

Athens had not been under Roman jurisdiction since the reign
of Leo III the Isaurian, but a papal bull of 1206 appointed a French
Catholic, Bérard, Archbishop of Athens. It placed the Parthenon
under the care of St Peter, and directed that it be run on the same
model as the Notre Dame of Paris. In this bull, and in his subsequent letters, Innocent III praised the 'ancient glory of Athens',
where Mary was now worshipped in 'Pallas' renowned citadel', and
stated that it was by the grace of God that the glory of ancient
Athens had not been forgotten.

The main physical contribution made to the Parthenon during
the Burgundian period was the renovation of a low bell tower, or

campanile; originally late Byzantine, it was built within the temple's porch (the south pronarthex), blocking a doorway, using blocks of a Roman monument. The tower would later be adapted as a minaret, so survives to this day, its spiral staircase leading the few visitors fortunate enough to be allowed up it to the roof line of the temple. An exonarthex was also created, by closing in the west porch at some point in the Frankish period, and a series of small chapels were added to the sides of the Parthenon, in the colonnade. The 1206 bull also made it clear that some structural changes were needed for liturgical reasons; in Byzantine churches a high *templon* screen divided the congregation from the altar, but this had to be replaced by the low balustrade that was the norm in Catholic churches. At some point the church's plate must have been replaced.

Since the Byzantines had heavily overtaxed the Greeks, in many ways Frankish rule was better for them, and the Franks were some-times perceived as liberators. To the Greeks it was merely a change of overlord, with the added benefit that the taxes they paid stayed with a local lord rather than going to far-off Constantinople. Michael Choniates paid a quick visit to the city in 1217, returning to his exile, but other Greeks, such as his nephew, chose to stay in Athens under the Burgundians.

With a new ruler came a new language, Latin, and a new name for the city. Like many other towns, Athens' name was corrupted from the Demotic Greek (εἰς᾽Αθηνας) and became *Satines*; it was called *Sethines* or *Setines* in official documents from 1278 on. Later, the Sicilian documents were in Latin, so it was referred to as *Athenae*. Under the Aragons it reverted to *Cetines* for the town and *Attenes* for the duchy, so that even in Latin it was *civitas Cetinarum* but the Acropolis was the *castrum Athenarum*. The Piraeus became *Porto Leone*, named after its monumental lion. Byzantine Greece had been called by the Crusaders the Empire of Romania, reflecting its history.

This period also marked the birth of modern archaeology, or more specifically Egyptology, but its catalyst was less a search for history than a search for mummy flesh, which at times was even more valuable than gold. Mummies, a term that derives from the word for tar (*mumia* in Persian, *moumiya* in Arabic), were named after the bitumen that was used in their embalming process by the ancient Egyptians. Mummies were originally stripped of their bitumen, but in succeeding centuries powdered mummy and even mummy flesh had become a valuable commodity for its perceived medicinal values. 'Pissasphalt' had been used for centuries in the Near East as a treatment for many injuries and illnesses, and mummy came to be a substitute for it.

There was an active market for powdered mummy in the west by the thirteenth century. The English Levant Company tried, unsuccessfully, to corner the market towards the end of the sixteenth century, and records preserve prices per pound for flesh in various Western cities. François I of France and many of his contemporaries wore little bags containing mummy powder, partly as an amulet, partly as a form of first-aid kit in case of emergencies. To the Muslims of Egypt, the lack of aversion these Christians had to eating human flesh, in effect cannibalism, was quite surprising, but they did not fail to take advantage of it. The high demand led to faking of mummies by substituting the corpses of the recently deceased.

Othon is last attested in Athens in 1225, leaving her in the hands of his nephew Guy. This Burgundian made Athens his home, so that under his rule the city flourished. His grandson Guy II (1287–1308) arranged a papal indulgence for visitors to his Parthenon church, which assisted the Athenian economy. He had made a dynastic alliance to an heiress who at the time had not yet hit puberty, and who died before producing an heir: a cousin, Gaultier, the Count of Brienne, became Gaultier I, Duke of Athens. He was known as a Defender of the Faith, but failed as a defender of Athens, and it was at this point that the Catalan Company entered the Parthenon's history.

The Catalan Company
at the Castell de Cetines (1311–1388)

Soldiers of fortune, mercenaries, mostly from Catalonia, made up what was known as 'La Companya Catalana', or the Catalan Company. Their name reflected their origins and their main allegiance was to the Catalan throne. In 1303 the Emperor Andronicus II Palaeologus had hired these Catalans to defend Constantinople. Five or six thousand of the company followed their leader, Roger de Flor, to Constantinople. As part of the bargain, Roger married Andronicus' niece, and was raised to the rank of Caesar of the Byzantine Empire. Upward mobility was not a twentieth-century invention. Although the Catalans fulfilled their side of the bargain, their increasing demands for money and land led Michael IX, co-emperor with his father, to have Roger assassinated. The Catalans moved south.

In 1310 Gaultier of Athens decided to hire the Catalan Company to defend his territory and to secure his borders. They won on the field for him, but again a dispute over money and land soon reared its head, and so war broke out. At the Battle of Cephissus on 15 March 1311, both Gaultier and those of the cadet branches of the family were killed on the field; only a handful of Franks survived. Cephissus was near ancient Orchomene, where Philip II had gained Greece, and Sulla defeated Mithridates, and there the duke was defeated by his own mercenaries. Gaultier's widow, Jeanne de Châtillon, barricaded herself in the Acropolis, but fled as soon as she was able to with her children.

Gaultier II failed in his attempt to reclaim Athens, but was for a year tyrant of Florence. Invited to take this position to defend the city from the Pisans (1342), he was soon expelled, and the date he left the city, the Feast of St Anne (26 July 1343), is still commemorated as the day of Florence's liberation. Its importance is emphasised by the number of times St Anne is present in Florentine scenes of the Madonna and Child. The expulsion itself is depicted in a fresco in the Bargello. Recorded as a citizen of the Venetian Republic in 1344, Gaultier II eventually became Constable of France, a position his maternal grandfather had held, and died at Poitiers in 1356 fighting the English.

The Duchy of Athens and Thebes was thus taken over by the Catalans and their followers; Athens became a military state, occupied by a company of mercenaries, but without a leader they trusted to reign. Though uncouth, the Catalans were wise men in that they knew themselves unable to govern; they turned to their former employer, Frederick II Hohenstaufen of Sicily. A man with a keen interest in the past, and who had undertaken some of the first excavations, Frederick appointed his five-year-old son Manfred as duke.

A series of dukes succeeded each other, but never set foot in Athens. The poverty of Athens is a theme that runs through the Catalan documents, just as it had through those of Michael Choniates. In 1348 the plague once again devastated the city, wiping out almost half the population.

The archives of the Sicilian House of Aragon were largely destroyed in the Second World War, but those of the Catalan branch of the family that took over are still preserved in Barcelona, making this one of the best documented periods of Athenian history. We know many petty details of the administration of Athens, though almost nothing about the Parthenon or its sculpture, other than that it continued to serve as the Catholic cathedral of Athens.

Catalan Athens was run for her dukes by their vicar general (*vicarius*). Under the Sicilians, the Catalans received no elevations, but under the Aragons they were sometimes ennobled and took a more active part in the running of the city. The duchy was made up of five municipalities, each with a bishop. The first Catalan vicar general was Berenguer Estañol (d. 1316), followed by Don Alfonso Fadrique of Aragon (1317–30), a natural son of Frederick II. Don Alfonso became a pivotal figure in fourteenth-century Greece, travelling widely and acquiring new territories, but when in Athens he made his home in the Propylaea palace of the Acropolis.

The names of only four castellans, the officials who were in charge of the Castell de Cetines, the Catalan name for the Acropolis, and thus had military control of the city, are preserved, although the articles of the company restricted holders of the office to a term of three years. The castellans would have been in charge of the upkeep of the Acropolis and of any renovations undertaken on it, but the Catalans seem to have added little to it during their time in Athens. Documents from January 1372 show that Peralta improved the fortifications, which, given the state of the duchy, was a wise precaution, and would save the city from a Turkish invasion in 1394. There are few traces of the Catalan Company on the Acropolis, although we know that the Parthenon was called the Seu de Santa Maria de Cetinas and had a dozen priests.

A parliament was held in Athens in May 1380. Although traditionally said to have taken place in the Parthenon, recent scholars have argued against this on the basis of lack of evidence. We do know that Romeo de Bellarbre presided over the parliament, so it is likely to have taken place on the Acropolis, and since there were no other buildings with rooms as large, until evidence to the contrary appears, it is safe to assume that the Parthenon was indeed its venue. Churches, the largest building in a medieval town, were often used as meeting places, and the medieval Christian was not as pedantic as we have become about the suitable use of religious buildings; for example, market stalls being set up in the aisles of Gothic cathedrals are well attested in France, despite Christ's example of throwing the money-changers out of the Temple.

Although it is assumed that the Propylaea had become a palace for the archbishop in the Byzantine period, the first reference to it serving as the home of the governor is in 1390. A small chapel of St Bartholomew was adjacent to the room which in Roman times had been a picture gallery (the Pinakotheke) in the north wing, and which served as a chancellery under the Franks. Little else is known of the Acropolis under the Catalans, but we know that after the Negroponte Truce of July 1319, between the Catalans and the Venetians, it was agreed that the former, who had been engaging in piracy, would temporarily withdraw their ships from the water and store the ships' tackle on the Acropolis. The last archbishop of the Catalan period, and probably the only Catalan to have held the position, was Antonio Ballester (1370–87), who like all his predecessors resided on the Acropolis, in a palace in the Erechtheion.

An interesting aside, in view of events at the end of the century, is to note that the Catalans could not will property to the Church, and any gifts made to the Church were instead used to fund fortification of the Acropolis. This law had been in place under the Burgundians in Athens, as in many other Eastern states of the Franks, and its justification was that there were so few Franks in the East, that if they started to give their assets away, there would have been nothing left. Although various popes had long protested against this, it remained in force; a petition was sent to Pedro IV asking him to revoke this law, but he rejected it.

* * *

While Catalan Athens was declining in the 1350s and 60s, the Ottomans were playing an increasingly important part in history to the east. Orchan, son of the eponymous Othman, fought on behalf of John VI Cantacuzenus, placing him on the Byzantine throne. Soon after, the Ottomans established a new capital at Adrianople in northern Greece. In 1363 the Turks captured Thebes. The hatred of some Orthodox for the Catholics was so great that at the fall of Constantinople, one leading Greek claimed the Turks' turban preferable to the Pope's tiara.

John V Palaeologus recognised Murad I as his suzerain, giving the sultan his son Manuel as a hostage. Gregory XI called the Council of Thebes in October 1373 to organise a crusade, but the various factions preferred to argue with each other than to unite and fight a common foe. Manuel II Palaeologus, John's son, later travelled west to raise support, but again in vain; he was desperate enough to spend a month at the English court in December 1400 as the guest of Henry IV. The years 1378–1417 marked the great schism of the papacy, when there were two rival popes at Avignon, and meant that no help was forthcoming from the West.

The plague of 1348 was one of the final blows to the Byzantine Empire, which by then consisted largely of Constantinople and some of its suburbs, with a few small outposts. Byzantine culture had flourished under the Palaeologi, a last swansong before its fall, but its jewels were literally pawned; John VI's coronation diadem, it was noted, held glass in the place of gems. Hellenic culture was rediscovered towards the end, and Manuel II started styling himself Emperor of the Hellenes, a title that earlier emperors had found abhorrent. Scholars were leaving for Italy even before Constantinople fell. The Ottoman Empire towards its end was known as 'the sick man of Europe', and the end of Byzantium, whose emperors had ruled the same lands, is best described by the same epithet.

During the early Catalan Company period, the great Arab historian Abulfeda (d. 1331) was praising ancient Athens as the cradle and library of Greek philosophy, but the records of the Franks seem to largely ignore the city at this time. A century earlier, after the sack of Constantinople, a manuscript of Aristotle's *Metaphysics* had found its way to Paris. The French were not ready for such advanced philosophy, and the University of Paris in 1210 ordered it to be burned, as they believed its study would lead to heresy.

Pedro IV had written in 1380 that 'the Acropolis is the earth's richest jewel, and of such worth that not a king in Christendom could create its equal'. The year before, his queen, Sibilia, had written to ask for relics of the Virgin from the Parthenon. They are not mentioned by later travellers, so she may have been successful in getting her hands on them; they may well lie to this day in a church in Barcelona.

In 1386 the Florentine Nerio Acciajuoli seized the lower city and in 1388 gained control of the Acropolis. Unlike the Catalan dukes who had never visited Athens, let alone lived there, Nerio made his home on the Acropolis, and so a new era in the history of the Parthenon dawned.

The Florentine Acropolis (1388–1456)

On 23 April 1358 Robert II of Naples, titular Latin Emperor of Constantinople, granted Niccolò Acciajuoli (1310–65), their Florentine Grand Seneschal of Sicily, the Lordship of Corinth as a reward for his services. The Acciajuolis were northern Italian steel-workers who had moved to Florence, where they turned their skills to gold and flourished as bankers in the twelfth century. By the early fourteenth century they had become a leading Florentine family, on a par with the Bardi, Pazzi and Medici. The Acciajuoli were bankers to the popes in Avignon, and through this connection wielded tremendous influence. Niccolò had little interest in his Greek lands, although he was buried in the Florentine Certosa, a monastery he had founded with their revenues.

He was succeeded by a cousin Nerio (Rainerio), who in 1371 became Lord of Corinth. Although the awarding of Greek fiefdoms was often seen more as a burden than a reward, when Nerio inherited he took on his possessions. In fact, Nerio increased his holdings by purchasing adjacent estates, but soon gold gave way to the sword and the banker turned warrior, seizing Megara from the Catalans in 1374. He then invaded Attica, first taking Piraeus, then the lower city of Athens (1385/6). The Acropolis fell on 2 May 1388, and Athens entered another stage in its history, under the rule of a Florentine banker. Nerio, wisely, chose to go to Thebes rather than linger in plague-ridden Athens, but would later be the first Lord of Athens since Othon to live in Athens. He remodelled the Propylaea to make it more in keeping with the style of contemporary Florentine *palazzi*, which continued to be heavily fortified in design centuries after the classical had become the style of choice in the rest of Italy.

Bartolomea, Nerio's elder daughter, was famed for her beauty. She had married Theodore II Palaeologus, third son of John V, and Despot of Mistras (1380–1407). In c.1250 the fortress of Mistras had been founded by a Frank, but he soon had to cede it to the Byzantines as part of his ransom. This last stronghold of Byzantium is worth visiting to appreciate Byzantine cities; much of the city we see today was created by Theodore's brother, Manuel II, who had been Despot of Mistras before him (1348–80). In 1388 another daughter, Francesca, married Carlo I Tocco, the Duke of Leucadia (1381–1429). One would like to think they married in the Parthenon as the Cathedral Santa Maria di Atene. If indeed they did marry in the Parthenon, the ceremony would have been conducted by Ludovico da Prato, the first Archbishop of Florentine Athens.

Unfortunately Nerio or Theodore II, which is not known, wanted to add Argos to their territories. The city was Venetian by then, so when Theodore seized it they were furious. In September 1389, despite a promise of safe conduct to negotiations with the Venetians, Nerio was captured and held to ransom. He denied involvement in the matter. After considerable pressure from his family and the papacy, and the payment of a ransom partly raised from stripping the treasures of the Parthenon, Nerio was released at the end of 1390, Francesca taking his place as a hostage. He also had to cede Corinth and Megara to Venice. At the same time Nerio paid tribute to the Turks for Athens, becoming their vassal, and clearly ignored the adage that a man cannot serve two masters, by serving, in theory, three.

Nerio was a philhellene, and exercised a policy of conciliation towards the Greeks in Athens. Under Nerio's half-Greek son

Antonio, Greek would even become the lingua franca of the city. One of his less successful policies in this respect was allowing Orthodox metropolitans to take up residence in the city, for the first time under Frankish rule. The first, Dorotheus, Nerio had to expel in 1392 for plotting with the Turks. Macarius, the second Metropolitan of Athens, went further, inviting the Ottoman general Timurtash to occupy the lower city in 1394.

Once again Athens became the capital of the duchy, with the Acciajuoli living in the Palazzo d'Acropoli, the stairway leading up to which Nerio rebuilt. His descendants would continue to transform it into a Florentine *palazzo*. The intercolumniation was filled in by panels, with windows at the top, to create extra rooms, but done in such a way that both the interior and exterior walls were ornamented by the ancient Doric columns. The rooms created were high, so some were subdivided by an additional intermediate floor level, doubling the space available. With its crenulations, the fortification style of the exterior was entirely in keeping with contemporary *palazzi* in Florence such as the Palazzo del Bargello.

A tower to the south of the Propylaea was added, twenty-seven metres high, and built using blocks from the ancient monuments of the Acropolis. Heinrich Schliemann funded the removal of this tower in 1874; some claim it was Burgundian, but scholars who were able to examine it at the time noted its similarities to contemporary Tuscan towers.

Nerio died in Corinth in September 1394. In his extraordinary will he left the city of Athens and his brood mares to the Parthenon, with special instructions for the care of the church's fabric and priests, placing them under the protection of Venice. He could not leave Athens to his natural son, and since all sources complain of the poverty of Athens, the gift of the city, while unprecedented, might not have been as generous as it initially appears. Interest in the Classical past was re-emerging in Italy at the time, and Nerio's love of the Parthenon may well reflect this new cultural movement. Many of the sculptures have evidence of a post-Byzantine whitewash applied to them, which may well have been part of this refurbishment.

In his will, dated 17 September 1394, Nerio specified funding for the refurbishment of the Parthenon; the silver stripped from the doors and the jewels from vessels, to meet his ransom, were to be replaced. He also asked to be buried in Santa Maria di Atene and for masses to be said there daily for his soul. Nerio raised the number of Latin priests from twelve to twenty to ensure that the requisite numbers of prayers were said. He also took care of the church in Corinth, though he was less generous with its endowments, leaving the city itself to Francesca. Nerio's soul was also to be cared for by masses in Florence and a weekly mass in Argos. The most lasting of Nerio's monuments was a poor hospital in Nauplia funded by his will, which remained in use into the twentieth century.

The same period that marked the rise of Florentine fortunes in Athens also marked the beginning of Ottoman domination of the Balkans. They defeated first the Serbs at Kosovo (1389). Then the Crusaders and Hungarians were routed by Bayezit at Nicopolis on the Danube (1396). In 1394, moving south, the Ottomans had seized Argos and threatened Athens, but Nerio bought them off with tribute. Timurtash Pasha led another charge against the Acropolis in 1397, occupying the lower city. Realising that he was unlikely to capture the fortress swiftly, and facing a Venetian force, he left. The Ottoman threat subsequently subsided as Bayezit was defeated and captured by Tamurlane.

Thus the Venetians held Athens from 1394 to 1402/3, during which time they spent two hundred hyperperi repairing the walls and defences of their citadel of Sythines of Athens. They ignored Nerio's will and cut the number of priests for the Parthenon down to eight, citing lack of funds, due to missing mares, and uncertain times as their excuse. They are unlikely to have honoured his other pledges to the fabric and chattels of the cathedral.

Under the Venetian interregnum we have our first long modern description of the Acropolis. It is written by Niccolò da Martoni, a Capuan notary, who visited Athens on 24/25 February 1395, on his way back from a pilgrimage to the Holy Land. He is the first visitor that we know of who asked to see ancient Athens, but since he was able to find guides who could explain the ruins to him, one can assume that others had also expressed an interest in them.

After a tour of the Roman remains, whose highlight was the philosophical schools, he went up to the Acropolis. He admired the marble entrance and proclaimed it as well made as that of his home town, though not as large. He walked through, counting the columns. Fortunately, the Parthenon was the same size as the cathedral in Capua, and so satisfied him. He wrote that it was impossible to imagine what kind of men could have built such a magnificent building. In his enthusiasm he over-counted the number of columns, and came up with a round figure of sixty. While it is easy to make fun of his maths, numerous small buildings abutted to the Parthenon at this time, and the intercolumniations were filled in, so counting might not have been as easy as it is today.

Inside, Martoni noted the two chambers, but did not mention the sculptures. He was more interested in the Christianity of the Parthenon than its pagan past, although his guide told him that the doors were brought over by the Greeks after the fall of Troy, and he duly recorded this.

Soon Antonio, the son of Nerio, decided to claim his birthright. He laid siege to the Acropolis after a 1402 revolt of the Athenians in his favour, which had handed him the lower city. During the siege, which lasted seventeen months, a historians' joke is that the starving men within the citadel ate every horse except those carved by Pheidias on the Parthenon frieze. In 1404 the Venetians on the Acropolis capitulated. Under his reign (1403–35) Athens was prosperous and were once again flourished. He died without a son, so the usual dynastic squabbles ensued between his widow and a young cousin. As a solution to the two claims, Murad, with the wisdom of Solomon, suggested they marry, so Nerio II married Maria, the Greek widow of his predecessor, and their son was his ill-fated heir. Nerio II was not initially a great success, and was briefly removed in favour of his brother Antonio II.

While out of power Nerio II returned to Florence, and was in the city during the Council of Florence. The Pope had insisted on union of the Catholic and Orthodox Churches before he would help the Byzantine emperor, and under the Orthodox system this could only be achieved by an ecumenical council. Eugenius IV invited the Orthodox representatives to the Council of Florence (1439–42), which was convoked to try to resolve the issues that prevented the union of the two Churches. Major issues were practical as well as theological; they included primacy, and the existence of Purgatory. The Roman Church had long since banned the marriage of priests and did not approve of the practice in the East, and the Orthodox prelates thought the Roman use of unleavened bread for mass to be barbaric.

The Orthodox Patriarch Joseph II died in Florence, and was buried in Santa Maria Novella. He and his emperor were also represented as the Magi coming from the East in the chapel of the Palazzo Medici-Riccardi, Florence (painted in 1459 by Gozzoli). John VIII Palaeologus proclaimed his Catholic faith in an attempt to gain Western support for his crumbling empire (6 July 1439), resulting in the technical union of the two Churches, and as a result of it Eugenius preached a crusade, which set off in 1444. It was crushed by Murad at Varna.

John's compromise was not enough to save Constantinople from the Ottomans. The council was of greater use to Italian culture than to Byzantine salvation, the seven hundred Greeks in Florence having contributed much that went towards creating the Italian Renaissance. Many scholars brought books that were not available in Italy and were much admired in the West. Gemistos Plethon (d. 1452), a celebrated Neoplatonist, and described by one traveller as the only thing worthy of praise in the entire Peloponnese, came from Mistras as a Byzantine lay theologian. He brought the first unadulterated copies of Plato seen in Florence. Even more importantly, Plethon brought a copy of Strabo's *Geography*; this led Columbus to accept the theory that the earth was not flat, and in turn led him to sail west towards 'India' in 1492.

Soon after the Council of Florence, Nerio II was back in his duchy, living in the Propylaea palace. He paid tribute for Athens to Murad II and to Constantine the Last, but under his reign the city continued to flourish both culturally and economically, so it was a small price to pay for one of the city's glorious periods.

The third important event of the Florentine period in the history of the Parthenon were the visits of Ciriaco de' Pizzicolli of Ancona

Renaissance drawings based on ones made by Ciriaco of Ancona

(c.1391–1455), who reintroduced the term Acropolis to describe the
castle of Athens for the first time in modern history. Ciriaco's first
visit was in April 1436, and his second, when Nerio II was again
duke, in February 1444. Ciriaco seems to have been the first since
Michael Choniates to have fully appreciated the history and beauty
of the ancient Acropolis, or at least the only one to have left a
record of it. In his time the Hephaisteion fell outside the city walls
with its four gates, and was separated from the Acropolis by fields.

When he visited the Parthenon, he recorded fifty-eight exterior
columns, counting the corner columns twice. More importantly for
us, he made sketches of the building and the sculptures, copying the
inscriptions. Most of these are now lost, although possibly one original and several copies are preserved. One copy, by Giuliano da
Sangallo, while highly fanciful and making the Parthenon look like
the Pantheon, shows that Ciriaco made much more extensive drawings of the temple than his preserved drawings would suggest. As
well as reintroducing the ancient name of the citadel, he provides
us with our first description of the Parthenon sculptures since

Pausanias, mentioning the metopes with a battle of the Centaurs, and the pediments, and drawing both along with the frieze, which he identified as representing Periclean Athens' victories. We know that Ciriaco had read Pliny's *Natural History* and Strabo (brought from Athens by Plethon), but he does not seem to be aware of Pausanias' description of the monument. His drawing of the west pediment shows Athena fighting a horse, so the central figures of Poseidon must have fallen out of the gable by then.

When Nerio died in 1451 he left Francesco, his young son by Maria, in the care of his second wife, Chiara. She in turn married Bartolommeo Contarini in the Parthenon in 1453. The Athenians, suspecting she intended to dispose of the young duke, asked Mehmet II to intervene. The Ottomans were by then rulers of Constantinople, and there Mehmet had been holding hostage Franco, the son of Antonio II. This Acciajuoli had managed to gain the sultan's favours through his bed, and Mehmet sent him to Athens as her last duke (1455–6).

Unfortunately, Franco could not keep the sultan's favour once out of his bed. He was in his turn besieged in the Acropolis by the Ottomans, and surrendered it on 4 June 1456 to Turakhan and his son Omar Athens. The same year Demetrius, Despot of Mistras, yielded his Peloponnese possessions to the Turks, as well as his only daughter Helen to the sultan's ever increasing seraglio, in exchange for some Aegean islands. Venice held on to several cities in the Turkish period, and only lost Crete in 1669, but 1460 effectively marked the end of the Byzantine Empire and its culture.

King Solomon's Mosque

Constantinople had fallen on 29 May 1453 to Mehmet II (1451–81), and the city was soon renamed Istanbul. After the capture of Athens in 1456, the Ottomans turned their attention to the Peloponnese. Other than a few mostly Venetian Latin holdings, mainland Greece was now part of the Ottoman Empire. The French and Turks became allies in the sixteenth century, signing an entente in 1536 where François I became the protector of the Catholics within the Ottoman Empire.

The fall of Constantinople traditionally marks the break from the medieval period to the Renaissance. Although an artificial date, since the beginning of the Renaissance was well under way in Italy, and did not begin until long after in England, it is a practical demarcation. Byzantine scholars opposed to Iconoclasm as a religious teaching had left for the West centuries before, and now more followed. These scholars renewed and continued the West's interest in antiquity, leading to the flourishing of Renaissance culture. Once the Franks lost Greece they appreciated it more. The Greek influx into Sicily and southern Italy is such that well into the twentieth century there was still a large Greek-speaking minority there; although they claimed to be descended from Ancient Greeks, they were in fact descended from Byzantines fleeing the Ottomans.

The first contact between the Turks and the Byzantines had been in Turkistan; many Turks were mercenaries in the Byzantine armies, and converted to Christianity, but most remained independent. In the second half of the thirteenth century a Turkic state was established in Bithynia by Ertughrul (d. 1281), after whose son Osman the Ottomans are named and trace their descent. They also claimed descent from Noah, and by the time of Mehmet II from the Byzantine Comnenes, via a scion who had supposedly embraced Islam in Konya and married a Seljuk princess. Bayezit had married a Germiyan princess, and much illustrious ancestry would also be claimed from this union. Once Mehmet had conquered the Byzantine world he felt the need to claim a connection to it to validate and reinforce his seizure of the lands.

Osman, the first Ottoman ruler to be described as a sultan, captured the lands to his west, lands that bordered the city of Constantinople, and it was to fight this sultan that Andronicus II had hired the Catalans to defend his city. Subsequent generations enlarged and embellished Bursa, their capital, making it not only one of the most beautiful Ottoman cities in Turkey, but also one of the best places to visit to get the impression of what an ancient city such as Rome or Athens would have been like. Ottoman policy at the time was that if cities surrendered they kept their rights and freedom of worship; if they did not, then the Christians became slaves. They taxed less than the Byzantines, so a surprisingly large number of cities chose to become part of his empire; in 1387 Thessalonica surrendered peacefully to him, as later would Athens.

Tamurlane defeated the Ottomans at Ankara in 1402, then sacked Bursa. Luckily for the Ottomans, after many victories, he decided instead to conquer China, and so returned to Samarqand. The Ottomans regrouped, and soon regained their strength in the region. Mehmet I built the beautiful Green Mosque in Bursa, and his son Murad besieged Constantinople in 1422. The siege failed, but this was only a temporary setback. Murad died in 1451, to be succeeded by Mehmet II, a man in whom more Greek and Serbian blood ran than Turkish.

Mehmet visited Athens in 1458, touring his newly acquired Acropolis fortress, and visiting the city's ancient ruins. The Orthodox metropolitan had fled, so Mehmet was greeted by an abbot, who gave him the keys to Athens and a tour of the city. In return the sultan exempted the abbot's monastery from taxation. Athens itself was administered by a *shoumbashi*, a relatively junior military official; his konak (palace) was in Hadrian's Library. In charge of the protection of the city was the disdar, the military governor, who lived in the Propylaea palace, and kept his family and seraglio in the Erechtheion.

The Ottomans expelled the Catholics, confirming the Orthodox Church in its possessions, and used the Church to maintain order within the Christian population and to collect taxes. The line the Church followed was to render to Caesar what was his, and to support the Ottomans; even in the nineteenth century, during the War of Independence the patriarch would preach against it. The Catholic Archbishop had lived in the Erechtheion, but the Acropolis became Turkish, and the Orthodox Metropolitan lived in the lower city; his palace was adjacent to Panagia Gorgoepikoos, the Little Metropolis that Michael Choniates had built, and which the Archbishop used as a chapel in his garden. The Orthodox Church unified the Greek population, and from the fall of Constantinople until the twentieth century Greekness would be associated with membership of the Church, not any link with the pagan past. The Church was in charge of the Greek population within the empire, and cared for both their spirit and their material welfare.

Ottoman sources praise this sultan's learning, and his love of ancient history. Mehmet II spoke Greek, and was far more cultured than many Western monarchs of the day; he probably knew more of Greek history than many Greeks living in Athens. He was genuinely interested in Athens, and fascinated by the city's past, calling it the City of Wisdom due to her ancient philosophical schools. Mehmet spent four months in Athens in 1458, returning briefly in 1460, and seems to have particularly appreciated the Acropolis, both as a fortress and for the way the hill had featured so much in the history he had learned.

Just as the earlier Christians had initially been reluctant to turn temples into churches, the new Muslim rulers were reluctant to convert churches into mosques, and most remained Christian churches. Several small mosques were built around the city, including

One of two Ottoman mosques that survive in Athens

the quite modest Fethiye Camii, or Mosque of the Conqueror (see above), on the ruins of an earlier church in the Roman agora, but the city changed little. Mehmet II, having added Athens to his domains, ordered that only the Parthenon be converted into a mosque, but that all other churches were to remain churches. Because of this, in 1830, after Greek independence, there were 120 Byzantine and medieval churches in Athens. Today only twenty-five are standing. Although there were many mosques in the pre-independence city, I know of only two Ottoman ones that are still standing; the Fethiye is used as a storehouse, and the other as a museum. The only functioning mosque is in a modern hotel.

Athens had first been subject to foreign rulers in the fourth century BC, and the following century had lost her independence, so the Ottomans were merely following the historical progression and replacing the Franks, another foreign power. The leap from Orthodoxy to Islam was not as great as it might initially appear, even in Constantinople; the Ottomans were enlightened tolerant rulers, and though they were Muslim, they did not suddenly impose a fundamentalist regime on Athens, nor were they particularly oppressive. In time many Greeks rose to high positions of state and would form a ruling class; the Greek Ottoman officials could be as unpleasant as some of their Turkish counterparts, and just as hated in Athens.

Byzantine Orthodox culture segregated the sexes, hiding women away in a separate part of the home, and allowing them so little freedom that it became routine for fathers to boast on their daughter's wedding day that this was the first time the girl had stepped out of the house. Women in the West were less confined, but still led relatively restricted lives at that time. Although the seraglio segregated the women and children from the men, this was not some sort of private bordello for the master of the house, and it merely continued the segregation of men and women that the Byzantines had practised, and which had also been the norm in Periclean Athens. Women left the seraglio only for visits to other homes, and to use the baths; even dining and worship were segregated among the sexes. The seraglio was sacrosanct, and officials could not enter it. In many ways Christian women were treated better than Muslims, and their punishments were less severe since they were not subject to Islamic law. The only women one saw walking around were the city slaves and Albanians, who were poor and had to work.

Athens was taxed fairly in this period compared, for example, to the Byzantine Empire; the Orthodox religion was freely practised, which it had not been under the Franks, and the right to appeal against unjust officials was also available. George Wheler speaks of such a delegation in the 1670s, when Michael Limbonas went to Constantinople, armed with gifts to gain an audience with the chief eunuch. The eunuch granted the Athenian request, and both the disdar and the voivode were replaced. Justice was not guaranteed even for Turks in the Ottoman Empire, but it could be gained even by Christians.

Another myth of Greek history is that religion and education were banned; although education was not widely available at this point, it had never been widely available either in Greece or elsewhere.

Few Athenians were educated, whether Ottoman or Greek, and for women the ability to read was restricted to the odd exception. The right to education and literacy are twentieth-century concepts, and education had always been a luxury. So Athens was more fortunate than many other Greek cities, with light taxes and for the most part enlightened rulers.

The Turks became known as the *Castrioti*, those who lived in the Acropolis *castro*, although the plague of 1555 did not differentiate between them and the Greeks as an inscription on a column of the Hephaisteion notes. The Turkish Acropolis was not all that different from the Frankish one, filled with repaired Periclean buildings that served new functions, and the space between these buildings crammed with the small homes of the Acropolis garrison.

The first priority of the Ottomans was to reinforce the Acropolis walls, so that they were more likely to withstand cannons, the new weapon which both the Turks and their enemies used. Crenulations were added to the walls and to the gates. The military governor moved into the old Florentine palace in the Propylaea, presumably adapting it to Turkish tastes in decoration; at some point the main passage was covered over and domed in the Ottoman style. The Erechtheion became the home of the governor's family and seraglio. The rest of the garrison were lodged in old Frankish houses on the rock, which presumably were rebuilt and added to over the years, with houses even crammed into the narrow strip to the south of the Parthenon.

A second wall was built around the base of the Acropolis, and an additional bastion was added on the west slope, below the Propylaea, to reinforce it. When the foundations of this bastion were pulled down, they proved to be made up of rubble and miscellaneous ancient architectural blocks and sculpture that had been gathered together from whatever was readily available. Cisterns were repaired and new ones created; munitions and food were stockpiled in case of siege.

The Parthenon did not immediately become a mosque, though it was converted into one a few years after Mehmet's visit. Mosques, like churches, generally face east towards Mecca, so structurally few changes were needed, but the most visible would be the piercing of the Attic sky by a minaret, built on to the old Byzantine tower in the south-west corner of the Parthenon. The square base of the bell tower was retained, and above it the cylindrical minaret was constructed, linked by a conical roof; from a balcony at the top of the minaret the muezzin would call the faithful to prayer five times a day. The Orthodox priests had previously rung bells and called the Christians to prayer – the sounds were not dissimilar – but this was now stopped so that it did not interfere with mosques' exaltations to worship. So the greatest changes to the city were the delicate minarets that now rose over Athens, and the sounds that were the result of these.

As in Hagia Sophia in Istanbul, and in other Byzantine churches that became mosques, the mosaics and frescoes of the Parthenon were whitewashed and plastered over. The sculptures of the Parthenon also seem to have been given another whitewash at this time. Due to a superstition the mosaic in the apse remained on view, for fear that covering it would bring the plague to the city. The frescoes of the Last Judgement in the entrance also remained visible.

Inside the Parthenon, the pulpit became the mimbar, and instead of sermons passages of the Koran were now read from it. The iconostasis had long been put out of use by the Franks, who had removed the panels between the columns, but its green jasper columns remained, as did the bishop's throne in the apse. A mihrab, in the east wall of the apse and pointing towards Mecca, was constructed. With time both the south and north aisles would fill with Muslim monuments. The wooden beams of the roof were carved with geometric motifs, a feature of Ottoman architecture, and more Islamic decorative borders were painted on the interior of the building. The old narthex is largely ignored by visitors, but this would have served the purpose of courtyards in other mosques, where the faithful purified themselves before prayer, washing and removing their shoes.

In the late sixteenth century a Greek, corresponding with the German Martin Kraus, wrote that two horses pranced over the entrance, and that myths of the gods were represented around the exterior. This is one of our first descriptions of the Parthenon sculptures. That there were now only two horses in the west pediment shows that the two in the southern part of the west pediment, seen in Ciriaco's drawings, were already gone by this date.

The Acropolis was still covered in earth at this time, and wild flowers grew among the buildings making it more picturesque. The number of ruins made stone readily available, and many of the houses in Athens were of stone, as opposed to the wood that was used in Constantinople, and which made the capital a firetrap. Athenian houses generally had a stone lower level, and a terrace above, supported by a porch; doors had two knockers, one for equals, the other for inferiors. Columns, marble blocks and other ancient remains dotted the city, and many of these were picked up to be used as building material, with *spolia* providing decoration.

The Turkish traveller Evliya Chelebi would later declare that nowhere else on earth were there as many wonderful things to see as in Athens, but by the end of the fifteenth century a German visitor declared Athens not worth visiting. Other Westerners would even question whether Athens still existed, or whether it was a mythical place like Atlantis, and few travellers were brave enough to visit.

Houses hugged the north slope of the Acropolis, and the administrative centre of the city was in the area of the old Roman agora. To the north were the two main bazaars, and many smaller ones, and here the locals would drink coffee and play chess. Attica was at the time of the conquest a mixture of around 35,000 Greeks and Turks, as well as the Albanians that the Franks had brought in to renew the declining population. By the time of Greek independence, Turkish was little spoken even by Turks.

The Battle of Lepanto, at the entrance to the Gulf of Corinth, was fought in 1571 between East and West. Pius V had organised a fleet of Western allies to meet the Ottomans; the Christian victory was overwhelming, and for a while stopped the continuous Turkish march westwards. Few travelled east to visit Turkish Athens in the first centuries of Ottoman rule. The Baron de Courmenin, the French ambassador to the Porte of Constantinople in 1630, described the Parthenon as undamaged by time, as if only recently built.

* * *

In 1667 Chelebi visited Athens; this well-born Turk had spent decades travelling, going as far north as Sweden, and would later publish an account of his travels. Chelebi particularly admired the Parthenon, which he described as one of the most beautiful mosques in the world, and which in his day was reputed to have been constructed by King Solomon himself. As a Muslim he had free access to the interior, and left us one of the few long descriptions of the Parthenon before it was destroyed.

The castle is ancient and simple in its construction, oriented from East to West upon a precipitous reddish rock in the middle of a plain. Such a fortress was never built on the face of the earth, so great is it and mighty, for it rises fully two hundred feet from the ground . . .

There are three gates one behind the other on the Western side; the distance between them being fifty paces. Inside the castle there are in all three hundred family houses, stone-built like forts themselves, all with tiled roofs. There are no gardens, but from all their windows and balconies and terraces can be seen the vineyards and flowerbeds, the sown fields and market-gardens of the plain . . .

In the middle of the fortress there is one mosque, marvellous and luminous, famous among the philosophers and travellers of the world. It measures two hundred feet by eighty. Within are sixty white marble pillars with shafts and capitals, all set symmetrically and in two storeys one atop the other.

But four columns between sanctuary and apse have shafts of ruby-red marble. Each one is a divine piece of artistry, an example of the philosopher's stone as it were, so shining and clean that it mirrors the colour of a man's face and is worth the whole of a country's taxes.

These columns which stand in the direction of the *mihrab*, support a large and magnificent baldaquin of aloe-wood, carved with all the skill of a goldsmith: he loses his wits who looks upon it. They say that beneath that aloe-wood dome the divine philosopher Plato hung a votive-lamp. And he set into the east wall of the mosque marble slabs as thin as paper, so that when the sun rose the slabs grew red, and the lamps inside the temple burned all the brighter, for they were drenched with turpentine and illuminated, they say, the whole interior. The infidel revered it all as magic . . .

Near the pulpit there are also four marble columns, green as emerald, carved with a variety of marvellous shapes and unimaginable flowers.

And upon six small columns engaged in the white marble columns of the colonnade, to the left of the green columns mentioned, the miraculous architect fashioned a white marble throne for divine Plato, which is enough to dim the sight of whoever in a small dome and there it is said that divine Plato, seated, taught the people and gave counsel. All around it are set marbles of coloured lattice-work.

The temple floor is paved in white marble blocks each ten feet square and so polished as to reflect the colour of a man's face.

The mosque has three gateways to the inmost sanctum. Between the outer and middle gate is a carved marble receptacle big enough to hold five men at once. In those days the founder of the temple gave his workmen wine to drink (shameless deed!) from here right down to the bottom. Now this bowl takes two horsehide skins of water. How large and tall men must have been in those days to drink to the very bottom of a bowl that holds two horsehide skins!

The ceiling of the intervening space is carved after a fashion pleasing to the Franks, and with carvings like those of Fahri Chelebi from Bursa. The middle gate is 40 feet high and its leaves are made of long cypress planks. In the days of the infidel all the doors and cornices were covered with golden ornaments and diamonds. Even today the places show quite clearly where they were attached . . .

Each of the shining white marble blocks in the walls of the mosque is as big as an elephant, and the marvel in all this is that no builder, however great his skill, can distinguish the places where they join. You would think each wall to be made all of one piece, and eighty feet high moreover. So smooth are the walls, and glistening, that they reflect the very smallest particle floating in the air, as well as the faces of the worshippers and their movements when they fall and rise again from their prostrations. In truth they are like mirrors, vast and single-surfaced. Yet another pleasant feature of this mosque is that there is no mortar: the blocks are held together by leaden and iron dowels only.

Around all four sides of the outer enclosure are sixty columns fifty feet high, not monolithic like those of the interior, yet as hard as you may look you will not be able to distinguish the joints between the drums.

Were we to describe every form and feature of this place, our writing would fill a whole book and the mind of man could not encompass it. It is like some impregnable fortress not made by human agency.

. . . Yet nonetheless there is no such magnificent mosque in the whole atlas of the globe. In civilized countries no sanctuary exists to equal it. May its construction remain eternal unto the completion of time. Amen.*

Around 1656 the disdar, Yussef Aga, had decided to celebrate a feast by firing, for amusement, cannon at the church of St Demetri at the foot of the Philopappos hill. On the eve of the feast the cannon were readied for the dawn attack and gunpowder prepared in the Propylaea, but during the night lightning struck the Ottoman dome over the passageway, igniting the powder. The Propylaea exploded, the Periclean building was badly damaged, and the disdar and his family were killed.

A letter of 1672 from Father Jacques-Paul Babin, a Jesuit, as well as some recently rediscovered drawings of his, provide the first detailed account of the ruins of the city. Babin thought of the Parthenon as highly as Evliya Chelebi had, praising the sculptures, and claiming that it surpassed even Justinian's Hagia Sophia.

* Although an old translation exists, it is highly inaccurate, and the only good English translation is in Kevin Andrews, *Athens Alive*, Athens 1979, pp. 68–77, from which this excerpt is taken.

I entered into the Mosque of Athens, which had been first built by the gentiles in honour of the Goddess Pallas, before the coming of the Son of God, then dedicated by the Christians to the Eternal Wisdom, after the prediction of the Apostles.

This temple, which can be seen from far away, and which is the most elevated building in Athens on the citadel, is a masterpiece by the best architects of Antiquity. It is about 120 feet long and 40 wide . . . It surpassed the church of Sophia built in Constantinople by Justinian, which otherwise is one of the miracles of the world: but I am informed that the murals inside are not plastered over and covered with slabs of marble, which in some places have fallen in from the upper levels, and that one can see bricks and stones, which were once covered in marble . . .

The Jesuits did not prove to be popular in Ottoman Athens, and soon the Capuchins, who established themselves in the city in 1658, became the leading Catholic order in the city. Babin's letter was, however, influential in the West and convinced several to visit. Many travellers stayed in the Capuchin monastery to the south of the Acropolis. There the monks provided shelter, and in 1669 they bought the small Lysicrates Monument, using it as a library. The city was divided into eight districts, one of which, Kandili, was named after this gem of a monument, then thought to be the Lantern of Demosthenes. The monument was identified as the Lantern of Demosthenes by Michael Choniates, and kept that appellation until the modern period.

Monks were responsible for the first plan of modern Athens, which influenced that of Spon (see below), and for a number of anonymous drawings of the Acropolis, made in the 1670s before the Venetian siege. These drawings show the Parthenon with windows jutting up through the Late Roman roof built in two sections, as well as the minaret of more recent Ottoman construction. All around are houses, filling all the available space on the Acropolis.

In 1676 Jacques Spon and Sir George Wheler spent six months in Athens. Both published books, recording much of the nonsense their guides told them. They were only allowed one visit to the

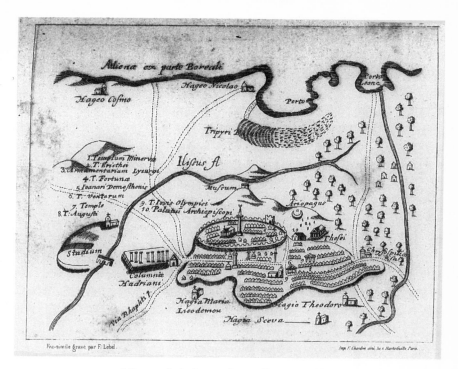

View of Athens from Spon, 1676

Acropolis, and then only after having presented lavish gifts of coffee to the Ottoman authorities; they were not permitted to make notes during their visit, having instead to rely on memory. They confused the old east entrance of the Parthenon with the newer western one, so reversed their pediments as described by Pausanias. Worse, they decided that two figures in the western pediment were later additions representing Hadrian and his wife Sabina. They noted that the metopes were rather damaged. Spon and Wheler did, however, provide one of the few guides to the city at that time, and a few years later when the Venetians besieged the Acropolis, the letters of Anna Åkerjelm show that the Swedes were reading Spon.

All travellers were potential spies, so few were allowed up on to the Acropolis at this time, and visitors were warned to keep away from it to avoid getting themselves into difficulties. Examining stones, let alone measuring them, even for antiquarian curiosity,

An anonymous drawing of the Parthenon as a mosque, c. 1670

seemed so odd to the Ottomans that it aroused the greatest suspicion. The Acropolis, though it had altered over the years, preserved most of the Periclean buildings intact, but their uses had changed; the Parthenon was a mosque, the Propylaea the military governor's palace, and the Erechtheion housed a seraglio. The military capabilities of the Acropolis would soon be put to the test.

The Decline and Fall of the Acropolis

Although the French had traditionally been allies of the Ottomans, Louis XIV had supplied the Venetians on Crete with troops in 1668. The Grand Vizier had publicly slapped de la Haye, the French ambassador, and diplomatic relations had been broken off; so for once the British were an Ottoman friend rather than a foe, and commercial treaties were signed. Louis, realising how costly a mistake this was commercially, appointed a new ambassador in the 1670s.

The Marquis de Nointel set off for Constantinople with a large entourage designed to create an impression. With him was an artist to paint the ancient marvels, and his orders were to bring back any antiquities he could. Nointel picked up pieces throughout his travels in Greece, Turkey and the Levant, and these are scattered among a number of French museums; many of them are exceptionally fine, but he was unable to get his hands on the Parthenon sculptures. An ambassador collecting was nothing new. In the early seventeenth century the Earl of Arundel had used the English ambassador to Constantinople to acquire pieces for his collection, as would Charles I. Ambassadors took care of trade and ran errands for leading subjects.

Even though Nointel did not bring the Parthenon sculptures back to France, what he left us of his trip is almost as valuable: drawings of the Parthenon sculptures before the explosion that destroyed many of them. The two weeks, or two months – sources differ – spent in

Athens led to a set of drawings of the Parthenon sculptures by an artist believed to have been Jacques Carrey. Although Carrey was not a great painter, he was a good draughtsman, and without his drawings it would be nearly impossible for us to reconstruct the arrangement of the surviving pedimental sculptures, or to know what the missing metopes represented.

Carrey's drawings illustrate the east and west pediments as they were preserved at the time, the south metopes, the east and west friezes, the middle section of the south frieze, and the eastern end of the north frieze. The metopes on the three other sides had been badly mutilated by the Byzantine Greek Christians, and so he did not bother drawing them. The central slab of the east frieze had been removed by the Christians, as had slabs 10, 17 and 18 on the north frieze, and two slabs of the south frieze were also no longer on the Parthenon. Cornelio Magni, who accompanied Nointel on his visit to Athens, noted the poor state of the pediments and of the metopes, though the frieze was in better condition.

A painting by Carrey shows Nointel in front of the Acropolis, surrounded by foreign consuls to Athens, and Athenian officials, both Orthodox and Turkish. Nointel praised the marvels of the Parthenon, declaring the sculptures more beautiful than any of Rome, at a time when Roman art was seen as superior. As an important diplomat from an Ottoman ally (once again), Nointel had several opportunities to visit the Acropolis, going first on an official tour, and then subsequently returning with his artists. On his return to court, Nointel advised Louis XIV to add the Parthenon sculptures to his collection to save them from further destruction by the Turks, but Louis preferred more complete statues, and was preoccupied with his latest mistress. Although Nointel did not publish an account of his visit, notes for a planned book and manuscripts by several of his associates survive, and these can give us an idea of what the Parthenon was like immediately before it exploded.

After the siege of Vienna in 1683, Pope Innocent XI formed a Holy League; often called the Last Crusade, its forces consisted of Poland, the Holy Roman Empire and Venice. The Venetians concentrated on the Peloponnese, where traditionally they had strong links, occupying most of it by 1687. Francesco Morosini, the Venetian who had held Crete to the bitter end, led this expedition. He was joined in the enterprise by Otto Königsmark, a Swedish count who brought with him a large entourage and many mercenaries. Today we can be grateful for the Swede's large retinue, for his wife's lady-in-waiting, Anna Åkerjelm, left us letters and a journal which describe many events from the campaign. Königsmark had previously fought the Turks in Hungary, and before that, as a student in Leipzig, he was known for having spoken, in Latin, of Athens' fate under the barbarian Ottomans. Ironically, his actions in the city would be more destructive than those of any Ottoman.

Morosini, like Caesar before him, stopped at Corinth and considered the idea of building a canal there, but again like Caesar swiftly abandoned the idea. The Metropolitan Jacob I had sent a delegation to Morosini in the Peloponnese asking him to capture Athens, which otherwise he would not have done, and always seems to have been reluctant to try. The Athenians now sent a second delegation to Corinth, and after many deliberations, the army marched on to besiege Athens, at the Athenians' request, in September 1687.

1687 medal commemorating the capture of Athens

The Ottomans, about 450 soldiers and 3,000 civilians, ensconced themselves on the Acropolis, and prepared to withstand a siege. The walls had recently been repaired, and the small Nike temple was pulled down to make way for a gunnery. Food and weapons were hoarded, and gunpowder was stored in the Parthenon, while the Turks moved into the houses that dotted the top of the Acropolis.

The Venetians took up positions on the small hills to the west of the Acropolis, opposite the only entrance. Although the Acropolis was solid and had withstood long sieges in the past, this was now the age of gunpowder and the Venetians started shelling the hill. Several of the Parthenon columns still show damage from that shelling.

A defector had told the Venetians that the Turks were holding their women and children, as well as their gunpowder, in the Parthenon mosque, but the shelling of the Acropolis did not stop. Just after

A column of the Parthenon that was damaged
in the Venetian siege

Fanelli engraving showing the Parthenon exploding in 1687

midnight on the morning of the 26th, Antonio Mutoni, the Count of San Felice – later described as 'a fool' – launched the artillery that fired the shell that hit the Parthenon. The Parthenon exploded, and a fire within it raged for two days. The Parthenon's marble architecture was structurally weak from the Late Antique fire, and the building exploded.

Eight columns on the north side and six on the south were completely destroyed, as was the wall behind them, and these pulled the sculpture down on to the ground. Most of the frieze and metopes on the long sides of the Parthenon fell off as a result of the explosion. Although the frieze blocks were larger and stronger and so some survived, the metopes were blown to smithereens. The east end was badly damaged, and the interior of the Parthenon was annihilated. As well as the destruction of one of the best-preserved Classical buildings, three hundred women and children lost their lives. The Ottomans soon surrendered, and the Acropolis became Venetian. The Parthenon lay in ruins, its sculptures largely destroyed.

The long walls and columns of the Parthenon had been blown out by the blast, the building losing twenty-one exterior columns, and what we see today is an early-twentieth-century reconstruction by a Greek engineer whose enthusiasm was unfortunately not paired with knowledge of architecture. The minaret collapsed, and the roof caved in during the fire. The interior was destroyed, with only stumps of some of the later Roman internal colonnade remaining. The mosque, church and classical treasury that had been the Parthenon all became a ruin for the first time.

The Acropolis the Venetians had held in the late fourteenth century had been mostly Byzantine in character, and the Parthenon near whole. The Acropolis Morosini ascended was in ruins, which he had created, with shells hitting and causing explosions in both the Erechtheion and the Propylaea. Count Tomeo Pompei was put in charge, removing bodies and clearing the ruins to make the rock accessible and inhabitable.

Because most of the long north and south walls were destroyed, so were the metopes and friezes they had held. A few blocks survived

1749 engraving of the Parthenon by Richard Dalton

(*Above*) An early photograph of the Parthenon taken soon after Greek Independence, showing the damaged interior and long sides, before reconstruction of the colonnade.

(*Below*) The Parthenon in 2004, largely reconstructed before the war. Work continues, in an attempt to undo the damage wrought by earlier restoration projects. The scaffolding will hopefully be removed in the next few years.

(*Left*) The north west corner of the
Parthenon today. The metopes seen
below the roof line are original fifth
century sculptures, not casts.

(*Above right*) Although the Parthenon was repeatedly changed, successive rulers repaired the
walls so that the Acropolis served as a fortress. The buttresses were added by the Burgundian
Lords of Athens after 1204 and are Medieval. From the ground one can barely see the roof
of the Parthenon. (*Below*) The site of the New Acropolis Museum is controversial due to
archaeological sites being destroyed during its construction, and opposed by many Greeks.

Alma Tadema's painting depicts Pheidias showing Pericles and leading Athenian citizens the newly built Parthenon. Although this is a creation of his imagination, it used evidence from excavations to show how the Parthenon might originally have been painted.

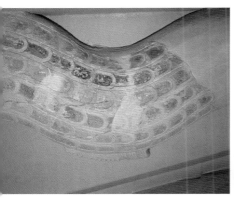

(*Left*) Archaic sculpture from the buildings on the Acropolis show how brightly Greek sculpture was originally painted. The building that this sculpture originally decorated was destroyed by the Persians when they sacked Athens. It was subsequently buried in the ground, which has preserved much of its pigmentation. The sculptures which remained on buildings were battered by the elements, and so rain washed the colour off them over the centuries.

(*Right*) A reconstruction made by the excavator of a Macedonian tomb at Lefkadia. The façade was articulated by architecture and painted, then buried under a mound which preserved it. Above the columns are faded metopes which copied the metopes from the Parthenon. (Reconstruction by Prof. Petsas, excavator)

A detail of a painting by Carrey, which shows the Marquis de Nointel and his suite meeting leading Athenians and Ottoman officials in Athens. In the background is the Acropolis, and the only painting of the Parthenon as a mosque.

Mehmet II was the Ottoman sultan who conquered Athens. An educated man, he read ancient Greek, and quoted Plato. Mehmet maintained close ties with Venice, and hired a Venetian artist, Gentile Bellini, to paint him and his court. Mehmet ordered that the ancient wonders of the city be preserved: only the Parthenon was turned into a mosque.

Selim III was Sultan at the time of the Elgin's embassy. He is shown here at his court in the Topkapi Palace, where Mary and Elgin were received both formally and informally. Selim saw ancient Greek sculptures as 'old stones' and could not understand why his Scottish friends would rather excavate the Acropolis than be showered with jewels.

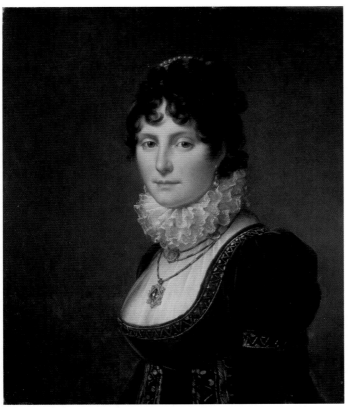

Mary Nisbet was Elgin's first wife. An heiress, she funded his acquisition of the Parthenon marbles, and used her powers of persuasion to get various British Navy captains to ship them back for her. Mary was very well educated, and so admired by the Sultan and his family that she was the first western woman allowed into the Seraglio to meet his mother and wives.

Lord Elgin as a young man. Although poor health was one reason he sought a post in Istanbul, the warm climate did not agree with him as much as he had hoped it would, and he lost his nose to disease there.

...uvel, the French consul, on the terrace of his house in the Agora. Fauvel acted as an agent for ...any collectors, but failed to acquire much of the Parthenon for Napoleon. Even the metope ...own in the portrait ended up in the British Museum (*below*). It was seized by Nelson at sea, and although Elgin offered to return it to Choiseul-Gouffier, the Frenchman declined.

Turner's view of the Acropolis.
Elgin had tried to hire the young Turner
but balked at the £400 p.a. the artist
asked for. Instead he hired Lusieri, an
artist otherwise forgotten by history.
This view owes more to the imagination
than to observation, and shows an over
large and too well preserved Parthenon.
The Medieval tower to the left would be
taken down later, its removal funded by
Schliemann.

The Elgin Marbles in the British Museum. A watercolour showing the way in which they were
first displayed, with leading artists and cultural figures vying to be depicted alongside them.

the fall to be buried in the ground, where they would later be excavated by Elgin. The south side suffered badly, and of the thirty-two metopes Carrey drew, all well preserved at the time, only eighteen are now extant; the south frieze suffered similar proportional damage, as did the north side. Carrey's drawings can be compared to those made by Richard Dalton in 1749 to show that through shelling and looting by Morosini and his army, the pediments were badly damaged. In the east pediment, figures K and M still had heads for Carrey, but by the time Dalton saw the pediment M was lost and K had fallen down. Figures U and V were lost, and figures S and T badly damaged. The back wall of the pediment was blown out by the explosion. The west pediment had suffered less from the explosion, since much of the energy of the blast had been absorbed by the wall between the cella and opisthodomus in the building. Morosini, by trying to remove some sculptures, greatly damaged the west pediment: figures D, E, F and G are lost, although fragments of E have been found, and figures H and M fell down.

At the beginning of 1688 the plague swept through Athens; the city's military value was negligible, and Morosini chose to abandon it. The Athenians gained little from this episode, and posterity lost the Parthenon. Before they left, the Venetians tried to take some souvenirs from the temple they had made a ruin; Morosini's engineers tied ropes around the west pediment figure of Poseidon to winch it down, but they dropped it, and it shattered on the ground, where Elgin's men would later find fragments. A second attempt was made, this time to remove the horses (figures A and L), but this too failed. Morosini had to content himself with bringing the Piraeus lion back to Venice, where it still stands to this day in front of their Arsenal, the lion being the symbol of St Mark.

One pedimental horse head, a Roman repair to the Parthenon rather than a Periclean original, made its way to Italy and is now in the Vatican Museums. Other soldiers in the army tried to take pieces of Athenian history home. A few years ago a head of a Lapith from a Parthenon metope was found in the water in the Piraeus, in a layer of stratification that matches up with Morosini's time. Another metope head dredged from the harbour is in the Louvre. Two heads brought to Copenhagen in 1688 match the figures on metope S4, now in London. Presumably other pieces did make it home with their new owners, but even if they are still preserved they have lost their provenance and, so, much of their value. The Turks had been anti-idols, so had cut off the odd head, but this looting for the sake of souvenirs was a new phenomenon, although it would be one that the Turks would continue when they retook the city, selling off heads and fragments of the Parthenon sculptures to affluent visitors.

The Ottomans regained Athens, declared an amnesty, and it was resettled. Fewer Turks returned, and whereas before the Venetians there had made up a quarter of the population, now they consisted of only 10 per cent of it. The Ottomans repaired the walls, and the Acropolis citadel was once again fortified. Building houses was a priority, and the scattered fragments of the ancient monuments made handy building material. The city prospered in the following century as trade and relations between East and West increased, and more and more visitors extended their Grand Tour to include Athens. In the early years of the eighteenth century, Demetrius Palaeologus led an expedition to Istanbul to the chief eunuch of the voivode; he spoke Turkish, and pleaded so eloquently that he was appointed in his place. Unfortunately, as a *rayah*, or Greek, Demetrius was liked by neither the Turks nor some Christians, so the first Greek leader in Athens for many centuries was murdered.

Eventually, by 1738, a smaller mosque was built within the ruins of the Parthenon, and it is this building that the travellers saw when they climbed on to the Acropolis to mourn the destruction of the Parthenon. The new structure was made of Parthenon blocks, and stood within the old cella, but was not axially aligned with it. Visitors could no longer see Pericles' building, but had to reconstruct it in their heads. The Erechtheion had been damaged in an explosion, the Propylaea had suffered the same fate, and the temple of Athena Nike was built into a bastion for Turkish guns. Above and around these ruins a jumble of Turkish houses, many presumably rebuilt after the Venetian shelling, covered the rock and gave it the illusion of a medieval village, with narrow alleyways and hundreds of roofs. This is the Acropolis that James Stuart would engrave, and the Acropolis that Elgin would see.

Stuart and Revett's view of the Parthenon, 1751,
through Ottoman houses and ruins

As the eighteenth century progressed, the visitors increased in number, and several scholars came out to visit, funded by the Society of Dilettanti. One of these was Richard Chandler, who visited Athens in 1764. Of the Parthenon he wrote: 'so much sculpture as is still extant . . . should be all likely to perish, as it were immaturely, from ignorant contempt and brutal violence'.

A few years before, in 1759, Athens had briefly had an Athenian Turk as the voivode; Tzistarakis built a mosque by the vegetable bazaar, next to the Library of Hadrian. This is one of only two mosques still standing in Athens, and is used today as a museum of Greek decorative arts. Nearby was a madrassa, a Koranic school, of which only the entrance gate survives, with an inscription commemorating its founding in 1721. The area around it, Monastiraki, still has stalls selling souvenirs, clothes and jewellery to tourists, and retains some of the bazaar atmosphere it must have had in the

Ottoman period, with shopkeepers calling out the quality of their wares to those that pass by. The Athens Chandler visited would have had a similar feel, and was still located to the north of the Acropolis. As he looked towards the hill he would have seen the Roman agora. The Tower of the Winds, which had been an Orthodox church, became a *tekke* or monastery for Whirling Dervishes in 1700, one of the sights of Turkish Athens. Since many of the great Classical cities – Troy, Ephesus, Constantinople and Halicarnassus – were in Ottoman hands, the idea of Athens as a Muslim city was not an aberration to Western visitors who travelled there. On the contrary, the Eastern 'flavour' added by the men's Turkish dress and the sounds of the muezzin calling the faithful to prayer at regular intervals throughout the day merely added exoticism to the experience.

In the West there had been a revival of interest in Antiquity. This Renaissance had begun in Italy, spreading slowly north, and increasing as more travellers saw the ruins of Rome. New excavations such as those at Pompeii and Hadrian's Villa at Tivoli were undertaken, bringing out complete Roman sculptures. More sculptures led to greater demand, and there became a sort of marble mania, where no self-respecting British or German gentleman could return from Italy without a dozen statues to decorate his residence.

In 1751 the Dilettanti sent a painter, James Stuart, and an architect, Nicholas Revett, to the East to study and measure temples, including those in Athens. In 1764 the society raised additional funds, which paid for visits by Chandler, Revett and the painter William Pars. Stuart and Revett eventually published several volumes entitled *The Antiquities of Athens*, which for the first time gave detailed and accurate images of the most famous Athenian monuments. Pars drew the famous illustration for their book where the Parthenon can be seen through the maze of houses on the Turkish Acropolis. These Athenian monuments were widely copied in England and Germany, often as garden follies.

In an age before photography made images available to all, Stuart and Revett were the source for the late-eighteenth-century gentleman who wanted to know what the Parthenon looked like, and it is from their book that Elgin would get his first sight of Athens and its antiquities. Chandler probably managed to acquire the two pieces of the Parthenon frieze, and part of a metope, which the Society of Dilettanti later gave to the British Museum. Other visitors acquired fragments, many of which have now been lost. The Turkish authorities, realising the pieces could be sold off to visitors for high prices, chopped off heads and hands to sell them off. If more of the Parthenon sculpture had remained on the Acropolis rather than being brought to London by Elgin, this may well have been its fate – to be divided among hundreds of private collections dotted around Europe.

The English were not the only visitors. The Comte de Choiseul-Gouffier visited Athens in 1776, returning later on his way to Constantinople, where he was appointed French ambassador to the Porte (1785–92); each visit is commemorated by an inscription on the Hephaisteion. Louis-François-Sébastien Fauvel was sent to Athens in 1781 as Choiseul-Gouffier's agent, and became one of the leading residents of Athens. Originally employed to make casts and to draw the ruins, his employer soon instructed him to buy anything he could. Long after Choiseul-Gouffier returned to France, Fauvel continued to live on the edge of the agora with his collection of Greek sculptures. He became an antiquities dealer, and there he continued to be visited by travellers long after Elgin and his men had left. Fauvel managed to gain permission to excavate around the Erechtheion, and Choiseul-Gouffier urged him to smuggle out some inscriptions.

A painting of Fauvel on his balcony shows him with a metope from the Parthenon and other sculptures. This metope had been removed thanks to a firman the sultan had issued in 1784, allowing Fauvel to remove sculpture from the Parthenon, although another was broken during his attempts at removal. This metope would be seized as war loot off the French, and although Elgin tried to return it to Choiseul-Gouffier, the offer was declined and it is now in the British Museum. Another metope now in the Louvre was acquired by Gaspari, the French consul in Athens.

Early in the next century, when Elgin's firman superseded Fauvel's, it would cover the Parthenon sculptures; the one Fauvel managed to get his hands on would eventually go to the Louvre. Another English visitor, John Morritt of Rokeby, tried to buy a metope in

1795, but failed. Although the Turks saw ancient sculpture as 'old stones', and referred to ruins as 'old walls', and most antiquities could be removed with permission in return for the right gifts, in the eighteenth century the Parthenon was still the exception and its sculptures could not easily be removed by visitors.

There was occasional unrest over the years, as in 1754 when both Christians and Turks rose up against the voivode, Sari Mouselini, and the latter had to take shelter on the Acropolis. Le Roy, the French architect who published engravings of the Parthenon, visited at this time, and the revolt made it harder for him to gain access to the hill. More serious was the Orlov uprising. In the early sixteenth century Peter the Great of Russia had declared himself king of his fellow Orthodox Hellenes, but offered no material help. The initiative for the creation of an independent Greek state began with Catherine the Great.

Catherine's first war with Turkey began almost by accident in 1768; troops chased some Poles across the border into Turkey, killing some Turks. Mustapha III used this as an excuse to declare war, encouraged by France. The British took the Russian side, helping the tsarina bring her navy around Europe from the Baltic to the Aegean, a feat never before undertaken. The fleet reached the Mani in May 1770, and then inflicted a crushing defeat on the Turkish navy at the Bay of Chesme off Chios. As part of the war Alexis Orlov encouraged rebellions in the Ottoman states. In August 1774 the new sultan, Mustapha's brother Abdul Hamid I, signed the Peace of Kutchuk Kainarji, which made Catherine protectress of the Orthodox Christians within the Ottoman Empire.

Catherine had been sympathetic to the Greek Orthodox, and in 1778, with the birth of her second grandson, her foreign policy took a new turn. While the Orlov revolts in Greece in 1770 mark the beginning of the Greek fight for independence, to the Russians they had been a ploy in the fight against the Ottomans. In 1778 Catherine chose to call a grandson Constantine, after the last Byzantine emperor, issued a medal proclaiming him Constantine III of Byzantium, and soon formed the 'Greek Plan'. Under this plan the northern Balkans would be an independent Orthodox state of Dacia.

Constantinople would be liberated, as would Greece, and they would form a new Byzantine Empire ruled by her grandson. Potemkin also had the idea of setting up a Jewish regiment who would free the Holy Land from the Turks and settle there.

The British, who had assisted Catherine in the first Turkish War, were unhappy with her increased power. They encouraged the sultan to declare war, which he did in August 1787. Joseph II marched into Serbia, and Potemkin led the Russian armies against the Ottomans in the Black Sea. In January 1792 the Russians and Ottomans made peace, the Treaty of Jassy confirming all Catherine's gains; but while she remained protectress of the Orthodox, there was no progress in terms of Greek independence. Catherine is said to have declared that she would not die until she had driven the Turks out of Europe, but in 1796 she did, and Greece was still a province of the Ottoman Empire.

The Orlov uprising had made no impact on Athens, where the people were too scared to revolt. Both the Turks and some Greeks retreated to the Acropolis, and the Turks became more wary of visitors. The Acropolis was a military fortress, so anyone trying to inspect it too closely was suspected of spying, but with the judicious use of gifts access was still possible. A band of Albanians sacked the lower city in 1778, following which new walls around Athens were built from scattered ancient monuments, but these were pulled down in the last century. By then many of the ruling class in the Ottoman Empire were Greeks, as were leading merchants, and Greeks were the powers behind the throne in Constantinople. Orthodox Greeks and Ottoman Muslims were buried side by side, as can be seen in a cemetery in Corinth recently excavated.

The French Revolution in 1789, the Terror that followed, and then Napoleon, all made it inadvisable to cross France. The French ambassador to Constantinople, Choiseul-Gouffier, was recalled, though his agent Fauvel remained. Italy soon became a military arena as Napoleon started encroaching on it, and so the eastern Mediterranean increased in popularity for visitors as previous favourite destinations became inaccessible. It was into this new political situation in the Mediterranean, where Napoleon was winning one victory after another, that Elgin came into the picture as the British ambassador to the Grande Porte in Constantinople.

An Embassy to the East:
Napoleon in Egypt, Elgin in Istanbul

The story of how the Elgin Marbles made their way to London involves Napoleon. Had he not disrupted a centuries-old balance of alliances in the Mediterranean, they are likely to have remained in Athens, sitting on the Acropolis rock where they had fallen off the Parthenon after the explosion of 1687. The Turks would have continued to use pieces of the Parthenon sculptures as building material, and to sell off others to visiting tourists. More would have been lost to us during target practice, in subsequent sieges, and they would have suffered like the material that stayed in Athens even under an independent Greece. Instead, they came to London to rest in the British Museum, by a circuitous set of circumstances that had made Lord Elgin an important man in Istanbul thanks to Napoleon's overwhelming ambition.

Having 'liberated' northern Italy from the Austrians and invaded the Papal States, Napoleon signed the Treaty of Campo Formio and returned to Paris at the end of 1797. Early the following year he was made 'commander of the army against England', and entrusted with an invasion. Realising that his troops were unlikely to succeed, Napoleon talked the directors into entrusting him with another mission, one he had suggested the previous year: the invasion of

Egypt. The primary aim was to acquire a rich colony, and to use it as a base to launch an invasion on the British territories in India. To appease Sultan Selim III, Talleyrand, the Foreign Minister, would go to Constantinople and sign a peace treaty, since war with the Ottomans was not intended. The Ottomans and the French had been allies since the sixteenth century.

Egypt had fallen to the armies of Selim I in 1517. Although nominally Ottoman, Egypt had been virtually independent for centuries, ruled by the Mamelukes, an elite of some 8,000 who formed the bulk of the army. When the sultan sent a governor, he was greeted by the Mamelukes with due honours, then imprisoned in his residence until the end of his term. These martial people originated from Albania and Circassia, and had regularly reinforced their number with recruits from their homelands. Like the ancient Spartans, they devoted their lives to war, investing most of their wealth in their equipment and training soldiers from childhood. But by the end of the eighteenth century the country was weak and their army was no match for new Western weapons.

On 18 May 1798 Napoleon set off from Toulon with his fleet, which included 167 scholars and artists whose purpose was educational, both to instruct the Egyptians, and to learn about Egypt. Along the way they were joined by a French fleet from Italy, and they stopped to capture Malta. The Ionian Islands had already become French territories, and would act as a base for the invasion. Napoleon, who had read the Koran on the voyage over, reached Egypt on 30 June. Alexandria was the only Mediterranean port in Egypt, but he did not want to attack it from the sea, so the fleet landed a little to the east. They disembarked that night, and by lunchtime the next day had seized Alexandria.

Leaving Kléber in charge, Napoleon marched south. A fortnight later he defeated the Turko-Egyptian army led by Murad Bey at the Battle of the Pyramids, then annihilated it in the Sinai Desert, thus gaining control of Cairo and Lower Egypt. Egypt was considered the 'navel of Islam', so this development was shocking to the sultan, as was the fact that the French invaders had long been Ottoman allies. Meanwhile, Rear-Admiral Sir Horatio Nelson, in a daring attack, destroyed the French fleet in Aboukir Bay on 1 August 1798, cutting off Napoleon and his 55,000 men in Egypt; they had no means of leaving, nor of getting supplies or reinforcements. Encouraged by this British success, in September 1798, the sultan ordered all Frenchmen in Ottoman lands to be imprisoned, including the French ambassador in Istanbul and Fauvel in Athens. Napoleon for the time being was trapped in Egypt, and thus had the time to reorganise and attempt to modernise Egypt. This he did with great success, creating institutions that would become the foundations of the modern state.

Dominique-Vivant Denon, a celebrated artist, followed the army into Upper Egypt, recording the monuments there. Denon's three years in Egypt produced numerous studies of the ruins, and he was made director of the Louvre on his return to Paris. The Pyramids at Giza were measured, and the sand around the Sphinx cleared. Some excavations were also undertaken, all with the purpose of acquiring antiquities to bring back to the Louvre.

Hieroglyphic inscriptions were copied but not understood. The breakthrough came in July 1799 with the discovery of a black basalt slab during building work at Rosetta. The slab was covered with an inscription in three scripts; hieroglyphics, demotic Egyptian and Greek. Since he read Greek, Lancret was able to identify it as recording the accession in 197/6 BC of Ptolemy V as Pharaoh. By comparing the Greek to the Egyptian, he was able to work out that the cartouches in the hieroglyphics contained names, and thus assign phonetic values to some of the hieroglyphs, which had until then been assumed to be pictograms.

The story of the Rosetta Stone is tangential to the story of the Elgin Marbles, but illustrates the value ancient remains could have, and the rivalry that existed between the English and French over their acquisition. After the British capture of Alexandria, the British and French generals, Menou and Hutchinson, fought over the antiquities the French had gathered together during their time in Egypt. The English claimed the antiquities as theirs under the terms of the surrender. Menou, aware of the value of the Rosetta Stone, claimed it as his personal property; Hutchinson decided that the stone was the most valuable piece, and agreed to leave the rest of their discoveries to the French in exchange for it. The French had copied the inscriptions, and a young linguist named Jean-François Champollion would soon decipher the hieroglyphics, thus unlocking the secrets of Egyptian inscriptions and history. He broke the code, realising that the hieroglyphics were a combination of pictograms, signs representing ideas, as had previously been believed, and signs that were phonetic and represented sounds.

Cut off from news as well as supplies from France, Napoleon was shocked to discover that Talleyrand had not gone to Constantinople as promised to make a peace, but that instead France and Turkey were at war. England was backing Turkey, who had declared war on France in the autumn of 1798. An Ottoman army was gathering in Syria to attack Egypt, and Napoleon marched his army into the Holy Land to meet it. Desperately short of supplies, after the unsuccessful siege of Acre he was forced to retreat. The Ottomans followed him back, and near Aboukir the Battle of the Nile was fought in July 1799. Although a decisive victory for Napoleon, news soon reached him of political turmoil in France. The country was now at war with most of Europe rather than just England, as it had been when he had left for Egypt. Austria had invaded Italy, and Corfu had fallen to a Turko-Russian fleet. The following month he left Egypt to return to Paris, again leaving Kléber in charge.

Thus this was the state of play when Thomas Bruce, the seventh Earl of Elgin and eleventh of Kincardine, was appointed Ambassador Extraordinary and Minister Plenipotentiary of His Britannic Majesty to the Sublime Porte of Selim III, the Ottoman sultan, towards the end of 1798. At the time George III was king and William Pitt First Minister. The Foreign Minister was William Grenville, a cousin of Pitt, and married to another Pitt.

There had been a vacancy for a new ambassador to Constantinople, and George III himself had suggested to Elgin that he apply for the post. The Prince and Princess of Wales were at war with each other, and so the king had taken a great interest in his granddaughter and heir Princess Charlotte, of whom he had custody. Martha, the Dowager Lady Elgin, was the little girl's beloved governess Eggy, one of the few people who ever showed the child any affection. Impressed with the exemplary way she was raising his granddaughter, the king was intrigued by the Bruce children, and asked his secretary to investigate further. Admiring Martha's parenting skills, George III took an interest in her son's career, and so Elgin won the influential post to the East, one that would make his name live on for centuries. The king went on to suggest that a suitable wife would also be an advantage to Elgin.

Although of ancient lineage, and descended from Robert the Bruce (1306–29), Elgin, who had succeeded to the earldom at the age of five, was not a rich man. He had, however, been well educated, both in England and in Paris, where he had studied law and met Benjamin Franklin. There he had argued that the Sabbath should be kept sacred, a theme that his future wife also kept close to her heart.

Elgin had succeeded in all three lines of employment open to a gentleman: the army, politics and diplomacy. In the army he had risen to the rank of lieutenant-colonel in Ireland by the age of twenty-nine, and five years earlier had been elected one of the sixteen Scottish peers that would sit in the Lords, where he had proven himself a natural politician, adept at bridging ideological differences. A first diplomatic stint in Vienna in 1791 at the court of Leopold II, where he had been sent by Pitt to be Britain's Envoy Extraordinary had been deemed a success, as had subsequent postings to advise the Austrians in Brussels in their battle plans against the French, and at the Prussian court in Berlin. In Berlin Elgin had been known for his great culture and his entertaining, though some even then had found him a cold fish. Therefore, he was felt to be suitably qualified for the position in Istanbul. He was encouraged to apply, and in November 1798 wrote to Lord Grenville:

> It has occurred to me as possible that it may be in your Lordship's intention to send to Constantinople an English representative equal in rank and situation to the Imperial and French Ministers at that Court. Should that supposition be founded I would venture to bring myself under your notice for that embassy (Historical Documents Commission, *Report on the Mss. of J. B. Fortescue Esq. preserved at Dropmore* (1892–1927) iv 359; St Clair, p. 1)

Elgin was appointed the following month, and soon began to make preparations for the journey. A bachelor, Elgin had been building a new Grecian-style house on his Scottish estate, Broomhall, designed by Thomas Harrison. Now that he had a home and a career, Elgin sought a wife, and managed to capture the hand of a beauty who had become the toast of Edinburgh society.

Mary Nisbet of Dirleton, the daughter of one of his neighbours, had the advantage not only of beauty and brains, but also of being the only child of one of the richest families in the country, and thus a highly desirable heiress. Mary's money may have been one of her main attractions, and made Elgin's acquisition of the Parthenon sculptures possible, but she was not spoilt – although lavished with affection as many only children often are. She was brought up to be aware of her surroundings and of the people on the lands that would one day be hers.

In addition, she was given a rigorous education, at a time when few women were, learning more than most boys at the time, and was fully versed in classical history and myth, making her an ideal companion for Elgin in his travels east. Although Elgin had the title, the Nisbets had the money, which in any age brought more power and respect. They were also well connected in terms of family relations, being kin to several dukes, and Mr Nisbet sat in Parliament. Mary herself had grown up in a far grander home than Elgin, one built for her father by Robert Adam, the leading architect of the day. Although Elgin's appeal to women, particularly the matrons of Berlin, is well documented, Mary was by far the better catch. In the long term Elgin might have done well to remember that all he had brought to the marriage was a good name and some charm, while Mary had brought wealth and connections. In 1799 these were automatically transferred to the husband, and divorce was almost unheard of. In a few years the Elgins themselves would change this, and open up new rights for women.

In the late eighteenth century communications were slow, and most news was passed through letters written by women. These letters were designed to inform and entertain, and to be read aloud to one's circle. Mary had been well trained by her mother, so she wrote home often, and many of these letters are still preserved. Thus this part of the Parthenon's history was funded by Mary's purse and recorded by her pen, making it as much Lady Elgin's story as that of her husband.

Elgin, in love, offered to remain in Britain rather than take up the post in Constantinople, if his chosen bride so wished it, but Mary, with the spirit of adventure that was so rare in women of her generation, rose to the occasion and agreed to accompany Elgin to the East. Of course, the marriage was firstly one of convenience, as was the norm at the end of the eighteenth century, when one chose a spouse based on rank and position, but the Elgins' letters show the love that soon grew between them, and the great deal of affection that Eggy and Poll, as they called each other, felt. Luckily, with the cash the marriage brought, Elgin was able to pay off the debts he had accrued during the construction of Broomhall, and the couple set off for Constantinople in style.

The diplomatic service under George III was quite different from the postings we have today under Elizabeth II. In 1799, when Elgin was due to depart, he was given a budget of £6,000 p.a., with which to pay his staff and expenses, and before he set sail he had to assemble his team. Elgin chose two private secretaries, William Richard Hamilton and John Philip Morier; the latter, having been born in Smyrna, knew Turkey quite well. A chaplain, the Reverend Philip Hunt, also joined the party, and borrowed heavily to finance his journey in the hope of making his fortune in the East, a theme that runs through several of his letters.

Harrison, Elgin's architect, was a great fan of the Grecian style, and considered Athenian architecture – or what he knew of it – to be superior to Roman, providing better models. Although there were by then many engravings of Athenian monuments available in Britain, there were no originals, so he suggested that Elgin have casts made, as these would greatly improve the arts in Britain. The idea was thus put to the government that the embassy should include artists, but this was rejected. Elgin would have to fund them himself, and he set about trying to recruit suitable painters. Among those he interviewed was a young Turner, who proved to be too expensive. In fact, Elgin could not agree terms with anyone suitable. Instead, the powers that be suggested a scholar for the party, there being a belief at the time that many ancient texts lay undiscovered in Constantinople libraries and Greek monasteries, and so Joseph Dacre Carlyle of Cambridge joined the party. An Orientalist, Carlyle secretly harboured plans to convert the Ottomans to the Church of England, and set off with Bibles in Arabic to implement his plan. All these people, the journey, a suitable palace and staff in Constantinople, as well as numerous gifts for the authorities, had to be funded by the ambassador himself, whose small stipend only went a little way towards covering his expenses.

Finally the group had been gathered together and the party set off from Portsmouth on the HMS *Phaeton* on 3 September 1799. Lady Elgin, pregnant with the first of many children she would bear Elgin, bore up quite well at sea considering her regular letters home to her mother spoke of her almost constant morning sickness. Laudanum, a blend of opium dissolved in alcohol, was her cure for this, and might go some way towards explaining her happy disposition on a trip the others found arduous. Elgin's men constantly complained of the conditions, and the captain thought Elgin's attachment to his wife most odd and 'unfashionable'. Elgin himself was thrilled with the potential opportunities of his mission, and delighted at how 'good-natured' his bride had turned out to be. Perhaps if we legalised opium once again, and made it available on the NHS, we too could all have happy marriages, and lower the rate of divorce.

Elgin's main purpose in Constantinople was to provide support to the sultan in the war against the French, whom the English planned to expel from Egypt, and to work towards improving British trade rights with, and access to, the Ottoman Empire. He was to build relations between the two empires. The French and the Ottomans had been allies for centuries, the former until recently providing the latter with military support, notably in their wars against Russia, so the break between the two countries was a new development and offered the British great new opportunities. Elgin was to step into this breach, forge new links with the Ottomans and gain as many concessions for the British as he could.

Napoleon fled Egypt during this same period, and his boat almost certainly crossed paths during the night with the *Phaeton* off the coast of Sicily. The Elgins stopped for a fortnight in Palermo, breaking the journey there. Nelson by the time of his Egyptian victory was already the lover of Emma Hamilton. The Elgins met this notorious ménage while in Sicily and paid their respects to Sir William Hamilton, British Minister to the Court of the Two Sicilies in Palermo. There the Elgins were entertained and went to parties, enjoying their last 'Western' socialising for several years. Of Emma Hamilton, Mary Elgin wrote to her mother on 4 October:

> I must acknowledge that she is pleasant, makes up amazingly, and did all she could to make me accept an apartment there, which I should have totally to myself. However I did not in the least scruple to refuse her Ladyship. She looked very handsome at dinner, quite in an undress; – my Father would say 'There is a fine Woman for you, good flesh and blood.'
> She is indeed a Whapper! and I think her manner very vulgar. It is quite humiliating to see Lord Nelson, he seems quite dying and yet as if he had no other thought than her. (Nisbet, p. 22)

Sir William Hamilton was a noted antiquarian as well as a diplomat, and he was able to advise Elgin on his artistic aspirations, while Nelson could brief him on politics and the military situation in the Mediterranean. In 1799 Hamilton, who had been British Minister to the Court since 1764, had had to flee into exile with the royal family after Napoleon's conquest of Naples, but luckily Sicily provided as many antiquities and volcanoes for him as Naples, the two being his twin passions. Sir William had acted as a dealer and guide to visitors to fund his own collections, the first of which he had sold to the British Museum. He had lavishly illustrated his collections with catalogues, and was able to advise Elgin on his own pursuits in the East, and help the new British ambassador to hire artists and mould-makers.

The first artist was hired in Messina. Giovanni Battista Lusieri, the King of Naples' court painter, had already illustrated the remains in Sicily, and had a certain fame at the time. Lusieri was hired for £200 p.a., as opposed to the £400 the young and little-known Turner had demanded, all work remaining the property of Elgin. Lusieri was to remain in Elgin's employ in Athens for two decades, although at the time he was hired it was assumed the mission would only last a few years. Largely forgotten today, Lusieri was considered a leading artist of his day. As Mary wrote home to her mother on 17 October

1799: 'I never in my life saw anything so beautiful as his drawings. My father would be delighted with them – so very superior to any we saw in London.'

With a lead artist now in their employ, Elgin sent him with his secretary, William Richard Hamilton, to Naples and Rome to recruit more artists. Napoleon, who had conquered much of Italy, had also stripped the country of many of its artists to work for him in Paris, so this was not an easy task. Hamilton was not able to hire all those he had hoped to, nor did he remain within the rather unrealistic budget he was set. Italy's museums were also bare, with most of their masterpieces by then embellishing Paris, for to Napoleon art was power, and once he had seized power he wasted no time seizing the conquered lands' art.

Hamilton managed to hire Theodor Ivanovitch, a Cossack, for £100 p.a.; Balestra, an architectural draughtsman, and his assistant for £125 p.a. for the pair; and two *formatori* to make casts at £100 p.a. each. Hamilton was also charged with hiring musicians for Mary Elgin. These all set off to follow the Elgins, but were delayed and did not arrive in Constantinople until May 1800, moving on to Athens in August.

The Elgins themselves left Palermo and sailed on towards the Bosporus, and were welcomed by Hassan Bey, the Capitan Pasha, at the Dardanelles, and lavish gifts were exchanged. This Turkish admiral was one of the most powerful men in the empire, a cousin of the sultan, their bonds cemented by his sister Hanum also being the favourite in Selim III's seraglio. Mary Elgin would soon be given the rare honour of visiting the seraglio, where she was befriended by Hanum. The next year even Selim's mother, the valida sultana, would welcome Mary and take her under her wing, the first foreigner to be granted this honour. Although gift-giving and ostentatious ceremonial displays were part of the etiquette of Ottoman life, the Elgins from the start became favoured guests and cemented a friendship with those close to the sultan which went beyond the usual civilities of diplomacy. The opulence of the Ottoman lifestyle was soon apparent and the elaborate giving of gifts almost routine, as Mary immediately noted, constantly given as part of daily life, and without need for any excuse or occasion.

Isaac then went and got some of my favorite [*sic*.] little round perfumes, he spoke to the Capt. Pasha who got up and went to a cabinet which he opened, took out a pretty gold enamelled box which he presented to me. We sat a little longer, and when we took our leave, the Pasha said I had not enough on, as it was cold; he sent for a new Indian shawl, not like Mrs Hepburn's, but a red colour richly embroidered, very ugly, but very valuable; they cost a great deal of money and are difficult to be got. You would have been delighted at his manner of giving me these things, it was not like giving presents, but as conversation turned upon perfumes, and cold, he produced these different things. (Nisbet, p. 38)

In the same way, when Elgin expressed interest in some ancient stones he saw, such as an inscription at Sigamon, these too were given to him. Ill winds held up the party near Troy, so they visited the site, Homer in hand, and acquired these first antiquities nearby.

After two months at sea, the *Phaeton* finally berthed in Constantinople, and the Elgins installed themselves in the British palace. A succession of Ottoman officials called and gifts were exchanged. Elgin was presented first to the Grand Vizier, and then to the sultan himself. Women could not take part in these ceremonies, but Mary, by then quite pregnant, was allowed to attend with her maid Masterman, both dressed as men – the disguise fooled nobody – and was presented as 'Lord Bruce'. The Ottoman acknowledged her, the first woman to have been granted this honour, and even bestowed gifts on her. The scene was unprecedented, and much talked of in letters of the day.

I am to be up early tomorrow morning to go to the Grand Vizier, Elgin has put me down in the List, *Lord Bruce*, a young nobleman. We sent a private message to the Vizier, by way of asking whether I might go. The dear creature sent back a most gallant answer, so, as he knows who I am, and as I am high in the procession, I think I have a chance of a nice pelisse. (20 November 1799, Nisbet, p. 48)

The following April she presented Elgin with a real Lord Bruce, George Constantine, as his heir.

Although Elgin made a success of his mission, much credit must be given to Mary, who was an even greater success, being accorded unheard of privileges such as access to the sultan's seraglio – she taught the women to reel – and the attendance of leading Ottoman officials such as the Capitan Pasha at her whist parties. The Capitan Pasha certainly seems to have become a fan of Mary's, regularly honouring her with his presence at her home, and sending a steady stream of extravagant presents, which she recorded in her letters home. He even asked her to teach him to play the piano. Her popularity with the court caused much resentment among other foreign missions that had not become as popular, but her spirit won the day.

> The jealousy this visit and the treatment I received, has caused here is quite ridiculous. Edinburgh is a joke to it.
> . . . the whole town is up in arms . . . that the Captain Pasha was coming to visit us – a thing that was never heard of . . . The foreign Ministers are as envious as they can hang in their skins; I really don't care what they say. I wonder what they will do, when I go to visit his Sultana and to the Seraglio, to visit the Grand Seigneur's Mother which I am to do, and nobody ever did but me? (28 January 1800, Nisbet, pp. 65–6)

The heat of Turkey had not been as good for Elgin's health as he had hoped; he developed a skin disease and lost his nose, which was probably not syphilis as Byron would later defame him by claiming. The loss was almost certainly a result of the huge quantities of mercury he was fed. Although mercury was used then as a 'cure' for syphilis, it was also given for almost every ailment from feeling tired to having a fever; Mary and the children were regularly fed large doses of it. Despite his disfigurement, Mary appears to have lost none of her affection for her beloved Eggy.

In 1800 Sir Sidney Smith arranged the Convention of El Arish in Syria, ending the war between the French and the Turks. Under this agreement the French would withdraw from Egypt, neither as victors nor the defeated, and be ferried back to France on British ships. Elgin immediately began making arrangements to implement this, but slow communications and Smith's technical lack of authority for negotiations on behalf of the British meant that the British initially rejected the idea of a convention, but then soon after accepted it. Various cross-messages agreeing and declining it between the three sides meant that war in Egypt dragged on for another year. The British and the Ottomans would inflict numerous defeats on Kléber's army, but in 1801 Egypt would return to the Ottoman fold.

Eventually, an independent Egypt would be carved out by Mehmet Ali, a Macedonian orphan, who had risen rapidly in the Turkish army. He fought at Aboukir, where the Ottoman army was decimated by Napoleon, but by 1804 had risen sufficiently to be named Pasha of Egypt. He remained in control of Egypt until 1849, ruling only nominally on behalf of the Ottomans, and at various stages trying to obtain Western support in his bid for independence. His son would later inflict great defeats on the Greeks in the Peloponnese during their war of independence, and after the failure of the Ottomans to hold Greece he would instead become ruler of Syria.

Although Elgin was blameless in the mess that resulted from the negotiations over the Egyptian situation, Napoleon seems to have seen him as personally responsible for the various problems involved in implementing the convention, and for the French defeat in Egypt. From then on Elgin became Napoleon's enemy. The Ottomans, however, credited Elgin with having brought peace and the return of Egypt, and Elgin's power at court increased.

Since France was the enemy of the sultan, Elgin's main objective was for Britain to become his leading ally, and it is at this point that Elgin enters history. Until Elgin the British ambassadors and consuls in the Ottoman Empire had been appointed and controlled by the Levant Company, as had relations between the sultan and Britain. In 1798 the British government had sent Smith to help the Turks, beginning the reconquest of Syria and Palestine from Napoleon on land. Choiseul-Gouffier had received the right to collect antiquities in thanks for French support of the sultan, and Elgin hoped to receive similar rights to bring back many ancient marvels to, as he often stated, improve the arts in Britain.

Soon after the birth of the Elgins' first child, Mary's parents arrived in Istanbul, after which the Nisbets set off on a tour of Greece. By August 1800 Elgin's artists had been in Athens, ready to draw and cast her monuments. They paid their respects to the British consul under whose protection they were, and also gave presents to the local Ottoman authorities who would provide them with access to the Acropolis and its monuments. The British consul, Ioannis Stamou Khondrodimas, was a Greek generally known as Logotheti, a title that reflected his official position as a tax collector for the Orthodox Church.

Athens was by then a small town of some 10,000 residents of mixed cultures and religions; half were Orthodox Greeks, a quarter Muslim although most were by then assimilated and primarily spoke Greek, the rest a mixture of Albanians and a few 'Franks', as Western residents were called. Just over a thousand homes nestled to the north of the Acropolis, within the 1778 walls, whose gates had been removed a few years earlier. Almost half the population is reputed to have fled during the tenure of the feared Hadji Ali Haseki, who had run Athens until 1795. The town was forty-third in the Ottoman Empire in terms of revenue according to British estimates, and was run by the voivode, who collected these revenues for the sultan, naturally also keeping a cut for himself.

The Louvre had been around for several centuries, but it rose to international prominence when Napoleon chose it as a depository for his Italian loot, as the Musée Napoléon, in 1801. The eighteenth century had seen the British Museum founded in 1753, and the Museo Pio Clementino in Rome in 1771. The Munich Glyptoteque would open in 1830, and these museums would be competing in their displays, all wanting to show off the best Greek originals to their public, to bring prestige to their countries as well as improving their arts in the age when the neoclassical was the ideal. At the end of the eighteenth and in the early years of the nineteenth century, the scale of these acquisitions was new and unprecedented, the tone set by Napoleon, and each country acquiring whatever it could get its hands on.

Although Elgin's removal of the Parthenon sculptures is now the most famous example of a museum gaining original sculpture from a Greek temple, around the same time the Bassae frieze also came to the British Museum, and the archaic Aegina pediments found a home in Munich. The French had tried to get their hands on the Parthenon, and when they failed resorted to piracy, seizing the *Venus de Milo* off a Turkish ship as the statue was on its way to Istanbul, having been bought by a Turk from the farmer who had discovered it.

Earlier travellers to Ottoman Athens such as John Morritt of Rokeby had expressed similar sentiments regarding antiquities: 'Some we steal, some we buy,' he wrote in a letter in January 1795. Elgin, as the official British representative to the Ottoman court, was far more scrupulous, seeking the necessary permits from the correct authorities. Choiseul-Gouffier, as ambassador to the Porte, had previously written to Fauvel of the Parthenon: 'Take away every antiquity you can, and do not lose any opportunity to remove from Athens and its surrounding countryside anything you can lay your hands on.'

Alas, Napoleon's invasion of Egypt had broken off relations between France and Turkey, so Fauvel did not succeed. During this brief period Britain and her ambassador, Lord Elgin, were in favour, and it was Elgin who would be permitted by the sultan to remove from the Acropolis those old stones in which the Ottomans had no interest. Elgin, like most others in his day, saw his removal of these Greek sculptures as saving them from destruction by the Turks and from the indifference of the Greeks who no longer cared for the glories of their past. Thus it was a quirk of history that allowed the sculptures of the Parthenon to come to the British Museum rather than the Louvre.

Work begins in Athens

Although Napoleon controlled Italy, and cut off visits by Grand Tourists over land, more adventurous visitors were able to go to Greece and Turkey, since the British navy had the upper hand in the Mediterranean. Only a few visited Ottoman territories, such as Egypt, the Holy Land and Turkey. The East was still an undiscovered land for the travellers, where 'over almost every door is an antique statue or basso-rilievo', as John Morritt said of Athens. In a letter home Morritt claimed that he soon planned 'to be in possession of one at least, if not more, of the alto-rilievos of Phidias which are over the grand colonnade' of the Parthenon. He failed in his quest to acquire some of the Parthenon marbles because of Fauvel's intervention. Many others also failed to bring home any of the Parthenon, and this is why they were later so critical of Elgin. It was jealousy pure and simple that embittered their tongues, for they too had looked up at the Acropolis, eyes dark with lust for its Periclean marbles, but had failed to persuade the Ottoman authorities to part with any quantity of them.

The Parthenon when Elgin's artists arrived in Athens and set eyes on it was a ruin. Much of the sculpture had been lost over the years as the temple's walls had come tumbling down through earthquakes, fires, successive rebuildings and, finally, the explosion of 1687. Barely half the sculpture Carrey had drawn in the 1670s survived in 1800 when Lusieri arrived in Athens, and much of that had been buried in the ground, under the homes the Turkish garrison built, where Elgin's team would find the carvings. Morosini and his soldiers had further damaged the sculpture after they had blown up much of the Acropolis, when they tried to hack off trophies and souvenirs of their devastating siege. Several of his soldiers, and then later visitors, had taken pieces of the Parthenon sculptures home with them, slowly eroding the monument by removing its decoration bit by bit.

Fauvel, in the later part of the eighteenth century, had also removed first a metope and then a slab of the frieze, on behalf of Choiseul-Gouffier, which he had shipped back to Paris. A second metope and assorted fragments which had still been in his house when he was imprisoned were confiscated by the Ottomans as war loot. Fauvel had been making good progress on behalf of Choiseul-Gouffier to accomplish what had been until then the dream of many Western visitors, and in which they had always failed, namely to save the Parthenon sculptures from destruction, and to bring them safely home to a Western museum.

Elgin's original aims had been more modest. He merely wished to bring back good drawn records of Athenian architecture, and with them casts of the architecture and sculptural decoration of the Parthenon. His acquisition of the Parthenon sculptures themselves was to come about largely by a serendipitous accident, as the political situation presented him with an unprecedented opportunity. Many had noted over the years how badly the ruins on the Acropolis were faring, sculptures being lost as they were hacked up and sold off piecemeal or burned for lime, and their condition in Elgin's day was noted by his chaplain, the Reverend Hunt, writing home to England in 1801:

> It grieved me to the heart to see the destruction made daily by the Janizaries of the fortress. They break up the finest bas-reliefs and sculptures in search of the morsels of lead that unite them to the buildings after which they are broken with wanton barbarity. (St Clair, p. 95)

Although Hunt was employed by Elgin, he echoes sentiments

expressed by numerous other travellers both before and after Elgin. Even travellers who claimed Elgin should not have brought the sculptures back to London agreed with this assessment, fearing that the sculpture would have been destroyed had it stayed in Athens. The original aim, however, had only been for Elgin's artists to draw and mould the sculptures. It would only be when the authorities prevented the artists from doing this, and demanded permission from the sultan, that the ruler would issue an edict allowing sculptures to be removed. This edict would be confirmed a second time by the sultan, and the sculptures were allowed to be exported over the next decade, so any suggestion that the removal of the Parthenon sculptures by Elgin's men took place without official permission by the legal authorities cannot have any validity.

One of Choiseul-Gouffier's metopes from the Parthenon was seized by the British, and accidentally found its way into Elgin's possession. Elgin, ever the gentleman, offered to return it to the Frenchman, but the latter declined, perhaps still smarting from his failure to acquire the rest of the marbles years earlier.

Even Elgin's old rival Choiseul-Gouffier had approved of what he had done, writing in 1809 in *Voyage Pittoresque de la Grèce*:

'il m'est difficile de les voir entre ses mains sans un peu d'envie; mais ce doit être une satisfaction pour tous ceux qui cultivent les arts, de savoir ces chefs d'œuvres soustraits de la barbarie des Turcs, et conservés par un amateur éclairé qui en fera jouir le public.' (Paris 1809, vol. 2, p. 85 f)

'it is hard for me to see them in his hands without feeling a little envy; but it must be satisfying for all those who admire the arts to know that these masterpieces were removed from the barbarities of the Turks, and preserved by an enlightened art-lover, and shall bring great joy to the public.'

These are gracious words from a gracious man, and it is a pity some of Elgin's countrymen could not admit their loss with such dignity. One of these, Edward Daniel Clarke, had met Hunt and Carlyle near Troy, where he had fallen out with Elgin's men over the site of Troy, and soon transferred his animosity towards Lord Elgin himself. In

Athens in 1801 Clarke set about collecting all he could get his hands on. He was rather proud of himself when he thought he had convinced the disdar to sell him what he thought to be a metope from the Parthenon, behind Elgin's back. In fact, this carving would turn out to be a much later relief when he showed it to experts, much to Clarke's embarrassment. At Eleusis, against the protests of the inhabitants who thought the statue guaranteed their harvest, Clarke stole a Caryatid without any sort of official permission. Although he later redeemed himself by giving his collection to Cambridge – along with a catalogue of attributions he gave his pieces which are so far-fetched they are almost funny – Clarke can never undo the damage his bitter tongue did to Elgin's reputation.

For this Clarke was the source of much misinformation given to Byron, and spread about London tales of what appalling damage Elgin and his men had done to the Acropolis. Byron wrote a poem that defamed poor Elgin, and the Greeks who demand the 'return' of the Elgin Marbles regularly repeat Clarke's silly stories to this day. Clarke was merely painting a false picture of the misdeed of a man he barely knew, and against whom, because of some chip on his shoulder, he had developed a vendetta. Clarke was jealous, and even his own brother did not agree with him, but instead readily helped ship the Elgin Marbles back to London. Alas, these lies and half-truths have clung to Elgin and to the story of how the Elgin Marbles were acquired, but they can be dispelled once and for all by retelling the story.

In August 1800 Elgin's artists arrived in the small provincial town that Athens had long been by then, and found lodgings at the foot of the ruin the Acropolis had become. They paid their respects to the voivode, the governor of the city, and to the disdar, the military governor who ran the Acropolis.

The Athens they visited was one where there was much freedom for the Greeks who lived there, some of whom were involved in the running of the city, and many of whom formed the administrative class in the Ottoman Empire. The archbishop was responsible for the Christians, as he had always been under Ottoman rule, with his own prisons and a grander residence than the voivode. The Orthodox

Greeks were not an oppressed people, and if anything most Ottomans in Athens had assimilated to their culture and spoke primarily Greek rather than Turkish. There was no clash between the Christian and Muslim cultures, but rather peace and a great deal of integration; the voivode had even married a Greek. The Greek war of independence was only a few decades away, but unrest was mostly in the Peloponnese rather than in Athens. Several foreign consuls, often native Greeks such as Logotheti, the British consul, assisted the increasing number of travellers who came to Athens, and provided lodgings. The French, who usually lodged with the Capuchins to the east of the Acropolis, were particularly well represented in this era, though at that time Fauvel and their leading lights were detained as prisoners of war.

The Acropolis itself was still a military fortress, and as such by Ottoman law owned by the government and thus ultimately by the sultan. The disdar, who resided on the rock, and the voivode as his immediate superior, were responsible for its upkeep as the home of the garrison and as a shelter in times of war, a status that the authorities would soon find themselves needing to invoke. The Periclean ruins of the Propylaea, the Erechtheion and the Parthenon were seen as just that, and had little importance to the Ottoman authorities other than as places to quarry a convenient supply of building blocks, and to chop off the odd section to sell to tourists. The Hephaisteion, on a small hill to the north-west, was still an Orthodox church dedicated to St George, as it had been for over a thousand years, but almost every other building that Pericles or Hadrian would have recognised was in ruins.

As in other citadels, such as Korone in the Peloponnese, the Turks had built their homes among the rubble on the Acropolis, reusing suitable blocks and constructing abodes following no particular order. The garrison worshipped in the small mosque which had replaced and been erected in the ruins of the earlier one in the Parthenon, and between all these structures were gardens in which fruit and vegetables grew. These were not enough to sustain the garrison, but could prove handy in times of siege, and the earth and plants on the rock must have made it look quite unlike the Acropolis we see today.

Stuart and Revett's engraving of the ruins of the Parthenon, seen above a maze of low roofs in 1751, must have been similar to the Parthenon Elgin's men saw when they arrived in Athens. Like many of those in the lower city, the houses on the Acropolis were built using any available material, and here they would have incorporated blocks from the Periclean structure reused for the walls, with sculptures set into these walls to provide additional decorative elements. The Propylaea, although damaged in the Venetian siege, was repaired and still served as a fortified gateway. The Erechtheion had fared less well; it was no longer whole enough to be a home and instead served for storage. The Nike temple had long been dismantled, its remains built into a Turkish battlement just before the Venetian siege. Nike did not bring the Turks victory, but ironically this reuse of the blocks helped preserve the temple.

For years ancient sculpture was believed to have been white, though in the later eighteenth and in the nineteenth century, through excavations, people were beginning to discover traces of paint on marble fragments. This caused a great shock, and even today many visitors to museums assume that the pristine white marble they see is how the ancients would originally have seen their statues. Elgin would have known that Athenian buildings may well have been coloured, for this was noted by Stuart and Revett in the first volume of their *Antiquities of Athens*, published in 1762. Scholars have identified minute traces of pigments on the Parthenon that have allowed them to identify the original colours of the Parthenon sculptures, though in Elgin's day the marbles were pale, and seem to have been covered in a neutral wash at some point in the Ottoman period, between the time the Parthenon church was transformed into a mosque and the time the Venetians shelled it.

The original floor of the Parthenon had survived the Late Antique fire, conversions into first a church then a mosque and, finally, the explosion. In the eighteenth century, however, all the paving slabs were removed from what had been the interior of the Parthenon, except those under the second smaller mosque. They were used as building materials, as was every other easily removable block of the Parthenon. What we see today is a reconstruction, and one that is far more 'whole' than the Parthenon in Elgin's day. Today's Parthenon was reconstructed before the Second World War by Greek engineers using blocks found around the hill, and again during the last years of the twentieth and first years of this century. Many of the blocks and columns we see standing today, two hundred years ago were lying around the Acropolis, or built into houses for the Turkish garrison dotted around the rock. When blocks were not removed for building materials, then they were dismantled to reach the lead used in their joins, since this lead was valuable for making bullets. This is the Parthenon Lusieri or Fauvel would have known, and the drawings of travellers show that the interior walls of the Parthenon, on top of which the frieze would once have been located, were no longer standing in 1800.

The Ilissos temple is another example of the effect of the swift decline in the condition of Athenian monuments. The temple, a small Ionic gem, was well preserved when Stuart and Revett visited in 1751, but by Elgin's time was destroyed. The temple lost columns as locals found that its drums provided an easy source of stone. The majority of inhabitants at the time were Greeks and they, as much as the Ottoman Turks, contributed to this slow attrition and destruction of classical monuments, it being human nature to use what is handy and available, just as the Byzantine Greeks had found it easier to convert some temples into churches rather than to build new structures.

In the eighteenth century travellers, increasing in number and all wanting to bring home a slice of ancient Greece as a souvenir of their journeys, added to the destruction of many monuments. Whereas before sculpture had been ground down and destroyed or burned to make lime, now canny locals realised that the same sculpture could be chopped up and bits sold off. Many pieces of the Parthenon, especially heads from the metopes which could more easily be broken off, were sold by the Ottomans and left the Acropolis in this way. Today, many of those fragments that left Athens piecemeal are now lost, their provenances forgotten, and had Lord Elgin not acted as decisively as he did, it is likely that much more of the sculpture would have suffered this sad fate. Some concluded, as poorly educated farmers in remote areas such as Afghanistan and Pakistan still do today, that the ancient remains must contain gold to be of so much interest to archaeologists, so they ransacked ruins, smashing up sculptures in the hope of finding mythical gold nuggets inside the ancient statues. Travellers returned home with their Parthenon fragments, but often once home lost interest in them just as modern travellers may lose interest in a sombrero or trinket they haggled over so fiercely on holiday. And even when the travellers did maintain their love for their ancient fragment, their heirs often did not.

A head from a Parthenon metope the Dukes of Devonshire had at Chatsworth was later given to the British Museum, as were some other fragments picked up by various travellers. More fragments were donated to other museums and are dotted around Europe, but even all these pieces of the Parthenon are only a small portion of the number of sculptures we know were brought back according to the travellers' own accounts. In 1902 a frieze block of the Parthenon was excavated, in an Essex garden of all places, its importance to an owner at one point having been so slight that he clearly thought it easier to bury it than to have it carted away. Chunks of the Parthenon sculptures have disappeared in this way over the years, and will hopefully be rediscovered some day, but none have come on to the art market in living memory. Leaving aside the almost certain damage many parts of the Parthenon would have suffered over the years had Lord Elgin not brought them back to London, this inglorious fate of lying hacked to pieces, dispersed and abandoned by a series of owners who lost interest in the sculptures, would have been worse. Lord Elgin was able to take advantage of the new order, step into the breach and so save the Parthenon marbles from almost certain destruction.

Lusieri, Theodor the Cossack, Balestra and his assistant, plus the two moulders, had thus all arrived in Athens in August 1800, and set to work. Their instructions were to draw and mould. They were also to collect antiquities if they could, but this was very much a sideline; recording what remained of the sculpture and architecture of the Parthenon was the priority. The disdar at one point would not let them on to the Acropolis, claiming that he had to preserve the modesty of the Ottoman women on it, and that, furthermore, recording was prohibited for military reasons. Wanting a large bribe in exchange for allowing them access, he claimed that Lord Elgin's team needed a firman, and so Lusieri asked Elgin to arrange one. Meanwhile, Lusieri and Balestra drew various monuments around the Acropolis. They drew the Hephaisteion, which was a church, and so under the jurisdiction of the archbishop, and the Lysicrates Monument, which was part of the Capuchin monastery, and to which they could not be denied access by the Ottomans.

The Ottomans did, however, make Fauvel's confiscated equipment, including scaffolding, ropes and a cart, available to the British team. Eventually, in February 1801, they were allowed on to the Acropolis, having been very generous with their gifts, and having agreed with the disdar to pay £5 per visit. This was a good rate, well negotiated, and less than the artist Edward Dodwell had had to pay for himself alone to draw. Theodor was quite creative in his depictions, restoring damaged sculptures, and rearranging the order of the metopes on the Parthenon to better suit his compositions. Other artists of the period used similar licence, sometimes emphasising decay to be more picturesque, or 'restoring' to give a better idea of the original; both are reasons why one must be careful when using drawings as 'evidence' for the state of the Parthenon sculptures. Unfortunately, many of the rather better drawings by Lusieri, the more talented and experienced artist, who became one of the sights of Athens sitting under his parasol on the Acropolis, were lost when the *Mentor* sank. Other Lusieri drawings were stolen by Clarke and published as his own, in Clarke's rather fanciful account of his travels.

Work began, but it certainly did not make much progress. Perhaps if the disdar had been less greedy and more welcoming to visitors, then Lord Elgin would not have had to seek a firman. If he had not needed a firman, he might not have brought the Marbles back to London, but history cannot be made up of such 'ifs'. As long as Elgin's team were drawing, all went well. When they erected scaffolding and tried to take mouldings to make casts, the authorities barred all visitors to the Acropolis and demanded another firman before they would permit any further work. Although this was probably a tactic to demand more money out of Lusieri, the Turks were also suspicious that the French might try another invasion within the Ottoman Empire. The French had recently invaded Egypt and were still fighting there, and so military zones such as the Acropolis were justifiably put off-limits to foreigners, who could all be potential spies. Elgin's team, who had barely begun work on the Acropolis, were forced to stop.

Carlyle, the scholar that the British government had attached to Elgin's delegation, was meanwhile continuing his search for ancient manuscripts in Orthodox and Ottoman libraries, with little success. He was also searching for the 5,000 Arabic Bibles he had shipped to Constantinople, which the Orthodox patriarch rather tactfully decided he had never received, wishing to preserve the status quo with the Ottomans; they did not approve of trying to convert Muslims, and punished apostasy with death. As part of Lord Elgin's attempts to bring about a peace between the French and Ottomans, and also to search for these missing classical texts, Carlyle accompanied the Reverend Hunt to Syria, travelling down through Turkey, in 1800.

By the spring of 1801 Hunt and Carlyle were back in Turkey proper, and travelling in the Troad, not having found a single lost ancient text. Instead, they decided to locate the site of the famed city of Troy, where the Greeks had fought for ten years for the beautiful Helen, the city whose fall is depicted in the north metopes of the Parthenon, in a prime location on the side most visitors walked along. The two Englishmen planned to do so by using a copy of Homer they had with them. It was there that they encountered and fell out with a group of British also trying to find the fabled city, under the leadership of the aforementioned Edward Clarke. The parties argued, Clarke felt slighted by Elgin's men, and seems to have maintained an increasing and disproportionate animosity towards them from then on. Later in Athens when he failed to get his hands on pieces of the Parthenon, he of course began his libels on Lord Elgin.

Hunt and Carlyle meanwhile travelled west to Greece, stopping at the monasteries of Mount Athos to continue their search for manuscripts. These manuscripts would eventually prove a problem to Lord Elgin, since he had signed off a selection Carlyle had borrowed from the Jerusalem patriarch resident in Constantinople.

After Athos the pair sailed down to Athens, where they met the Nisbets, returning from Constantinople and on their way back home to Scotland.

Although Hunt had hoped to see great progress made by Lusieri and the team, the artists were still barred from the Acropolis. They could neither draw the Parthenon sculptures nor make casts of them. Persuasion was to no avail; Hunt and Carlyle were allowed on to the Acropolis to visit, but the artists were not. Hunt realised that a firman was their only hope, and returned to Constantinople determined to get one. In May the Nisbets returned to Scotland, with antiquities they had collected and been given, including a throne presented by the Orthodox archbishop. Carlyle's mission was over, now that he had a few manuscripts and could show that there were no more lost classics to be rediscovered in the East. He too set off for London.

By the beginning of 1801 Napoleon had subdued all his enemies other than Britain and Turkey, and he turned his attention to his army trapped in Egypt. General Menou, who was by then in charge of the French forces in Egypt, was a better administrator than a fighter. The British landed at Aboukir Bay on 8 March. The French sailed along the coast from Libya, Cato's March in reverse, but were unable to land, and so the French in Egypt surrendered to the British General Sir Ralph Abercromby. The French surrendered on the same terms as they had earlier, under the Convention of El Arish. In September of that year the British navy shipped them back to France.

Egypt returned to the Ottomans, who had power in their nominal province for the first time in centuries. When this victory was announced in Constantinople great celebrations were held for the recapture of Egypt, and the sultan Selim III was awarded the epithet 'the Conqueror'. As a sign of respect to the British, the sultan even acknowledged Mary Elgin during the celebrations, the first woman an Ottoman sultan had ever publicly honoured in this way. Lord Elgin instantly became the most important foreigner in Constantinople, and as such could wield great influence; he was awarded honours and plied with gifts, as was Mary. Although modern scholars emphasise the gifts presented to the Ottomans, gift-giving went both ways and all officers of the British forces who had taken part in the campaign were generously rewarded by the sultan.

Elgin was granted almost any request he made, mostly rather modest and unselfish ones. He was able to arrange for all Maltese slaves in the Ottoman Empire, Malta being British at the time, to be freed. He also persuaded the sultan to free the French-held prisoners in the empire, including Fauvel in Athens and the French representative in Constantinople. While the French representative had been imprisoned since 1798, the British had made the French palace their residence, and this meant that Lord Elgin had to find a new home in Constantinople for his embassy. The sultan granted Elgin a suitable plot of land in the city worth £9,000, and a further £8,000 to fund construction. Balestra was brought from Athens, where he was not in any case making progress on the Acropolis, to design a new British palace. Ironically, this was a copy of Elgin's Scottish seat, Broomhall. One of Elgin's aims for his embassy to the East had been to find models for the architecture of his Scottish home. In Turkey he found himself commissioning a reproduction of that very house, in all its neo-Grecian splendour, to be built in Istanbul. Finished long after the Elgins had left, both this new Broomhall and the French embassy fell victim to a conflagration in 1831.

In May 1801 a first firman, allowing Elgin's artists access to the Acropolis, was sent directly to the voivode in Athens. Now lost, it was already out of date by the time it arrived in Athens, due to long delays in its journey from Constantinople. At that time the French navy was again gathering at Toulon, and Lord Elgin informed the sultan that the British suspected the French were planning to invade Greece. The Acropolis was reinforced to withstand an attack, ancient marble blocks from the Parthenon and other Periclean monuments being used to do this. Military fortresses such as the Acropolis were immediately closed to visitors, so in effect Lord Elgin himself had been the cause of his own artists being denied access to the Acropolis.

Hunt, Carlyle and the Nisbets arrived in Athens soon after the artists had been ejected from the fortress for a second time in May 1801. Although the two Englishmen had managed to make the journey from Constantinople, the firman had not, showing how slow Ottoman communications could be. Elgin was by then losing interest in his earlier attempts to bring Athenian architecture back to Britain, and almost gave up. The Nisbets' enthusiasm in Athens spurred him on, and when Hunt returned to Constantinople he too, full of praise for the work going on, pushed Elgin to obtain a second firman.

Hunt outlined in a memorandum all that he hoped to see in this new firman. He wanted the artists to be given access to the Athenian Acropolis so that they could freely draw the temples and make mouldings of the elements; he wished to be allowed to excavate a little to explore further the structure of the buildings; and finally he wished to be allowed to take away any ancient remains that did not compromise the fortification walls of the Acropolis as a military fortress. By 6 July the Ottoman authorities had agreed to all these requests, and the Cayman Pasha confirmed this in a letter. Only the lines preventing Elgin from removing anything from the walls were omitted. In effect, Elgin was given carte blanche to take whatever he liked from wherever he liked on the Acropolis. Although the original imperial order is now lost – it had been handed over to the voivode in Athens, not kept by Elgin's men – an Italian copy made at the time has survived. Italian was the language Westerners and Ottomans communicated in, since Venice had several colonies within Ottoman territory, and traded actively with the empire. This copy gives the text of the second firman, and was brought back to England by Hunt. It survives as part of the Hunt Papers, now owned by William St Clair.

The Grand Vizier was still in Egypt, so his deputy, the Cayman Pasha, issued the document on behalf of the Ottoman government, and in accordance with the wishes of the sultan, the supreme authority in the empire, whose word was final. The French had been defeated thanks to the assistance of the British. Lord Elgin and the British were being showered with all manner of honours and gifts, and so this request, for what the Ottomans saw as no more than a few broken bits of old stones, must have seemed trifling and trivial to the sultan. The Ottomans had heard stories of British eccentricities, so if Lord Elgin wanted stones from the Acropolis rather than being heaped in gold, the sultan was delighted to oblige.

There was only one difference between what Hunt had hoped for, and what Elgin was granted: the exclusion from removing material from the walls was omitted by the Ottomans, thus giving them more than they had asked for, and sanctioning all that Elgin's men later did.

One word in the firman led to differences in interpretation – the word translated as 'qualque'. Elgin's men took it to mean at least 'some', and since the Ottomans later granted export licences for the marbles removed, they too must have intended this use of the term. The firman is not particularly precise about what is described, in a slightly derogatory way, as stones the Ottomans thought little of, and 'some stones' is the way in which the Turks regularly referred to ancient ruins, and even whole ruined cities. The firman was generous, and sanctioned the removal of anything Lord Elgin wanted from the Acropolis. The Elgins were delighted, and Mary Elgin wrote to her parents on 9 July:

> I am happy to tell you Pisani [the interpreter] has succeeded à merveille in his *firman* from the Porte. Hunt is in raptures, for the *firman* is perfection, and P. says he will answer with his whiskers that it is exact.
>
> It allows all our artists to go into the citadel, to copy and model everything in it, to erect scaffolds all around the Temple, to dig and discover all the ancient foundations, and to bring away any marbles that might be deemed curious by their having inscriptions on them, and that they are not to be disturbed by the soldiers etc, under any pretence whatever. Don't you think this will do? I am in the greatest glee, for it would have been a great pity to have failed in the principal part, after having been at such expence [*sic*]. (Nisbet, pp. 97–8)

Hunt's memorandum, Mary's letter to her parents and the Italian translation all tally. So, contrary to what some Greek scholars now claim, the firman fully allowed the legal removal of the Parthenon sculptures by Elgin. On the next day, 10 July, Elgin wrote to Lusieri in Athens telling him that they had permission to start excavations.

I should wish to have example in the actual object, of each thing, and architectural ornament – of each cornice, each capital – of the decorated ceilings, of the fluted columns – specimens of the different architectural orders, – of metopes and the like, as much as possible. Finally everything in the way of sculpture, medals, and curious marbles that can be discovered by means of assiduous and indefatigable excavation. This excavation ought to be pushed on as much as possible, be its success what it may. (A. H. Smith, Lord Elgin and his Collection, *Journal of Hellenic Studies*, 36 (1916) p. 207; St Clair, p. 99)

After the problems they had had in implementing the first firman, the Reverend Hunt himself delivered the second one to the voivode in Athens, to make sure that it arrived, and that its terms could immediately be put into action, setting off from Constantinople in mid-July to do so. Hunt was accompanied by an Ottoman official, Rachid Aga, to make sure the highly esteemed Lord Elgin's wishes were clear, and even more importantly that the sultan wished them to be granted; the Ottoman official was to see that Elgin's men were well treated, and the imperial order obeyed. They arrived in Athens on 22 July, having stopped to pick up a few antiquities along the way, and Hunt was welcomed by Logotheti as a guest in his house.

Two other British visitors were in Athens, Edward Dodwell and William Gell. Friends of Hunt's, they were also conveniently both artists, so they have left us valuable contemporary pictorial information about Elgin's work in Athens. The Elgin artists were already back up on the Acropolis, drawing alongside Dodwell and Gell, though they had been having the usual difficulties in gaining access. Hunt visited the voivode, along with his companion from Constantinople, bearing the firman. The voivode apologised for the problems the artists had been having, blaming the disdar as governor of the fortress, and promised free access to the Acropolis for all Englishmen. He reassured them that he would fully implement the terms of the firman, assisting Elgin's artists in any way he could.

Hunt, having by now had some experience of the Ottomans, knew that it was important to seize the opportunity while it was there. He hired Greek labourers and set about collecting inscriptions on the Acropolis, bringing them down to the city. Among those inscriptions were some that would later prove to be the accounts of the building of the Parthenon, others that were later inventories of its treasures. Next, Hunt began excavating, digging into the ground, and clearing the many centuries of debris that had accumulated around the ancient monuments. Where he could reach them, he dug down into the foundations, beginning with the Erechtheion's famous Caryatid Porch.

Once Hunt had brought the firman to Athens, all in the city, Greeks and Turks, as well as the authorities, cooperated with him. As well as the sultan's firman, a series of official decrees were issued locally in Athens by the voivode in support of Lord Elgin's work. When the matter of access and the disdar's previous interference was resolved, work could not have proceeded more smoothly, with all assisting in any way they could. Logotheti gave Elgin the pieces that were in his own house. Various Greek Athenians were happy to sell Hunt the bits of sculpture and inscriptions they had lying around at home. Some even started their own little excavations around Attica, hoping to find more objects with which to supply this mad Englishman intent on buying bits of broken old stones. The Greek Orthodox archbishop also allowed Hunt and Elgin's agents to take antiquities off Church lands.

Hunt did not limit himself to Athens, but travelled around Greece, looking for rediscovered but unappreciated antiquities. He made a tour of the region in his diplomatic capacity, to offer reassurance to the local pashas that the British would help the Ottomans against any French invasion. The pashas in turn were happy to help him in his quest for antiquities. At Mycenae he thought about bringing back the famous Lion Gate, but decided against it. Lord Elgin and a later traveller brought back some architectural elements from the Tomb of Atreus, and these are now in the British Museum. At Eleusis Hunt identified the Caryatid, and thought of adding her to his collection, but the locals protested, so he did not. Later, Clarke was not so considerate of their feelings.

The eastern end of the south colonnade of the Parthenon had been badly damaged in the seventeenth-century explosion, and then continued to crumble in the subsequent century. Since most of the columns were no longer standing, nor were the majority of the metopes that had once been placed above them. One metope had already fallen down to earth in a storm. Only seven more metopes of the Centauromachy, the metopes that had not been defaced by the iconoclast Byzantine Greeks, were still on the building. The disdar had already allowed Fauvel to remove metopes, and now gave permission for Hunt to do the same. There was some brief discussion of whether this was indeed allowed under the terms of the firman. The voivode, having spoken with Rachid Aga, the Ottoman official who had accompanied the firman from Constantinople, ruled that it was allowed.

So on 31 July 1801 the first of the metopes to be removed by Hunt was taken down. Drawings make it clear that the state of preservation of the Parthenon meant that the metope was not 'hacked' from the building, as some now claim. Rather, the slab with the sculpted reliefs was easily lifted out of its slot within the architectural framework, causing no damage to it. A second metope was removed the next day, and both were taken to the British consulate. There they were drawn, before being taken to Piraeus and shipped off, on their way to London within weeks.

The terms of the firman were fully investigated when the British government bought the Elgin Marbles and entrusted them to the British Museum. Even earlier, in Athens at the time of the work, in any uncertainty over the phrasing of the firman, the voivode followed Hunt. He took the option more favourable to the British, as he had been told to do by Rachid Aga. The voivode did so knowing that the sultan had meant to be generous to Elgin, and showing also that in general few Ottomans in any case cared for broken old stones.

Although legally and officially approved, the work was smoothed by the exchange of many gifts, the Ottoman custom. The permission to remove material he was interested in had been the sultan's gift to Lord Elgin. Like many documents written in a foreign language and centuries ago, the terms of the firman are open to interpretation, but the terms the sultan had intended were clearly not exceeded. Nor were they seen to have been exceeded by the Ottomans, who issued subsequent firmans confirming the legitimacy of the work carried out by Elgin's men, and by allowing the collection to be exported.

In 1749 Richard Dalton had drawn the west pediment of the Parthenon, showing twelve figures *in situ* in the gable. In 1800, when Lusieri arrived in Athens, there were only four figures still in that same gable, and two of those had lost their heads within the previous thirty years. Five blocks of the frieze James Stuart had seen in the mid-eighteenth century had vanished by Elgin's day. Fauvel had made a cast of another frieze block in 1790, which by 1800 had also vanished. The situation with the metopes was similar.

As Elgin would later tell Parliament in 1816: 'Every traveller coming added to the general defacement of the statuary . . . And the Turks have been continually defacing the heads; and in some instances they have actually acknowledged to me that they have pounded down the statues to convert them into mortar' (*Select Committee Report*, p. 41).

One Turk, whose house was compulsorily purchased so that excavations could take place beneath it, laughed at the British, claiming he had long ago ground up the statues he had found under the house, making mortar out of the Periclean gods. As even Hobhouse, the travelling companion and friend of Byron, who hated Elgin and spent many years disparaging the latter's work, noted: 'If the progress of decay should continue to be as rapid as it has been for something more than a century past, there will, in a few years, be not one marble standing upon another on the site of the Parthenon' (*Journey through Albania*, p. 339).

Much of the sculpture Elgin brought back to London was lying on the ground or excavated from the ground. The frieze blocks, for example, could not all have been removed from the building, since drawings show that the walls that once stood under it were no longer standing in Elgin's day, and so we must conclude that it was therefore on the ground.

Abutting the west end of the Parthenon there had been a small Turkish house, home to one of the garrison. Hunt bought it, pulled the house down, and began excavating under it, beneath the west façade of the Parthenon. The expense proved to have been a good investment, for they soon found many of the pedimental statues, which had fallen out of the gable and on to the ground in the 1687 explosion. When the Turks rebuilt their homes on the Acropolis after the explosion, they had simply built over these figures, thankfully not chopping them up to make building blocks.

To the south of the Parthenon, much of the south frieze was found, along with a few more pieces of the pediment figures. The central block of the east frieze and of the Panathenaic procession, the scene with the folding of the *peplos*, was found built into a wall, where it had been drawn by Henry Hope in 1799. Given that it was removed from the temple when the old east end, above which it had been since Periclean times, was remodelled as a Byzantine Greek church by the Christians, it is a miracle that it survived all those years in such good condition.

The frieze blocks were heavy, and it seemed a colossal task to bring them back to London whole, their sheer weight making this a daunting task. Since many of the backs of the blocks were heavily damaged by the explosion, and since these backs were plain and unadorned, Hunt ordered that they be removed. This too is now seen as a deed of great vandalism by some modern Greeks, but if they had remained whole, the frieze blocks would never have arrived in London. They would now be as destroyed as those that stayed in Athens.

Although this action meant that the frieze blocks could not be put back on the Parthenon, very little of the Parthenon was standing in 1800, and certainly far less than the constructed modern version we see today. The possibility of rebuilding the unloved ruins of the Parthenon would never have entered the minds of these early travellers. It seemed imperative to save the Parthenon sculptures, rather than to dream of restoring a structure that was in ruins. The Parthenon is now being rebuilt using modern blocks by modern Greeks; but though the form of the original building might one day rise again, the pollution in Athens prohibits the sculptures' return to their original location, so whether Hunt did more harm than good remains a moot point. He saved the frieze blocks' sculpture from destruction, even if he had to cut off the backs of the blocks to do so.

Elgin tried to enlist the help of the British government in shipping back the Marbles, asking for a ship or two that might be passing to help. Alas, a suitable navy ship large enough was not available, so Hunt could not implement his most ambitious plan, which was to bring back to London the entire Erechtheion. Hunt did remove one Caryatid, now in the British Museum, and it is tragic to compare her marvellous state of preservation with that of her poor sisters left in Athens, statues whose features and details are nearly worn away by pollution, and who now have to reside in a gas-filled box, their condition being so poor and their marble too fragile to expose to air. The copies on the Erechtheion today had to be modelled from the figure in London, not those in Athens.

Dodwell and Gell were on the Acropolis in 1801, thanks to Elgin's firman, and at the time were greatly encouraging the work his men were undertaking, and seemed to approve of it. Dodwell would return in 1805, providing us with more drawings of the period. Later he

Caryatids from the Erechtheion in London (left) and in Athens (right), showing the deterioration in their condition since 1801

turned turncoat, claiming he had seen much damage; unfortunately for Elgin, by the time Dodwell published these claims in 1819 he was following Byron's lead and making up things he could not possibly have seen, as he was not in Athens when much of the sculpture was removed from the Acropolis.

Edward Clarke had arrived in Athens in October 1801. After his meeting with Hunt at Troy, he had decided to make Elgin his mortal enemy. Unfortunately, he was the one who told Byron scurrilous tales about Elgin, defamatory stories that Byron chose to repeat in *Childe Harold* (published 1812). Clarke himself would cause great devastation to the village of Eleusis by removing her Caryatid, a figure the locals associated with the bounty of their harvest. Rather ironically, it was thanks to Elgin's help that he was able to bring this piece back to England on a British warship.

Clarke had tried to buy a Parthenon metope from the disdar – and under Hunt's nose – but instead bought a later Roman relief at an over-inflated price. This only increased Clarke's bitterness towards Elgin, and the chip on his shoulder soon turned into a quarry, and it was in that quarry that he found the nonsensical and libellous 'facts' that he later fed Byron. Clarke bought some pieces of the Erechtheion's architecture, but these are now lost. He tried to lure Lusieri away from Elgin and into his own service, but failed. Perhaps Clarke's greatest achievement came about by accident. He brought back an Egyptian sarcophagus from Alexandria, now in the British Museum, which a young scholar has recently and very convincingly argued was the sarcophagus reused to bury Alexander the Great.

Hobhouse, Byron's companion on his first trip to Greece, left us drawings that are often used to show the 'vandalism' of Elgin, and the poor state in which he left the Acropolis. The drawings of the Parthenon are not accurate, as they do not even show the pedimental sculptures we know remained on the building well into the 1970s, long after Elgin's day.

These pediment sculptures that remained have an interesting history, and show the importance of checking original sculpture instead of merely reading much later secondary sources. Figures C and D of the west pediment depicted Cecrops and his Daughter, and date to the original phase of the Parthenon. In 1671 Wheler and

Spon identified them as depicting Hadrian and his wife Sabina, and dated them as belonging to a later Hadrianic restoration of the building in the second century AD. Stuart and Revett repeated the story in *The Antiquities of Athens* (1751), so Fauvel also thought them to be Roman. Hunt followed suit and left them behind in Athens. Nobody bothered to look at the sculptures themselves, or knew enough about Greek sculpture, to date them to the classical period as Greek originals. In 1795 these two figures and one other were the last of the sculptures in the pediment to still have their heads. By 1801 only one of these still had their head, and soon there were none.

In December 1801 a brig Elgin had bought, the *Mentor*, took ten cases to Alexandria and brought back William Richard Hamilton. He had been in charge of shipping the French safely home, and then undertaken a tour of Egypt with Clarke. On this tour Clarke had acquired the Alexander sarcophagus. Although usually overtly imaginative in his attributions, in this sole case he might have been correct. Alternating with returning the French army to Napoleon, Hamilton had shipped some Egyptian antiquities back to London, including the Rosetta Stone. This was one of the pieces found by the French, but which they handed over to the British when they relinquished Egypt. Hamilton stayed on in Athens, to await the arrival of his patron.

Elgin reigned supreme among the foreign residents, the aims of his mission accomplished more fully than anyone could have imagined, with both the British government delighted and the sultan over-joyed. Now it was time for Elgin to take a holiday, have some fun, and to go see this famous Parthenon, which he had heard so much about. The Turks found the Westerners' habit of travelling for pleasure the height of eccentricity. Their love of old stones they understood even less, but in this matter the sultan was happy to indulge Elgin's whims.

To everyone else in Constantinople this would have seemed a just reward for a favoured diplomat, representative of the country that had just helped them rout the French from Egypt. Far more shocking to the Ottomans, where hierarchy and ritual ruled their lives, was the fact that the sultan and his family embraced the Elgins so warmly. The sultan's mother welcomed Mary into her home, and the sultan spoke to Elgin, not through a series of lesser officials, but directly and face to face. As Mary described the incident:

> Never was anybody received in the stile Elgin was, at his audience. As soon as he appeared before him, and was going to begin his speech as is the custom, the Sultan himself began speaking, a thing that was never before done – looking at E. and making an inclination of his head. His speech was the most flattering thing possible, saying how much he was indebted . . . the Sultan again addressed himself to E. paying him a handsome compliment. Colonel Graham and Hutchinson both say it was more like a conversationé [*sic*] than an audience. (8 October 1801, Nisbet, p. 133)

The Firman

A firman was needed for Elgin's artists to continue working on the Acropolis, and so such a firman, drafted by Hunt, was granted by Selim III to Elgin and his agents in May 1801. Only a copy in Italian, translated below, survives, but it is clear that everything Lord Elgin had desired was given.

Sultan Selim III's gratitude to, and affection for, Elgin were such that he even gave the Scot antiquities from mosques in Istanbul, such as the porphyry sarcophagus that now holds the remains of Robert the Bruce in Scotland. Although the firman allowing Elgin to remove material from the Acropolis has not been found in the Ottoman archives, other documents have been found in the Basvekâlet Arsivi which record gifts of antiquities in Istanbul. Elgin is described by Selim as his 'beloved friend Elchy-Bey', to whom the sarcophagus from the mosque of Osman, a colossal Egyptian beetle, and other ancient remains were given. The sarcophagus was originally probably in the church of the Holy Apostles, demolished in 1453, and had held the remains of a member of Constantine the Great's family. As the property of a mosque, the sarcophagus could only be given to Elgin by the sultan. Such a transaction would have been seen as a greater gift from the sultan than permission to remove sculpture from Athens.

This English translation was read into the minutes of the 1816

Select Committee. It had been presented to Parliament by the Rev. Hunt himself – the man who had accompanied the original from Constantinople to Athens

It is hereby signified to you, that our sincere Friend his Excellency Lord Elgin, Ambassador Extraordinary from the Court of England to the Porte of Happiness, hath represented to us, that it is well known that the greater part of the Frank (i.e. Christian) Courts are anxious to read and investigate the books, pictures or figures, and other works of science of the ancient Greek philosophers: and that in particular, the ministers or officers of state, philosophers, primates and other individuals of England, have a remarkable taste for the drawings, or figures or sculptures, remaining ever since the time of the said Greeks, and which are to be seen on the shores of the Archipelago and in other parts; and have in consequence from time to time sent men to explore and examine the ancient edifices, and drawings or figures. And that some accomplished *Dilletanti* of the Court of England, being desirous to see the ancient buildings and the curious figures in the City of Athens, and the old walls remaining since the time of the Grecians, which now subsist in the interior part of the said *place*; his Excellency the said Ambassador hath therefore engaged five English painters, now dwelling at Athens, to examine and view, and also to copy the figures remaining there, *ab antiquo*: And he hath also at this time expressly besought us that an Official Letter may be written from hence, ordering that as long as the said painters shall be employed in going in and out of the said citadel of Athens, which is the place of their occupations; and in fixing scaffolding round the ancient Temple of the Idols there; and in moulding the ornamental sculpture and visible figures thereon, in plaster or gypsum; and in measuring the remains of other old ruined buildings there; and in excavating when they find it necessary the foundations, in order to discover inscriptions which may have been covered in the rubbish; that no interruption may be given them, nor any obstacle thrown in their way by the Disdar (or commandant of the citadel) or any other person: that no one may meddle with the scaffolding or implements they may require in their works; and *that when they wish to take away any pieces of stone with old inscriptions or figures thereon, that no opposition be made thereto.*

We therefore have written this Letter to you, and expedited it by Mr Philip Hunt, an English gentleman, Secretary of the aforesaid Ambassador, in order that as soon as you shall have understood its meaning, namely, that is the explicit desire and engagement of this Sublime Court endowed with all the eminent qualities, to favour such requests as the above-mentioned, in conformity with what is due to the friendship, sincerity, alliance and good will subsisting *ab antiquo* between the Sublime and ever durable Ottoman Court and that of England, and which is on the side of both those Courts manifestly increasing; particularly as there is no harm in the said figures and edifices being thus viewed, contemplated and designed. Therefore, having fulfilled the duties of hospitality, and given a proper reception to the aforesaid Artists, in compliance with the urgent request of the said Ambassador to that effect, and because it is incumbent on us to provide that they meet no opposition in walking, viewing, or contemplating the figures and edifices they may wish to design or copy; or in any of their works of fixing scaffolding, or using their various implements; It is our desire that on the arrival of this Letter you use your diligence to act conformably to the instances of the said Ambassador, as long as the said five Artists dwelling at Athens shall be Employed in going in and out of the said citadel of Athens, which is the place of their occupations; or in fixing scaffolding around the ancient Temple of Idols, or in modelling with chalk or gypsum the said ornaments and visible figures thereon; or in measuring the fragments and vestiges of other ruined edifices; or in excavating, when they find it necessary, the foundations, in search of inscriptions among the rubbish; that they be not molested by the said Disdar (or commandant of the citadel) nor by any other persons, nor even by you (to whom this letter is addressed;) and that no one meddle with their scaffolding or implements, *nor hinder them from taking away any pieces of stone with inscriptions* or figures. In the above-mentioned manner, see that ye demean and comport yourselves.

(Signed with a signet.) SEGED ABDULLAH KAIMACAN

A typed document in Medieval Italian was found amongst the Hunt Papers, and is now in the private collection of William St Clair. It appears to be the original on which the above was based, and has been reproduced in his book, *Lord Elgin and the Marbles*.

The Italian text would have been the official version drawn up by the dragoman, the Ottoman court translator. The Italian is medieval and full of abbreviations, but quite clear. The document is largely one continuous paragraph over three pages; the language used is rather stilted, and the grammar poor.

The Italian word used for 'the ruins' is '*ghiaja*', which literally means gravel; although sometimes translated as rubbish, it was the word used in Italian translations of Ottoman documents to refer to ancient ruins. In modern Italian it means 'grandmother' although I assume that the voivode did not use this interpretation. '*Qualche pezzi di pietra*' can mean some pieces of stone, or more correctly 'any' in Medieval Italian.

The document could not be more explicit in showing clearly that Lord Elgin had the full blessing from legal government to undertake the work he did on the Acropolis, and to remove any material he wished to. Almost no other acquisition of antiquities is as well documented, nor as legal, during any other period in history. As soon as Hunt delivered the letter to Athens then Lusieri and his men could begin work on the Parthenon sculptures.

The Elgins arrive in Athens

In the spring of 1802 Lord and Lady Elgin visited Athens. This journey had required permission from London, which had been granted soon after the firman. Then Mary's pregnancy had delayed the trip, so that they finally arrived in Athens in April. Many marbles had already been loaded on to ships and sent off to London by the time the Elgins visited, but they were present to see some items removed from the Acropolis, as Mary wrote to her mother on 2 June. In the ten months since the firman had been granted, approximately half the material that would become the Elgin Collection had been excavated and brought down from the Acropolis. This included all the pieces of pedimental figures that had been dug out of the ground, twenty blocks of the frieze and seven metopes, as well as assorted architectural elements from the Parthenon.

Before returning to Constantinople the Elgins toured Greece, adding to their collection as they visited ancient sites. They visited the pasha of the Peloponnese in Tripolis, where they were entertained and gifts exchanged. The Elgins were given permission to remove any antiquity they wanted from the Peloponnese, and the freedom to excavate where they wished. A voivode in the Peloponnese allowed Elgin to excavate at Mycenae long before Schliemann, and some pillars from a tomb were brought back, although again it was decided that to remove the Lion Gate involved too great a feat of engineering for too little reward. The Elgins also stopped at Marathon, where they continued some excavations on the site of the great battle, which had been started by Fauvel and Choiseul-Gouffier. They appreciated the importance of Marathon, even if modern Greek politicians do not. Unfortunately, the excavations at Marathon were never completed, and the site was destroyed a few years ago by the Greek government to accommodate a rowing lake for the 2004 Olympics.

Constantinople was in a state of turmoil due to troubles with the neighbouring Pasha of Roumelia, and the arrival of the plague. Instead of going straight there, the Elgins sailed back at a leisurely pace, stopping at Delos and Smyrna, and only arriving at the Porte in September 1802. It is a pity they could not have stayed longer, finished their excavations at Marathon and Mary Elgin written more of her charming letters, so that we would have more details of Lusieri's summer work on the Acropolis. Soon after, Mary gave birth to a third Bruce, and the couple decided to return to London, Lord Elgin feeling satisfied that both his diplomatic and cultural missions had been satisfactorily discharged. Plans were made to leave Constantinople at the beginning of 1803, and the Elgins set sail for England on 16 January.

After Elgin had left Athens six more frieze blocks and two metopes were brought down off the Acropolis by Lusieri. Excavations yielded another block of the Parthenon frieze and several from the small temple of Athena Nike. The Nike blocks had been built into, and were found within, the seventeenth-century fortifications of the Acropolis, so these, if any, are the only pieces that it can be argued broke the terms of the memorandum Hunt had originally proposed.

The Nike temple blocks that were brought back to London, now in the British Museum, are highly unusual in that they are one of the few examples of decoration on a Greek temple that depicted a near-contemporary historical event, a battle from living memory, the Greek victory over the Persians at Marathon. This is exceptional in Greek art and shows the importance the ancient Athenians had placed on their great victory over the Persians.

Architectural elements from all the major buildings on the Acropolis were gathered, to furnish examples of the architecture which could be copied back in England. Although the modern Greek people place less importance on these blocks, the government has asked for their return as a matter of priority even over the sculptures, since they are needed in the reconstruction of the Parthenon as a tourist attraction. While some architecture blocks are in museums, some have been incorporated into other structures, such as Renaissance *palazzi* in Venice, and the Greek government after independence gave the people of America a block of the Parthenon to be incorporated into the Washington Monument. They argue that these blocks are vital parts of the Parthenon and necessary for rebuilding the structure. The US government has declined to tear down the Washington Monument, which they see as a symbol of American democracy, in order to help the Greeks with this request, suggesting that a modern marble block could easily be used instead.

When Lord Elgin was back in Constantinople he was given further firmans and letters which confirmed the legitimacy of the work his men had undertaken in Athens. Elgin sent these to Lusieri, who in turn gave them to the voivode in Athens in October 1802. Officials visiting from Constantinople inspected the Acropolis fortifications the following month, and do not seem to have had any problems with the work undertaken. The sultan and his officials clearly condoned the excavation of the Acropolis and the removal of sculptures on Elgin's behalf, since they not only sanctioned it in a series of official decrees, but they also inspected the citadel in Athens in November 1802, and found no fault there.

In July 1801 the French prisoners within the Ottoman Empire had been transferred to Constantinople, and they included Fauvel from Athens. Elgin gained their release, and so in effect set himself up for difficulties when Fauvel returned to Athens, and when the French government returned to favour with the Porte. While he had been imprisoned in Constantinople, Hunt and Lusieri had not been as gentlemanly as Elgin, and had tried to get their hands on Fauvel's collection, housed in the Capuchin monastery. They failed. Since Lusieri had been using Fauvel's equipment on the Acropolis, the news that the Frenchman was returning to Athens as consul must have caused the Sicilian some consternation.

In October 1802 France and the Porte signed a treaty of peace, and in December a new French ambassador, Count Sébastiani, Napoleon's cousin, arrived. The two states had resumed their old friendship, as if the invasion of Egypt had never happened. Although the Elgins remained favourites of the sultan, Britain did not. Fortunately by then most of what would become known as the Elgin Marbles were already off the Acropolis.

Slowly they had been moved down to the Piraeus, and were being loaded on to passing Royal Navy ships, to make their way back to London. Most ships did not sail straight for London, so the Marbles made their journey via a variety of exotic ports such as Alexandria, Halicarnassus, Smyrna and Malta. Even as a British ambassador, getting his cases on Royal Naval vessels was not an easy task for Elgin. Mary was more successful, using her 'persuasive powers' on men who had been at sea for many years and so were more susceptible to her charms. Another load was shipped aboard the *Mentor*, which sank off Cythera in September 1802. Hunt, by then back in Constantinople with Lord Elgin, immediately left for Greece on board HMS *La Victorieuse*, to the rescue. The Marbles were soon salvaged, and since most of the cases that fell into the water had contained mouldings rather than sculptures, the damage was minimal.

Christmas 1802 saw the arrival of Captain Clarke, brother of the pesky traveller. His ship, HMS *Braakal*, ran aground in the Piraeus. Hunt saved the ship by persuading the Ottoman authorities to pull it off the rocks. In return this Clarke, clearly a better man than his brother, helped ship out as many cases of Marbles as his ship could carry – forty-four in all. Most of the Marbles had now left Athens, the city's monuments had been measured, drawn and recorded, and the best sculptures saved. By the end of 1802 Lord Elgin's planned work in Athens was almost complete. Just before he left Constantinople for good, he received a final set of letters from the Grand Vizier confirming and ratifying his work in Athens.

Although most of the work in Athens had been carried out, and the artists dismissed, Lusieri remained to finish the mission. Hamilton was on Cythera salvaging the cases that had sunk with the *Mentor*, and Hunt also remained a few months longer in Athens. The salvage operation cost Lord Elgin about £5,000, and when all the cases were safely on shore Nelson dispatched a ship to collect them. Lusieri continued to take his role as Elgin's agent seriously, and in 1803 added more marble metopes and frieze blocks from the Parthenon to the collection. In 1803 Lusieri also removed a Caryatid from the Erechtheion, his earlier plan to ship the whole temple back to London having proved a little unrealistic.

Robert Smirke, an artist Elgin had rejected for his mission, was now in Athens and one of the first to start criticising Elgin's work on the Acropolis. He wrote a melodramatic account of the Parthenon groaning in misery as the Marbles were removed, but seemed happy enough to take some of the Erechtheion himself. Smirke's Erechtheion pieces are now lost, as are the fragments taken by Clarke, but his angry journal, written in bitterness at not having been part of Elgin's team, unfortunately has not suffered the same fate.

Although Byron too would later add his voice to the criticisms of Elgin, and do so with great effect, when he had been in Athens he wrote in his diary on 8 January 1810: 'When the Turks want lead, they disjoint a part of the marble structures and find the object of their search in the juncture of the marbles. During the time that Lusieri was away, on account of the short war, nearly half of the south wall of the temple of Erectheus [was] pulled down.'

Fauvel did not return to Athens until January 1803, but once he was back he soon created enough problems to make up for all the time he had been locked away. Elgin had by then left Istanbul, so could not come to Lusieri's rescue. Lusieri remained in Elgin's employ for many more years, sometimes being paid, occasionally producing a drawing. Lusieri's loyalty to Elgin and determination to finish his work was admirable, though without an ambassador to protect him, and Elgin's bankers becoming less willing to advance credit, this became harder.

Over the next two decades the two agents would continue their rivalry, which at times descended into a farce worthy of Aristophanes. As amusing and ridiculous as much of the behaviour of these two boys was, we must gloss over it. Fauvel tried to seize Elgin's remaining

Marbles, but was unable to do so as he could not find a suitable ship on which to whisk them away.

The salient point of their rivalry is that they would divide the city into two camps: the Lusieri–British propaganda on one side, the Fauvel–French on the other. All visitors would be pushed by fate or by chance into one or the other. Those who fell into the hands of Fauvel would be fed dark tales of Elgin's misdeeds, and this is where the story of his having lost his nose to syphilis began. The visitors would return to London, and so the fables would be repeated to all who would listen, embellished with each retelling, just as they are still repeated today by those who wish to spread anti-Elgin propaganda and lies.

The Earl of Aberdeen, the future Prime Minister, managed to acquire a piece of metope and some architectural elements of the Parthenon while in Athens in 1803. He had tried to buy part of the frieze, but failed. Aberdeen would later try to suggest that the Parthenon sculptures Elgin had brought back were rather inferior works, which yet again sounds like bitterness, and one suspects that had he himself managed to get his paws on them, the sculptures would have been transformed into marvels. Aberdeen's Parthenon fragments, like those of so many other travellers, are now lost, perhaps because he did not appreciate them enough to care for them.

In February 1804 Lusieri stopped removing sculpture from the Parthenon. This was largely due to a lack of funds, and partly due to Fauvel's interferences, rather than as a result of a change of heart from the sultan. Instead, he resumed his excavations around the building, and elsewhere in Attica. Over the years visitors to Athens increased, but they found that Lusieri and Elgin had a near-monopoly on material from the Acropolis. Their thwarted attempts to collect turned to bitterness; many of those who later condemned or criticised Elgin had themselves tried to acquire pieces of the Parthenon, and been unable to do so.

Finally, in 1805, there was a locally issued ban on all digging by the new voivode. Lusieri kept on drawing, but acquired no new material. Elgin's credit had run out, and since he was in a French prison he could do nothing about it. Instead, Lusieri concentrated on shipping the sculpture to England, where they became the Elgin

Marbles. Fauvel regularly tried to get his hands on the few Marbles left in the Piraeus, but Lusieri thwarted his attempts and kept them safe.

As Elgin would write to Lusieri, 'The slightest object from the Acropolis is a jewel,' and he had indeed managed to save for posterity many jewels from the Acropolis that might otherwise have been lost.

Clocks exerted a great fascination on many Eastern people, whether Ottoman sultans or Chinese emperors, as Matteo Ricci found. And so Elgin commissioned a clock for Athens. It arrived in the city in 1813, and was erected on top of a tower the following year. For years the clock stood above the city, until it was struck by lightning. Most Athenians at the time valued this gift far more highly than they did the crumbling Parthenon on the Acropolis.

The Legality of Elgin's Actions

It is easy to revise history through the use of hindsight. Elgin is often criticised for having negotiated the acquisition of the Elgin Marbles from the Ottoman sultan rather than from the Greeks. Greece at the time was a province of the Ottoman Empire, and not a country, nor had it ever been a country before. Elgin could not have known that Greece would fight a civil war and claim independence, just as one could not today imagine Native Americans breaking free from the United States and creating a separate state on Manhattan Island, or the Aboriginals staging a revolt in Australia and seizing power. The Ottomans were the legal government at the time: they had control of Greece and they were the authority in the region. To say that Elgin could have, let alone should have, foreseen Greek independence is ludicrous.

In the fifty years before Elgin removed the Parthenon sculptures from the Acropolis, almost half of the sculptures we know had still been in existence and recorded in 1750 were no longer extant in 1800. Most of these losses can be attributed to the Ottoman Turkish garrison living on the Acropolis, hacking up pieces to be used as building blocks. Some can also be attributed to the removal of small bits by travellers, who took the fragments without the permission of the Ottoman authorities and the sultan; most of those pieces are now lost.

The story of the acquisition of the Elgin Marbles is complex. I would argue that Lord Elgin legally acquired them from the legal government at the time, and that he did so with their full approval. The Greeks would argue that he didn't, because even if he did legally acquire them from the Ottomans, they claim that the Ottomans had no right to let him have them. They also go one step further for good measure, questioning whether he had even legally acquired them from the Ottomans. The point of contention is the firman, the ultimate legal authority within the Ottoman Empire.

Elgin was, as we know, a favourite of the sultan, who allowed him to have items from his own personal mosque, something otherwise unprecedented. When Elgin wished to remove some sculptures from the Acropolis, the sultan willingly granted this wish, which is clearly stated in the firman. Elgin represented what was at the time the Ottomans' most powerful and most active ally, and in addition to this he and his wife had made some powerful friends at court. If the sultan wanted Elgin to have some old stones, under the law of the Ottoman Empire, then Elgin was legally allowed to have them.

Once we remove the doubt that there was no firman and examine its text, the main point of contention according to the restitutionists is the use of the word '*qualque*' in the Italian translation. As previously stated, the Greeks today would interpret this as allowing only 'a few' stones to be removed, basing their translation on current Italian, rather than on the Italian used before and around 1800, when it more usually meant 'any'.

Hunt's memo, on which the firman was based, states that these stones could be removed as long as they did not interfere with the walls of the fortress. These lines were omitted from the firman itself. The firman states that they can take anything they dig up or find within the '*ghiaja*'; literally gravel, but a term used by the Ottomans to denote ancient ruins.

Many of the pedimental figures Elgin's men removed were excavated. Some were found in the ground, most were found in the heaps of rubble that dotted the surface of the late Ottoman Acropolis. A handful of pedimental sculptures were still on the building, and these were removed from the gables. Whether or not the firman allowed

Elgin to remove the sculptures still on the Parthenon itself was a point raised by the voivode. He consulted the Ottoman official, who had come from Constantinople with the firman, and the official confirmed that the firman allowed Elgin to remove anything he wished from the buildings on the Acropolis.

Numerous people have tried to question the legality of Elgin's acquisition of the Parthenon sculptures. The leading legal scholar who has examined the dispute is Professor John Merryman, Sweitzer Professor of Law at Stanford University, as well as a professor in the Art Department. He has argued that, since the Ottomans had controlled Athens since 1460, their claims over the artefacts associated with the Parthenon and on the Acropolis were legal and recognisable. He has also argued that since Elgin had obtained written permission, in the form of a firman, which was the most formal kind of permission available from the government, he, Lord Elgin, was allowed to remove the Marbles. Elgin received another firman allowing him to export the Marbles from the Piraeus. This later firman in effect confirmed Elgin's permission to remove the Marbles. Therefore, the fact that Elgin was allowed to export the Marbles he had brought down off the Acropolis legalises his claim to the Marbles.

Merryman also believes that had Elgin not taken the Marbles, and had Napoleon also not removed them, then the Ottomans would almost certainly have destroyed them. The Ottomans caused enough damage to the Acropolis during their tenure of it and, in the decades between Elgin's removal of the sculptures and Greek independence in 1831, it was the scene of a great deal of fighting. The Ottomans had in the past used several of the buildings to store gunpowder and ammunitions, and they had damaged the buildings when the gunpowder exploded. It is highly likely that more damage would have occurred to the sculptures had they remained in the Acropolis. They could have been used to build further fortifications, in the same way that the temple of Nike had been taken down and used for Ottoman fortifications during the Last Crusade.

Merryman further suggests that had the Marbles been dispersed piecemeal to dozens of travellers and collectors, many of them would have been lost. So Elgin's removal had the benefit of keeping the majority of the sculptures together, as well as preserving them. He states: 'One can admire the Greekness of the Marbles and respect their specific cultural importance to Greeks without concluding that they belong in Greece' (Merryman, p. 1916). It should, however, be noted that Merryman is highly suspicious of the idea of cultural nationalism, seeing it as something tinged by its use by the Nazis in Germany. He adds: 'Lord Elgin, contrary to the attacks on his reputation today, seems to have acted in good faith, and out of the genuine desire to preserve what the Ancient Greeks had created.'

The British Committee for the Restitution of the Parthenon Marbles claims that 'ownership' of the Marbles is no longer an issue, and that the Greeks only want 'a loan' of them. However, this does not mean that the Greeks accept British ownership, as the last Minister of Culture made clear when he wrote to the *Sunday Times* in 2005 claiming that the Greeks did still legally own the Elgin Marbles in London. The loan requested is also a permanent one, which seems to defy any rational interpretation of the word 'loan'. If we wanted to call in this loan, and return the Marbles to London, do we honestly believe that the Greek government would ship them back to us?

In terms of Elgin's actions, we must stop looking back retrospectively, and with hindsight, judging him by the standards of our own day. Elgin could never have known that Greece would soon gain independence, nor could he have foreseen that over a century and a half later the Greeks would suddenly decide that the Parthenon was of great importance to them. Elgin only saw that the Parthenon sculptures in Athens were being damaged, and he saw that if he did not succeed in removing them from the Acropolis they would soon be destroyed – as proved to be the case with many of the sculptures he left behind.

Other travellers before Elgin brought back pieces of the Parthenon sculptures; over the years some of these have been lost, but many others have found their way to the British Museum. A point worth making is that those sculptures which were removed from the Parthenon in the eighteenth century are even better preserved than the Elgin Marbles removed at the beginning of the nineteenth century, which in turn are, of course, in much better condition than the pieces which stayed in Greece. Almost all the small pieces of the Marbles hacked off by the Turks and sold to travellers have disappeared. If Elgin had not brought the Marbles back en masse, this would have continued and many more would have been lost to us.

To the British Museum

On 16 January the Elgins and their staff set sail from Constantinople on the HMS *Diane*. On 25 March the British and French signed the Peace of Amiens, so the journey home should have been uneventful. By May 1803, however, war had once again broken out. On their way home the Elgins visited Athens once more, then made several more stops before reaching Rome. They spent Easter in the city, discussing the Marbles and their possible restoration with Canova. The great sculptor strongly objected to any restoration, arguing that no living sculptor, not even himself, could possibly equal the skill of Pheidias. Elgin, probably more swayed by his empty purse, concurred. For this, we can all be thankful, for such an action would irreversibly have damaged the Parthenon sculptures.

The Elgins continued their journey from Rome by land, arriving in France in early May. On 18 May war was declared, and Napoleon ordered all British men to be imprisoned. Ambassadors normally had diplomatic immunity but, contrary to all rules of war, the Elgins were held under house arrest in Paris. Napoleon, who had wanted the Parthenon marbles to add to the glories of his new Louvre Museum, and who blamed Lord Elgin personally for his defeat in Egypt, would take a keen interest in the Scot. He even wrote several letters ordering that Elgin be treated harshly. Elgin would later claim that Napoleon had offered to free him in exchange for the

Parthenon sculptures, but those were by then on their way to London.

The Elgins were allowed to live in Paris, and to visit, rather than be held prisoner, Elgin having given his word that he would not try to escape. In July they were given permission to move to a spa for the sake of his health, where they were joined by Hunt, and finally met Choiseul-Gouffier. Choiseul-Gouffier had been allowed to return to France by Napoleon, although he did not regain his properties. Even the piece of the Parthenon frieze Fauvel had managed to ship back to France had been confiscated, and was now in the Louvre. A metope and some other smaller antiquities had been returned to him.

At the beginning of 1804 the first large shipment of Marbles from Athens arrived in London. Elgin was still in France at the time, so his mother arranged to store the crates with various friends. To save money, Elgin even wrote to her suggesting giving the Marbles to the government. Instead, his agents carried on spending, even buying cases of antiquities at a customs clearance. One of those crates contained a Parthenon metope seized by Nelson. Around the same time Elgin and Choiseul-Gouffier were in France discussing the fate of the latter's collection. Some years later Elgin would try to return the metope to the Frenchman, but Choiseul-Gouffier's pride made him decline.

Elgin unfortunately, and through no fault of his own, became caught up in anti-British propaganda while the two countries were at war, and so at the end of the year was imprisoned in Lourdes fortress, where he was kept in particularly harsh conditions. Napoleon seemed determined to punish Elgin for every British transgression during the war. Eventually he was allowed to return to Paris in the spring of 1805, although his mental health appears to have deteriorated, and this in turn would lead to the breakdown of his marriage. Elgin had taken out his anger on Mary. The Elgins' son, William, born the previous year in France, died. Mary, pregnant again, was allowed to return to Scotland to bury him. She was accompanied by a neighbour, Robert Fergusson, to whom she had turned for support.

Back in Britain Mary kept working to gain her husband's release. A year later, in June 1806, Elgin returned to London, having signed

a paper agreeing to go back to Paris whenever the French government requested him to. This agreement meant the end of his diplomatic career, since he could not be posted as a British ambassador
when the French could on a whim demand his presence in Paris.
As a gentleman he was bound to honour his word to do so.

In 1806 Britain and Turkey were technically at war, since Britain
supported Russia, whom the Ottomans were fighting. Large portions
of Elgin's Marbles were still in Greece, along with other items the
Scot had collected. Lusieri fled, and Fauvel stole many of the more
portable items from Elgin's collection. Lighter objects were sent to
Paris, but the Marbles were heavy and needed a strong ship for their
transportation. Elgin offered the government this group of sculptures, if they would send a British warship to seize them from the
Piraeus; they declined. The following year, whilst Britain and the
Ottoman Empire were still at war, the Ottomans according to some
critics of Elgin – hardly reliable sources – apparently claimed that
Elgin's actions had been undertaken without permission.

The various states at war soon realigned their alliances, and by
January 1809 Britain and Turkey were again at peace. By February
1810 the British were once again in favour. Elgin's actions were
deemed to have been authorised by the sultan. A new firman was
issued by the Ottomans, and he was allowed to export the last of the
Marbles. Now that Britain was once again a favoured ally, Elgin's
actions were considered to have been undertaken in good faith and
with the full permission of the Ottomans. This last firman arrived in
Athens in March and confirmed the validity of all the work undertaken by Lusieri as Elgin's agent, both on the Acropolis and within
the Ottoman Empire. If the terms of an earlier firman had been over-
stepped in any way, as some critics of Elgin claim, its results were
certainly now retrospectively legalised and accepted by the sultan.

Fauvel made one last attempt to steal the Marbles from Elgin.
Despite much evidence to the contrary, of which he was only too
aware, Fauvel was the first to question the validity of Elgin's work.
Fauvel only tried this tactic on a local level and failed, because
everyone knew that the two men had been rivals. Fauvel was
Elgin's competitor in the acquisition of the Marbles, but he did not
dare to go as far as question the firman with the authorities in

Constantinople as he knew that there too he would have been rebuked. The thwarted collector instead began to spread rumours in Athens, which would later be picked up by gossip-hungry travellers and spread through Europe.

This was of course the time when Byron first visited Greece. Byron and Lusieri were on the best of terms in Athens. It helped that Byron was infatuated with Lusieri's fifteen-year-old brother-in-law, showering the boy with gifts in exchange for sexual favours. On 8 January 1810, he and John Cam Hobhouse first went up on to the Acropolis, leaving this description of the mound after Elgin's work there:

'With Mr Lusieri, paid a visit to the Acropolis. The *propylæa* or gates, five of them seen at entrance, but filled up with stones the gate of entrance now. Just where it was anciently, pillars of the Parthenon double with *relievos* on the frieze, above capitals of the second row. This before you get into the temple – in the temple you see the door entering it, but not so large as formerly, the ancient marble pavement with pillars to the right but all thrown down to the left. Immense masses of columns scattered about. On the right, the fading vestiges of the daubings of the Greek church.'

On 11 April 1811 Byron sailed to Malta on the *Hydra*, with the last five cases of the Elgin Marbles, and his catamite. Lusieri stayed on in Athens, continuing to excavate and draw, dying just before the Greek War of Independence erupted. He was buried in the Capuchin monastery in Athens.

Napoleon had been shown the fragmentary frieze slab in the Louvre's basement in January 1802 and insisted this marvel be immediately restored and put on display. Napoleon's interest in the Parthenon meant that the French were determined to ship back the antiquities Fauvel had collected. A ship, *L'Arabe*, was sent to Piraeus to collect the rest of the Choiseul-Gouffier collection for the nation, including the other Parthenon metope Fauvel had managed to get his hands on. War had broken out as it was returning to France, and so by the rules of war at the time the ship was considered fair game, and was seized by HMS *Maidstone*. She was taken to Malta and her cargo auctioned, though the antiquities were sent to the government in London by Nelson. The government did not want to buy

The one frieze block that reached the Louvre was heavily over-restored, and so damaged, on the personal orders of Napoleon

the sculptures, Mr Christie the auctioneer thought them not worth auctioning, and so they remained at Customs House.

Eventually, after he had been released by Napoleon, Lord Elgin found the Parthenon metope. As a sign of goodwill he tried to return the metope to Choiseul-Gouffier. Their two agents in Athens had taken rivalry to the realm of comedy, but the two collectors had tried to help each other in captivity in France despite their years of dispute. Elgin made a futile request to Nelson, asking that he return Choiseul-Gouffier's antiquities to the Frenchman. Choiseul-Gouffier asked Napoleon to free the Scot. Neither succeeded, but both had behaved like gentlemen.

The sole metope Choiseul-Gouffier had managed to bring to France was auctioned by his heirs and bought by the Louvre. Today it is displayed to the right of the frieze maidens. On the other side of the frieze block are a head from the frieze, a badly corroded metope head which had been fished out of the Piraeus waters into which it had been dropped by one of Morosini's army, and a head possibly from one of the pediments. The gallery in which they now reside is lined by a corridor that leads from the Victory of Samothrace to the Venus de Milo; both these women are considered 'highlights' of the Louvre and constantly surrounded by visitors. During the several mornings I have spent with Choiseul-Gouffier's Parthenon sculptures, I have never seen them admired by more than a handful of people.

Back in London, Elgin rented a house on the corner of Piccadilly and Park Lane, and built a temporary pavilion to shelter the Marbles. The cases were opened, and his hard-won treasures exhibited from June 1807 to almost universal acclaim. A large body of Greek sculpture was displayed in the West for the first time, and the triumph of Greek art over Roman was proclaimed. John Flaxman, the leading British sculptor, immediately declared them to be 'very far superior' to all the Roman sculpture he had seen in Italy. The president of the Royal Academy, Benjamin West, added his voice to the praise, declaring the sculptures 'sublime'. Applications from artists to sketch the Parthenon sculpture came pouring in, and soon there was not enough room in the pavilion to accommodate their many admirers. In Georgian Britain people expected to be allowed to visit the homes and collections of their peers, just as Elizabeth Bennet looked around D'Arcy's house when she was touring the region.

A few dissenting souls were not so enthused with Elgin's collection. Richard Payne Knight, a collector and scholar as well as an MP, preferred small bronzes to marbles, on the basis that most great Greek sculptures had originally been cast in bronze rather than carved in marble. Although his small bronzes were as much copies of the lost originals as later Roman marble sculptures, he transferred his dislike of copies to the Parthenon Marbles on the basis that these too were in marble, and so must be inferior. As illogical as this opinion appears to us today, at the time Payne Knight was a man of considerable influence, and so this view was adopted by others. Within days of Lord Elgin's return to London, Payne Knight was condemning the Marbles as Roman, sight unseen, to Elgin's face.

Payne Knight had never been to Athens, had seen few Greek originals, and the Elgin Marbles themselves were still in their cases, so his judgement was issued on art that he had never seen but still condemned. The two pedimental figures of Cecrops and his Daughter, which Elgin left behind in Athens, were at the time thought to be Roman additions. In fact these two statues are Greek originals, but Payne Knight took this concept of a later dating of the Parthenon pediments to the extreme. Even once he had seen the Elgin Marbles, he still declared them all to be Roman and branded them as distinctly inferior works. Unfortunately Payne Knight was influential among the Society of Dilettanti. Lord Aberdeen, who had seen the sculptures in Athens, but was a thwarted buyer of them, added his voice to the dissent. The fools would continue to disparage the Parthenon sculptures for the next decade, and Payne Knight's reputation would suffer irreparable damage because of this lack of judgement.

The norm would have been for the sculptures to have been dropped off in Rome to be restored, and then shipped on to London. Because of Napoleon's invasions, Elgin did not follow this course. Although restoring the sculptures, by adding heads and re-carving worn surfaces, was discussed, fortunately for posterity these plans were soon abandoned. The Neo-Classical style and taste was giving way to Romanticism, a theory under which the sculptures' broken state was seen as part of their charm. Byron, as ever, took Romanticism one step further. He had wanted the sculptures to stay in Athens, and to slowly fall apart on the Acropolis, rather than for them to be saved for future generations. To Byron a crumbling ruin was Romantic; a museum was not.

Antonio Canova was considered one of the great sculptors of his day, and fortunately he was against restoration of the Elgin Marbles, and his views prevailed. Other leading sculptors were approached by the peer to restore the Marbles, but they were equally reticent about doing so. In the end Elgin found that he could not in any case afford to pay for the work, and so the Marbles were spared this form of vandalism which ruined so many others.

Mary, tired of bearing children, asked to be spared the burden of further pregnancies. Her husband, scared of losing his only son and not having an heir, refused. Elgin, his mind twisted by his time in solitary confinement in France, for the first time began to behave in a particularly unpleasant way. He leapt to the conclusion that Mary was having an affair with Fergusson, and against all advice pursued a case for divorce, hoping to get his hands on his wife's money on behalf of his children. Since the money belonged to the Nisbets, and Mr Nisbet was still alive, Elgin failed in this enterprise. Although there is no evidence of any impropriety on Mary's part, Fergusson subsequently married her to preserve her reputation, and the two really do seem to have lived happily ever after.

Mary no longer provided seemingly endless funds, as she had done during the marriage, and so Elgin found himself heavily in debt. To exact revenge he alienated their children from their mother, an estrangement that would last several decades. His career was over. Under the terms of his parole from France it would have been difficult to appoint him to any diplomatic post, when he could be summoned to Paris at a moment's notice. Elgin lost his seat in the Lords in 1807, and his ill-health made a military career equally impossible. Elgin had to face the fact that after a brilliant start, his public life was over and his purse empty. His income had always been limited for a man of his rank, but now he was almost poor; as William St Clair pointed out, his £2,000 a year would not have made him a catch to an Austen heroine. Out of this small sum he also had to pay off the huge debts which had resulted from his embassy to the East.

In 1810 Elgin offered the collection of antiquities he had acquired to the British government. Although some now claim he only did so because of his new poverty, this had been his plan all along, and is clear in letters throughout. The British Museum expressed an interest in the collection, and Elgin published a pamphlet on their acquisition to bolster the sale, a text that remains one of the prime sources for the Marbles' history. Elgin provided the government with a list of his expenses. One can argue that the deal proposed was less a sale of the sculptures than a negotiation over reimbursement of his expenses. Elgin could easily have sold them to a private collector – even Napoleon – for far more money.

Lord Elgin estimated his expenses in the enterprise as £62,440. He asked the government not to buy the Marbles, with a profit on the transaction, but merely to acquire them in exchange for his expenses. After the Napoleonic Wars, Britain's economy was in the grips of a recession. The sum seemed huge to many politicians, who failed to appreciate the Marbles, and feared having to justify the expense to a British people who were going hungry because they could not afford bread. The Paymaster-General countered with an offer of less than half that sum, and Elgin declined. Meanwhile the second half of the Marbles arrived in London in May 1812, and he moved his collection to Burlington House, although the arrangement there was far from ideal.

In 1805 an Act of Parliament had bought the Townley Collection of Roman Sculpture for £20,000. The Townley Collection was initially argued to be superior to the Greek Parthenon marbles, since the sculptures were whole and could be used as models by artists, whilst the Elgin Marbles were broken and so of less use for copying. The arrival of the Elgin Marbles in London marks a turning point in Western perceptions of ancient art and culture, when Greek art came to be regarded as superior to Roman. Later, when the British Museum would send expeditions in search of sculpture, they would send these to modern Turkey in search of Greek originals, rather than to Rome, which had been the main hunting ground of collectors in the eighteenth century seeking ancient sculpture.

Various sums were mentioned as being the 'market value' for the Elgin Marbles. Most of them were extremely modest, particularly in light of the sums that had recently been paid for the far inferior Bassae frieze by the British, and the Archaic Aegina pediments by the Bavarians. Elgin was offered far greater sums by private collectors, and by foreign governments, but declined in favour of pursuing his preferred option of seeing the Marbles in the British Museum. Eventually he would prevail in this wish, but not before his reputation had suffered at the hands of rivals, and he had fully satisfied the government of the value and legality of his collection.

Charles Cockerell was one of the leading archaeologists working in Greece. In 1811 he had bought the Archaic pedimental sculpture of the Temple of Aphaia on Aegina, from the local Greeks who had found them, for £40. Although the legality of the move is highly questionable, the following year he auctioned them; the British representative arrived too late to buy them, so they went to Ludwig of Bavaria for £8,000. The Aegina marbles were in a more Archaic style than the Parthenon, considered more primitive in an age that did not yet appreciate primitive art, and so were less appreciated at the time. They were smuggled out of Greece in a transaction of highly suspect legality, the same year that the last of the legally acquired Elgin Marbles arrived in London. In 1812 Cockerell obtained a firman to excavate at Bassae in the Peloponnese. A Classical temple of Apollo yielded a frieze depicting battles against the Amazons and the Centaurs. Despite having legal permission, Cockerell was unable to prevent the Ottomans from smashing the beautiful example of one of the earliest Corinthian capitals he found there. The frieze was bought by the British government for £15,000 and deposited in the British Museum. Shorter and cruder in quality, the Bassae friezes should have helped to set a market value for the government's purchase of the Elgin Marbles.

Byron published *Childe Harold* in 1812. Using poetic licence and huge exaggeration for dramatic effect, the barely known Byron set himself up with this poem as a David to Elgin's Goliath in the cultural milieu of London art circles. Although Byron was considered a rogue and a scoundrel, not the sort of man one would have to dinner, few could resist the fun of some scandal, and so Elgin's name is still associated with these libels. We now know that much of what Byron said was neither true nor accurate, but calumnies such as Elgin's having had syphilis are still repeated today. Byron's poems were satires upon the travellers, and collectors, so hardly objective; satiric poems by their very nature work better when one only presents one side, and when one attacks rather than praises. Although Byron had written *Childe Harold* in Athens, most of his time in Pericles' city had been devoted to a treatise in which he had more interest and which he preferred researching: *Sodomy Simplified*. Byron was already considered bad, but people had not yet realised he was also mad and dangerous to know, so his verses carried a little weight.

> But who, of all the plunderers of yon fane
> On high – where Pallas linger'd, loth to flee
> The latest relic of her ancient reign;
> The last, the worst, dull spoiler, who was he?
> Blush, Caledonia! Such thy son should be!
> England! I joy no child he was of thine:

Thy free-born men should spare what once was free;
Yet they could violate each saddening shrine,
And bear these altars o'er the long-reluctant brine.

But most the modern Pict's ignoble boast,
To rive what Goth, and Turk, and Time hath spared:
Cold as the crags upon his native coast,
His mind as barren and his heart as hard,
Is he whose head conceiv'd, whose hand prepar'd,
Aught to displace Athena's poor remains:
Her sons too weak the sacred shrine to guard,
Yet felt some portion of their mother's pains,
And never knew, till then, the weight of Despot's chains.

Cold is the heart, fair Greece! That looks on thee,
Nor feels as lovers o'er the dust they lov'd;
Dull is the eye that will not weep to see
Thy walls defac'd, thy mouldering shrines remov'd
By British hands, which it has best behov'd
To guard those relics ne'er to be restor'd.
Curst be the hour when from their isle they rov'd,
And once again thy hapless bosom gor'd,
And snatch'd thy shrinking Gods to northern climes
    abhorr'd.

                        from *Childe Harold*, canto II.

John Galt also wrote satiric poems about Elgin, while trying to follow in the Earl's footsteps as a collector by seizing the cases that were waiting to be shipped back in the Piraeus. His private letters make it clear that the sculpture would have been in grave danger had they remained in Athens, Galt acknowledging that Elgin had saved them. In public Galt, like Byron, was trying to be deliberately controversial, and Elgin as a cuckold without a nose was an easy target.

Byron found a ready ally in Edward Daniel Clarke, who was willing to defame Elgin in any way possible. Elgin's removal of the Parthenon sculptures was condemned as barbarism since Clarke had failed to purchase any for himself. Like Baron Munchausen's, Clarke's own less legal seizures on the other hand were glossed over or became great deeds. Dodwell added his condemnation, though he too had taken pieces of the Parthenon sculpture. The Viscount de Chateaubriand did the same, whilst also picking up a few of the Parthenon's sculptures when the opportunity presented itself. The French of course almost unanimously condemned Lord Elgin at the time; the man had been given what they had desired, and long sought.

Few of those who condemned Elgin were objective, and most did so because he had succeeded where they had failed. Robert Fergusson, Mary Nisbet's second husband, was a leading scientist and an MP, and so influential. He may well have been behind many of the attacks. If so, then Elgin deserved this for the shabby way he had treated Mary during their divorce.

On the other hand, Ennio Quirino Visconti carried far more weight. Visconti had run the Capitoline Museum in Rome before Napoleon had brought him to Paris to become Director of the Louvre. Elgin asked Visconti to come to London and write up his opinion of the Marbles, which the Italian was happy to do in October 1814, the highest praise for them flowing from his pen. Even Elgin's old rival Choiseul-Gouffier had approved of what he had done, as noted earlier.

Canova visited the Elgin Marbles in November 1815, and was ecstatic in his praise. He conservatively estimated them at £100,000, a sum which is likely to have reflected their true value on the art market in Italy, since Canova had long been involved in supplying Roman sculpture to visiting Englishmen. Around the same time the Bassae frieze arrived in London. Payne Knight had been instrumental in its acquisition for the British Museum, and tried to claim that it was wholly by Pheidias and far superior to the Parthenon sculptures. History has proven otherwise, and even at the time few agreed with him, and began to mock the dandy Payne Knight's reputation behind his back.

Ludwig of Bavaria sent agents to make overtures to Elgin, desperate to buy his whole collection. Elgin insisted on giving the British government first refusal. A few odd pieces from Greece subsequently arrived in Britain and made their way to Broomhall. The Parthenon sculptures had never been intended to 'decorate' his Scottish seat, and so stayed in London, garnering admiration which increased each month, and which in theory should have increased their value.

The first set of discussions over the sale of the Elgin Marbles had been delayed, because Napoleon's brief return to power in France had given the government other priorities. In 1816 the British government set up a Select Committee which looked into a possible purchase. Unfortunately both Lord Aberdeen and Richard Payne Knight, neither a fan of Elgin, were on the committee. Payne Knight suggested an offer for the collection of £15,000, which was deliberately meant to be insulting. Elgin was dragged into various 'scandals' involving missing drawings and borrowed books. He should not have been blamed for either, but as British ambassador at the time, he was.

On 16 February Lord Elgin presented his petition to Parliament, requesting that the British government buy his collection of antiquities on behalf of the British Museum. The petition was granted, to Elgin's delight, but they could not agree how much to pay him for them. Britain was at the time in the grip of a depression, and the wisdom of spending government money on stones rather than bread was raised. Although art is the realm of the educated, politicians have always known that the people preferred bread and circuses. A Select Committee was therefore set up to discuss the issue of cash, and exactly how much money should be handed over to Elgin.

On day one a complete history of the acquisition of the Marbles was taken. Day two went into details of Elgin's outlay and expenses, which had now risen to £74,240. Elgin had earlier offered the Museum the sculptures as a gift if they met his expenses. Their subsequent sale was thus a bargain for the government, costing them far less. The validity of the firman was discussed, argued, and then accepted. Elgin was found to have legal title to the marbles that now bear his name, and so he also had the right to dispose of them in any manner he wished.

William Richard Hamilton, by then a civil servant who had been involved in returning Napoleon's looted art to Italy, was called as a witness since he had been employed by Elgin. He valued the collection conservatively at £60,000, as well as confirming the story of

the acquisition. Artistic experts all praised the quality and importance of the sculptures.

Payne Knight came next. He declared the Parthenon sculptures
as being of little value. Broken, their surfaces gone, and largely
Roman repairs rather than Greek originals, was his verdict. He
claimed that the architectural elements were more valuable than the
sculptures. So he valued the whole collection at a new figure of
£25,000, claiming disingenuously that they would fetch less than
half that sum at auction. Lord Aberdeen, in yet another *volte face*,
praised the sculptures this time, but valued them at £35,000. He
confirmed the damage the Ottoman garrison was doing to the
Acropolis, so supporting the argument that Elgin had saved them.
The Rev. Philip Hunt was also a witness, producing the Italian copy
of the firman still preserved today. The original he pointed out that
he no longer had, since he had given it to the voivode in Athens.

The hearings lasted a fortnight, and the committee then produced
a report. Although it accepted Elgin's actions as legal and having
safeguarded great sculptures, the report recommended only £35,000
for the purchase of the Elgin Marbles. Lord Elgin wanted Britain to
have his collection and he was desperate for money. He had to accept
the offer, and so Parliament voted him the funds by a narrow majority.
Various creditors in turn claimed this sum. Elgin ended up with
neither his marbles, nor the money. A subsequent Act of Parliament
confirmed the nation's ownership, and entrusted the Elgin Marbles
to the care of the British Museum. The Museum took possession of
the Elgin Marbles in August 1816, and put them on public display
the following January.

In 1817 Choiseul-Gouffier died. The British Museum claimed the
metope Elgin had earlier offered the count; his heirs auctioned the
second panel which he had managed to hang on to. The single
metope from the Parthenon was bought by the Louvre for 25,000
francs (around £1,050) making a mockery of the sum paid to Elgin.
The architect Henry Inwood, who would later build St Pancras with
its Caryatid Porch modelled on the Erechtheion, brought back more
architectural elements of the Parthenon, selling them to the British
Museum for £40 in 1819.

In London a thousand visitors came to see the Marbles each day, and the galleries were filled with artists studying and drawing them on Tuesdays and Thursdays. The Marbles came to be highly influential on both British and European art, becoming part of our greater cultural heritage when they entered the British Museum. Just as the Elgin Marbles had been a diplomatic gift from the sultan to his beloved Elgin, by 1819 casts of the sculptures became themselves diplomatic gifts and were sent to many European courts. The Museum made casts of new pieces that were found in Athens, adding these to Elgin's casts and originals, as well as to other original fragments of the Parthenon sculptures that entered the Museum over the years. Countless Regency and Victorian monuments were inspired by the Parthenon sculptures in the British Museum. Others used printed versions of the frieze to decorate interiors, or casts if they could afford it.

For many sculptors of the time, who learned by copying, studying casts was considered almost as useful as being able to see the originals. Napoleon III later had made three casts of Trajan's Column; one, now in the Victoria and Albert Museum in London, is far better preserved than the original. In 1819 the Louvre offered the British Museum the metope they had bought from Choiseul-Gouffier's heirs in exchange for a set of casts. Strangely the Trustees declined this offer, although in 1840 the Louvre sent them an original head they had acquired which matched a block of the Parthenon frieze that the British had.

Medieval sculpture was coloured, as were buildings such as cathedrals. On some medieval sculpture it survives, though rarely on buildings. The Regency scholars were aware that the Parthenon marbles would also have been coloured, but they chose to ignore this aspect, which did not appeal to their tastes, and so have formed our own vision of the Parthenon today through their aesthetics. Although many are shocked when they learn that the Parthenon was once painted, it should be stressed that it was never garish, but was rather more subtle.

Greek art became appreciated, studied and famous only when it came to museums in the West. The final triumph of Greek art over Roman, and our appreciation of it, is entirely due to Lord Elgin and the collection he brought back from his embassy to the East.

*   *   *

Elgin married again in 1810, but the second Lady Elgin was not as rich an heiress as Mary had been, so he was still in considerable financial difficulties. His second wife gave him eight more children. His son with Mary died, and the present Bruces are descended from this second union.

In 1820 Elgin was back in the Lords as one of the Scottish peers. The following year he and Byron joined the fledgling Philhellenic Committee, which supported an independent state of Greece, and raised funds towards this aim. Creditors continued to hound Elgin, so he moved his new family abroad, and settled in, irony of ironies, Paris. His daughters eventually shared Mary's fortune, but it seems to have brought them no more happiness than it had brought their father.

Byron too left London in disgrace, never to return. After a separation from his wife, and a rumoured affair with his sister, he fled to Italy in 1816. Eventually he made his way to Greece, to witness and encourage the War of Independence. Byron has become one of its heroes, a favourite of modern Greeks, who fortunately have not read Hobhouse's diaries, and so do not know how little he really thought of them. He went to join the independence fighters at Missolonghi, although he never took part in the war itself. He arrived on 3 January 1824, and died there of a fever rather than in battle, on 19 April. Byron had left Italy to yet again flee from an affair and by accident fell into the pantheon of eternal glory.

Earlier French ambassadors had tried to remove the Parthenon sculptures but failed. Elgin was able to do so because of the great favour shown him by the authorities in Constantinople. This favour was only partly due to his position as a representative of the British, and mostly because of the way he and his wife had charmed the Ottomans and ingratiated themselves with them. Royal Navy ships had also been involved in transporting the Marbles, but Elgin had paid for the use of these, and so it was found that he had not acquired them on behalf of the British, nor abused his diplomatic position in doing so.

What is surprising is that Elgin's ownership as a private individual rather than as a British representative had not been challenged more fully, given the amount of government resources he used in forming his collection. One can argue that perhaps the amount of expenses he was refunded by the government, in proportion to what he had spent bringing them to London, was seen to reflect the use of British rank and resources. This might be looking at the situation through modern eyes and using contemporary standards in hindsight; Georgian London appears not to have found what Elgin did to have been in any way an abuse of his position.

During the first two decades of the nineteenth century most of the major monuments in Athens suffered great damage. When war broke out, their condition deteriorated further. The Erechtheion, immediately to the north of the Parthenon on the Acropolis, was almost destroyed and what we see today is largely a reconstruction. Had more of the Parthenon marbles stayed in Athens, we would have fewer of them today. The two remaining pedimental figures that remained, Cecrops and his Daughter, lost their heads to the collections of Dodwell and of Fauvel; both in turn are now lost to us, although one hopes they might one day turn up in an estate sale.

Fauvel started to sell off his collection piecemeal, with the present location of many of the items unknown; they are missing, presumed destroyed. The disdar gave Cockerell a piece of the frieze (S1), which is now also in the British Museum. Quite a few of the fragments of the Parthenon sculptures acquired by other travellers did eventually make their way into museums, and some are now in the British Museum. Fauvel would be turning in his grave if he knew that today the Parthenon sculptures are often referred to by the generic catch-all phrase the Elgin Marbles.

When we compare the casts Elgin had made in 1801–2 with sculptures he left in Athens, we can see only the tragedy of a steady deterioration in their condition. The Parthenon sculptures suffered during the last decades of Ottoman rule in Greece, and continued to crumble under an independent Greece. Most were finally removed from the building in the last few years, although some of the original sculptures are still on the Parthenon, and continue to be the victims of Athenian pollution and acid rain.

London meanwhile, at the helm of the British Empire, became a new world where art and culture, funded both by the Industrial

Revolution and by colonies, flourished. Waterloo was portrayed as a new Marathon, where the small kingdom of Britain had defeated the larger Empire that the tyrant Napoleon had created. In this analogy Britain became a new Athens of the north, and Napoleon was no better than the barbaric Persians. In gratitude the nation gave Wellington a magnificent house, No. 1 London. Although the Wellington Arch at Hyde Park Corner is Roman in style, the friezes on the arches adjacent to the house, and linking it to Hyde Park, are decorated with copies of the cavalry from the Parthenon frieze. Napoleon may have based his brief hegemony on the Roman Empire, but Britain chose to model herself on the flowering of democratic Athens. The British Museum became a temple to the Muses, and just to the north a new philosophical school, University College London, was founded. But as in ancient Athens, so in modern London, these new institutions and ideals remained the prerogative of the elite not the masses for much of the nineteenth century.

The 1930s cleaning in the British Museum

In the British Museum the Elgin Marbles were moved from a temporary exhibition space to a permanent gallery, and then finally to a new wing whose construction was funded by Joseph Duveen. The displays were re-arranged regularly and after long debate the walls were repainted in a variety of colours that were thought to create a better backdrop for the sculptures. And they were regularly cleaned. A few years ago a cleaning undertaken in the 1930s became notorious when a British scholar described it as almost an act of barbarism. Since many of the British arguments for keeping the Marbles are based on the Museum's custodianship and care, this was obviously a serious accusation, and became an integral issue to the debate over their ownership and location.

In December 1999 the British Museum organised a conference to debate this 1930s conservation of the Parthenon sculptures. A number of Greek archaeologists and scientists presented papers at the conference, which sounded authoritative, with scientific terminology and electron microscope close-ups. The British Museum in the 1930s had clearly removed the original fifth-century paint and surface of the sculptures, those scholars argued at great length. The British Museum had by this point already apologised for the 1930s cleaning, which although harsh, and would not be undertaken today, was considered an acceptable technique at the time. Similar techniques were used in Greece on major monuments and are used in Italy to this day. If anything the Hephaisteion, also a fifth-century Doric temple in Athens, is far better preserved than the Parthenon. Yet the Greeks in the late 1950s used the same technique to clean it that later they would condemn the British Museum for having used in the 1930s. The technique is still used by some Italian museums to this day. Arguments continue over how to clean art, with condemnations of various techniques.

Many British archaeologists did not speak, and criticism of any Greek was even open to a charge of racism. I rather foolishly put my hand up, and pointed out what to me was an intrinsic problem. The brown sludge that the Museum had removed in the 1930s, and which the Greek scientists claimed had been the original fifth-century surface of the Marbles, covered the fourth century BC repairs to the Parthenon sculptures, the Hellenistic repairs to the Parthenon sculptures, several sets of Roman repairs to the Parthenon sculptures, as well as the iconoclast Christian defacing of the sculptures by the Byzantine Greeks. This puzzled me. How could an apparently original fifth century BC surface cover a sixth-century AD surface, which post-dated the creation of the Parthenon by over a thousand years? Let alone a fifteenth-century surface?

Although the Duveen Galleries were built in the 1930s to give the Elgin Marbles a wing of their own, and a permanent home in the British Museum, unfortunately because of the outbreak of World War II the Marbles could not be displayed there. The Marbles were not hidden away, as some Restitutionists claim, to hide any 'damage' caused by the cleaning in the 1930s. Rather the Marbles were put into storage to protect them from the bombs that Hitler and the Nazis were dropping on London almost daily. The Duveen Galleries, like many London buildings, were damaged during the Blitz. After the war it was not considered a priority to reopen the British Museum fully, nor to put the Parthenon marbles immediately on display. The government quite rightly thought that it was more important to try first to repair the infrastructure of the city, and to create housing.

During the war, the National Gallery in Trafalgar Square was also emptied of its art, which was sent to Wales for safe keeping. Instead it was used for concerts and for exhibitions of modern or contemporary art. The public were not happy with this development and complained to the director, Kenneth Clark. A solution was found, by which only one old master painting was shown each month. When the siren sounded and danger seemed imminent, the painting was moved down to the basement, and when the all-clear was sounded it was brought up once again to be exhibited to the public. This was the novel solution found to bridge the compromise between safeguarding the paintings in the keeping of the gallery, whilst at the same time providing the public with access to them.

Joseph Duveen, later Lord Duveen, was one of the great art dealers of the twentieth century. He can also be characterised as a rogue. Duveen made his money based on the simple observation that Europe had a lot of art, and Americans had a lot of cash. One could argue that Duveen, who later became a trustee of several Museums, paid for the British Museum galleries that housed the Parthenon marbles almost as a penance for the great works he had exported to America. Duveen built with this new wing a temple to the Marbles; the twentieth-century secular version of the Renaissance church built by a Medici to save his soul. In many ways this is appropriate as the cult of art and taste has replaced the cult of God and religion.

The Elgin Marbles were eventually restored to the Duveen Galleries and these were reopened to the public in 1962. Since then the Elgin Marbles' galleries have been permanently open, and are one of the highlights of the British Museum, seen by the vast majority of the 4.6 million visitors the Museum receives each year free of charge. In addition to the main Duveen Gallery, there are also slip galleries by the display. These hold smaller fragments of the sculpture which could not be added to the display of the main frieze, and architectural elements of the Parthenon. Reconstructions and panels also clarify the history of the Parthenon in terms of education.

It should also be made clear that the British Museum and the Greek Archaeological Service have very good relations. The British

Museum curators and the archaeologists who work on the Acropolis, such as Professor Manolis Korres, often collaborate. If the two sides did not cooperate as well as they do, it would not have been possible to solve some of the mysteries and problems associated with attempting to reconstruct the Parthenon. Several Greek archaeologists I have spoken to are quite happy to see the Elgin Marbles remain in the British Museum. The claims to return them to Athens are made usually by the Greek government.

The Debate over the Elgin Marbles: who owns them, and where do they belong?

At the beginning of the nineteenth century Elgin was given permission by the Ottoman sultan to take any sculptures he wished back to London. Today the debate over where the Elgin Marbles should be housed has become increasingly heated. The Greeks and restitutionists claim that the Marbles can *only* be appreciated in Greece, a form of cultural nationalism. The British Museum however argues that it acquired the marbles legally and has cared for them well.

Until recently this has also been a one-sided debate, in which restitutionists made claims and few stood up to them. The British have a strong sense of fair play; if we have wronged someone, we want to right the wrong. Thanks to the overwhelming nature of the campaign, public opinion has turned in the last decade towards returning the Elgin Marbles to Athens. Unfortunately this reversal is based largely on arguments which have little basis in fact. It is fashionable these days to apologise for any perceived wrong of which we might have become retrospectively guilty. If we continue along this path, then sooner or later we will end up apologising to the Greeks for saving the Parthenon sculptures, expressing our regret that Elgin brought them to London instead of leaving them to be destroyed in Athens.

The debate over the Elgin Marbles has been raging for more than twenty years, since Melina Mercouri became Minister of Culture in 1983. In 1981 Mercouri, a Greek actress, decided to enter politics. She sought the advice of the PASOK party leader, Prime Minister Andrea Papandreou, and chose to make the Marbles her cause. Soon afterwards, she turned up at the British Museum, with camera crews in tow, and demanded that they immediately be returned to Athens. Mercouri, with the dramatic flair of a diva, threw herself on her knees in a gallery and kissed the floor, declaiming her love of the Parthenon. 'This is our history, this is our soul,' and 'They are the symbol and the blood and the soul of the Greek people', are the kind of statements she liked to make. A curator, ever the English gentleman, helped her up, whispering *sotto voce*: 'These are beautiful sculptures, Mrs Mercouri, but the Elgin Marbles are in the next room.'

As early as June 1816 Hugh Hammersley, an MP, first proposed that they could be returned to Athens, should there ever be an independent Greece. During World War II, as part of Nazi anti-British propaganda in Greece, Hitler and Goebbels initiated a campaign to demand that the British return the Parthenon sculptures. The first demand by the Greek government was made in 1965. It did not ask specifically that the Elgin Marbles be returned to Athens; instead it demanded that all the Greek antiquities, anywhere in the world, should all be immediately repatriated to Athens, the only place they could possibly be appreciated. This demand was universally ignored.

Subsequent demands have been made for the Bassae Frieze in the British Museum, the Victory of Samothrace and the Venus de Milo in the Louvre, and assorted other works of art, which are all also presumably 'unique'. In 2005 some Greek individuals, backed by a national newspaper, even tried to claim items in Afghanistan and Iraq, on the basis that they had been made there by people of Greek origin over two thousand years ago. Clearly the demands for the repatriation of the Elgin Marbles are not unique; nor are the Elgin Marbles a special case. One fear expressed by curators is that if they were returned, this would create a precedent, with other countries claiming that art was illegally acquired and should be returned to them. But, according to Christopher Hitchens, 'the precedent argument is unusually silly. For one thing, the Greeks do not want anything else "back".' It is good to hear that Mr Hitchens can guarantee the actions of future Greek governments.

The Department of National Heritage examined the issue of the Elgin Marbles in September 1996. It concluded that under Article 1 of the First Protocol of the European Convention, the British Museum could not be compelled to return the sculptures to Athens unless it were paid financial compensation, and that this compensation must bear some relation to the market value of the Marbles. The Department also thought that in returning the Marbles to Athens, the British Museum would be failing to fulfil its duty to the public interest. Given that a mediocre Roman Venus can fetch £7–8 million at auction, it is not surprising that the Greek government has not yet suggested buying the Marbles back from the British Museum. The Cultural Committee of the Council of Europe also recommended that the sculptures should remain in London as Athens is too polluted; they were in addition concerned that they would not be adequately preserved in Athens.

An investigation by the Culture, Media and Sport Committee of the House of Commons which began in October 1999 found that there was no reason to change the status or location of the Parthenon sculptures in the British Museum. After Labour won the general election in Britain in 1997, the Elgin Marbles were the subject of one of its first policy statements. Chris Smith, then Minister of Culture, came down with a firm 'no' to the question of returning them.

Recently the Greek government changed tactics. It is now asking for a permanent 'loan' of the Marbles to Athens. It is almost impossible for the Trustees of the British Museum to answer this Greek request satisfactorily, because the Greek government is not asking for a loan in the normal sense of the word, meaning that it would borrow the sculptures for a few years and then return them. It wants a permanent loan: for the Marbles to move to Athens until the end of time. What it is in effect still demanding is for Britain to give up the Marbles, thus substituting one word for another with an entirely new meaning. So this supposed new policy initiative on the part of Greece, which gives the impression that it is willing to compromise to help resolve the dispute, is of course nonsense. If it decided not to return the Marbles to London at the end of the loan, there would be nothing anyone could do about it.

Robin Cook suggested in 2004 that if Britain returned the Elgin Marbles to Greece, then the Greek government would support our bid to host the Olympic Games in 2012. He seemed prepared to give up one of our great cultural treasures, for a possibly greater chance of gaining an Olympic bid with Greek support – in other words our heritage was to be exchanged for short-term political advantage. Cook's proposed swap was met with near-universal derision. One of the key tenets of the Olympic movement is that the Games are not used for political purposes. As Lord Melbourne, the nineteenth-century politician, remarked: 'God help the Minister that meddles with art.'

In many countries archaeology is politicised. In most Greek excavations Slavic pots and layers are routinely ignored, since the Slavic era in Greek history is one that the Greeks would rather not acknowledge. Greece, although it prides itself on its heritage and emphasises the classical past to the exclusion of all other eras, is by no means the worst example. Many people criticise Israel, which seems to behave as if might is right, and uses archaeology to validate the Jewish historical claim to the region. Jewish antiquities are preserved, and Christian ones sometimes, since these have economic benefits as tourist attractions. Muslim and Ottoman monuments, however, are treated in a more cavalier way. During the siege of Nablus the Israeli army destroyed Ottoman buildings. Those buildings were built by Muslims and are the cultural heritage of the Palestinian people in that area. Some would argue that in doing this, the Israelis thus were trying to deprive the Palestinians of their cultural heritage. The National Socialist Party in Germany were probably the most extreme example of using art and archaeology for political propaganda. For all these reasons cultural nationalism is reviled today.

Some xenophobic Britons claim that the Elgin Marbles can *only* be appreciated in Britain which is perhaps as extreme as the claim that they can *only* be appreciated in Greece. The British Museum's Trustees and Director argue with more sophistication that the Elgin Marbles are better seen in the context of other civilisations and cultures, such as the Egyptians, Syrians and Chinese, in the Museum.

The Greeks think that the Elgin Marbles are better seen in context in Athens, within the framework of the city that once created the Parthenon. In the British Museum the Elgin Marbles are one of the most important exhibits, and there they have become an integral part of British culture. Poets and painters have been inspired by them, and each day thousands of visitors admire them. Millions each year visit the Elgin Marbles in London; only a few museum employees have seen the majority of the Parthenon sculptures in Athens in recent years, since most of them were locked away in their storerooms rather than on display.

After the Parthenon sculptures were acquired from Elgin in 1816 and displayed in the British Museum, they were greatly admired. Many who had previously praised the superiority of Rome were suddenly confronted with Greek originals and found themselves instead praising the ideals of classical Greece. This led to a movement of philhellenism in Western Europe. This philhellenism not only provided the Greeks, in their attempts to gain independence from the Ottomans, with men willing to fight, but also with money to buy weapons and to support the war. It also led to the recognition of an independent Greece by the West. There was no nation of Greece before the British helped create it in 1833, and the presence in London of the Marbles certainly contributed to this process.

The Parthenon sculptures which Elgin brought back have been in the British Museum far longer than Greece has existed as a country. In those two centuries they have in turn become part of British heritage. In the British Museum they act as ambassadors of Greek culture in Britain. The city state of Athens which created the Parthenon no longer exists, but in the last two centures, while in London, the Elgin Marbles have had great impact on English art.

Henry Moore's reclining sculptures, which have become icons of modern British art of the twentieth century, were influenced by the reclining figures from the Parthenon pediments he saw in the British Museum. This continues to this day, influencing a new generation of British artists. When Selfridges was being refurbished a few years ago, to mask the scaffolding, the management commissioned a work of art by Sam Taylor-Wood. She created a continuous frieze of artistic figures of today, such as Elton John, and said that the Parthenon frieze in the British Museum was one of her main influences in the creation of that work. Are the Parthenon sculptures really *only* of relevance to Greeks, or could we reasonably claim that the Elgin Marbles can now be considered part of British cultural heritage too?

The British argument rests mainly on reason. Had Elgin not brought them back, the Elgin Marbles would no longer exist. Had the British Museum not cared for them, we would have lost an integral part of our world heritage. The Greek claims on the other hand seem to suggest that sentiment and love of the past are above the rule of international law and supersede the fact that the British Museum acquired the Marbles legally. Many Greeks think that romantic claims about their blue Attic skies will sway us, and for years unfortunately they have.

The British Museum's statement concerning the legal status of their collections is, in contract to the melodramatic Greek appeals, rather dry and far less touching. It reads:

> The Trustees hold the British Museum's collections under the terms of the *British Museum Act 1963*. This legislation prohibits the Trustees from permanently disposing of objects unless they are duplicates of others already in the collection or are 'unfit to be retained . . . and can be disposed of without detriment to the interests of students'. It does, however, provide for objects to be loaned for public exhibition, having 'regard to the interests of students and other persons visiting the Museum, to the physical condition and degree of rarity of the object in question, and to any risks to which it is likely to be exposed'. Any decision in connection with a loan request takes all of these aspects into account. The Trustees may not make 'permanent loans', although renewable loans are possible.

The Greek government and the British Committee for Restitution of the Parthenon Marbles routinely demand that the Elgin Marbles be returned to Athens – or be 'loaned' permanently to Athens, and every time the Director of the British Museum is legally required to answer 'no'. Neither the Director nor the Trustees of the British Museum can 'return' the Marbles as they hold them in trust for the nation. Even if the Trustees of the Museum ever wished to return the Marbles, they would not be able to do so, because the Museum is governed by this Act of Parliament. Only another Act would enable the British Museum to dispose of part of its collection. The British Museum's official response to the new Greek demands is that the Trustees do not loan objects that are considered iconic and central to the collection, such as the Rosetta Stone and the Elgin Marbles; this rules out a permanent 'loan'.

Few cultural issues are clear-cut. There are grey areas in the debate over the rightful home of the Elgin Marbles, just as there are grey areas about the validity of the antiquities market. The moral and legal arguments involved in the issue are both complex and exceedingly simple. Western museums would argue that they would be empty if everything had to be 'returned'. Although it is reasonable to return stolen goods, for example, the art that the Nazis confiscated from many Jewish families before and during World War II, surely one has to draw the line somewhere, and create a statute of limitation for restitution, otherwise where would one begin? Jerusalem for example was sacked first by the Babylonians, and then later by the Romans, who carried off and melted down the Temple treasures. Should the modern Italian government today be made to 'return' the Coliseum, whose construction was funded by loot from the Temple in Jerusalem, to the modern state of Israel?

Should we return looted art in chronological order to Greece, starting with the first items removed from the country by the Romans, and work our way forwards? The sculptures from the temple of the Apollo Sosianus in Rome for example, which are still preserved today, are known to have come from a temple in Greece. Should they be returned to Athens, or is 2000 years a reasonable limit, after which we should not demand the restitution of works of art? Should art created by ancient 'Greek' people in the region that now comprises the modern Albania, for example, remain in Albania, or be returned to Greece? These all sound like ridiculous arguments, but many of the arguments involved in restitution debates are equally absurd. The numbers of potential claims are limitless.

In many ways both the Greeks and the British are fighting over the Marbles using many of the same arguments, each claiming that they belong to their country; both morally and legally. The simple answer is that the Elgin Marbles belong to the whole of humanity. The Greeks and the restitutionists claim that the British are trying to hang on to the Parthenon sculptures in London because they represent our glorious past, when we had an Empire and colonies. On the other hand, ironically enough, the Greeks themselves have turned the Parthenon into a symbol of Greekness that represents their own 'glorious' past, the time when Athens had a great Empire, when the Athenians subjugated fellow Greeks, slaughtered and crucified those who objected. So, to the Greeks the Parthenon has also become a symbol of their own great imperial past, when the Athenians stole from other nations they had subjugated through warfare, loot which they used to fund the building of the Parthenon, a structure that they in turn used to house this tribute.

'. . . the time has come for these Marbles to come home to the blue skies of Attica, to their rightful place, where they form a structural and functional part of a unique entity.'

Melina Mercouri

'The Parthenon without the Marbles is like a smile with a missing tooth.'

Neil Kinnock

These quotes, and others like them, give the misleading impression that the sculptures in Athens and those in London would be brought together to form a whole with the building for which they were created. If only the British stopped being so stubborn, and gave us back our Marbles, then we could rebuild the Parthenon – this is the impression restitutionists give; the sculptures would be put back on the Parthenon. Professor Anthony Snodgrass, a leading restitutionist, has claimed that 80 per cent of the Parthenon is preserved and can be found up on the Acropolis.

In fact it is highly unlikely that much more than half the Parthenon's blocks and architectural elements have survived. Some were taken to the British Museum, and the Greeks would like these back. For those pieces, I can see the *theoretical* validity of the claim, and would not be devastated if they were returned to Athens. But other blocks made their way to Venice as ballast over various centuries, and as mentioned before Professor Michael Vickers has identified some of these built into various *palazzi* in Venice. These blocks are obviously a problem, as is the block given to the people of the USA, and incorporated into the Washington Monument. Would the Greeks want us to destroy beautiful Renaissance *palazzi* and a major national monument? At the moment they are demanding the return of *every* piece of the Parthenon.

In terms of the sculpture, at most half is preserved. Previous estimates suggested that 60 per cent of the exterior frieze was preserved. Since we now know that there were friezes planned within the porches, and so there was probably more than previously thought, less than 50 per cent of the original frieze is preserved. Of this portion half is in London, and half is in Athens. Therefore, integrity is not a good argument in favour of reuniting the Marbles in London with the Parthenon, because it would not be possible to do so – the Parthenon sculptures will never again be whole, no matter how many computer-graphics seek to persuade us. The Greek Archaeological Service has long ago abandoned the idea of returning the Parthenon sculptures to the Parthenon itself.

Archaeologists in fact regularly ask for the very opposite to happen. They plead that the Greek Archaeological Service remove the last remaining sculptures from the building. Of course if pressed, the Greeks will agree that the Marbles, if returned to Athens, would be housed in a museum there, just as they are housed in a museum in London. One can question why it should be considered more satisfactory to see the Parthenon sculptures in a museum in Athens than in a museum in London. The sculpture would have no more context in a museum in Athens than in a museum in London. If it is the duty of the Greek government to bring the two together, in order to 'preserve its cultural heritage in its totality', perhaps it should start by preserving what it already has?

The marbles in London and Athens could not be displayed side by side at this time, because those in London are in good condition, while those in Athens are not, many sitting in storage, yet more awaiting conservation. Even the museum that is intended to house them has become controversial. The construction of the New Acropolis Museum has twice been stopped by the Supreme Court in Athens. After these defeats in the courts the previous PASOK government simply ignored its own Supreme Court.

At the moment more people can appreciate the Elgin Marbles for free in the British Museum than would pay to see them in Athens. The British Museum is free of charge, and it has been demonstrated repeatedly and quite clearly that people visit museums which do not charge admission fees far more often than those that do. Greek museums are, on the other hand, open relatively sporadic hours and have large admission fees. Even if every tourist visiting Athens bothered to go to the Acropolis – something few do – it would still receive fewer visitors than the Elgin Marbles in the British Museum.

Two years ago a small hand was broken off by a thief and stolen from the Bassae frieze in the British Museum. Because the Bassae frieze was a Greek sculpture, the Greek government protested vociferously to the press. It has been rather more reluctant to admit that pieces routinely go missing from museums in Greece. Sometimes this is in well-publicised burglaries, such as at the Tegea and Corinth museums. Unfortunately more often the pieces are very simply 'lost' in storerooms, and quite regularly these thefts are not noticed until spotted by scholars in auction catalogues. In November 2003 the British Museum held a conference entitled 'After Actium' where scholars presented information about recent Roman excavations in Greece. One of the most exciting papers presented an Augustan altar found at Nicopolis. The altar had been found after the war. A new excavation of this site began in 1995, by which time ten of the twenty-six blocks decorated with sculpture that had been previously known were now lost.

Although Professor Evangelos Venizelos, the previous PASOK Minister of Culture, has claimed that reuniting two halves of the sculpture would make study easier, this is not my experience. When I was studying material for my Ph.D. on Greek architectural sculpture I was denied access to more than half the material I needed to see in Greece. Sometimes institutions couldn't find the pieces, at other times perhaps they simply didn't want a foreign scholar seeing

them. Greeks might argue that this is because there is such an overwhelming quantity of material in Greek museums, but in Italian
museums, which have similar amounts of material, the storerooms
are organised and it is possible – in fact quite easy – to gain access
to material.

The way Greece cares for its past has improved in recent years,
but it might be better if Greeks put their own house in order, before
they criticised the British Museum over its small failings.

The Marbles are famous mostly because we argue over them. They
are not famous because they came from the most famous temple in
antiquity; the Parthenon was a beautiful building, but important
only to the Athenians, not to all Greeks. The exterior frieze of the
Altar of Zeus from Pergamon, now in Berlin, is a finer work of
Greek sculpture but less well known, because the Turks have not
launched a campaign seeking for the Pergamon Altar to be returned
to Turkey.

Although there are many wonderful museums in Athens where
the Greek share of the Parthenon sculptures could be housed, for
the last decades the majority of these have been in an inaccessible
basement store-room, to which scholars and tourists alike are denied
access.

Some of the sculptures remain on the building. Others were
removed as late as 1993, but still have not been fully conserved,
and were only recently shown for the first time in a temporary
display (2004). The concrete cast that replaced the original frieze
on the building, like the Caryatids on the Erechtheion, were respectively fashioned after casts Elgin had made and a figure Elgin had
brought back to London, since the sculpture in Athens is in such
poor condition. Some of the pedimental figures sit forlornly in a
gas-filled box. They were removed in 1977, by which point they
had become too delicate to have contact with air. Despite this, the
remains of the frieze were not taken down until 1993. Other original fifth-century sculpted metopes remain on the Parthenon to this
day, being eaten away by pollution and acid rain.

So, if some Greek fairy godmother could wave a magic wand and
send the Elgin Marbles back to Athens tomorrow, they could not
even be displayed with the Athens Parthenon sculptures. The

Athens pieces are in such bad condition that if the two were ever displayed next to each other, this would cause considerable embarrassment to the Greeks and seriously bring into question their custodianship of what they themselves describe as their greatest cultural treasures.

When some of the west frieze was put on display in 2004, this was done quietly, and without fanfare. Anyone looking at it, then looking over at the frieze blocks moved to the museum in the nineteenth century, would be horrified at its poor state. Anyone who saw the condition of the west frieze in Athens next to the Elgin Marbles in the British Museum would immediately decide that the Marbles in London should stay there.

Equally shocking is the condition of the east frieze blocks in Athens, which have suffered far more from overzealous 'conservation' and cleaning. Given the criticism that the Greeks level against the British Museum for overcleaning in the 1930s, the bright colour of these Athens blocks was surprising, even shocking. Their matt, bright white surface makes them look like casts rather than real marble. I mentioned this to Michael Daley, Director of ArtWatch UK and an expert on restoration, who has studied the Parthenon sculptures. He suggested to me that their surface was probably the result of a very aggressive cleaning, and that their matt look was characteristic of chemical or abrasive cleaning agents or steam-cleaning.

In the former, the white, apparent 'cleanness' of the surface is usually the result of marble being etched into countless irregularities. This roughness has the effect of scattering light-rays and thus producing greater optical brightness. Abrasive cleaning treatments also sacrifice surviving, historical surfaces in order to excavate the whiteness that lurks below the raw material. High pressure steam cleaning is usually less injurious to the marble surface itself than other treatments (though it can cause cracking) but paradoxically it produces the same optically misleading (and sculpturally unfortunate) effect. That is, it blasts away the particles of stone, dirt – or whatever – that lodge between the marble's crystal components and thereby unify its surface. Without this material, 'cleaned' marble acquires a rougher, more granulated (i.e. sugar cube-like), light-scattering surface.

Michael Daley's objection to these supposed 'conservation' treatments is that, injuries that may result to the sculpture apart, *all* have the unfortunate consequence of drawing undue visual attention to the *surface* of the stone and thereby undermining a proper 'reading' of the sculpture's *forms*. In sculpture, form is bounded and articulated by surfaces but *is not synonymous with them* – in much the same way that in drawing and painting, shapes are bounded and articulated by lines. The British Museum has to disclose information about the Parthenon Marbles in London under the Freedom of Information Act. There is no such law in Greece, and curators have not been forthcoming about past cleanings of the Athens marbles, so we will never know what was done to them over the years. We only know that the Greeks continued to 'clean' ancient sculpture with steel chisels long after the British abandoned this technique as too abrasive.

Who owns our Heritage?

Collecting art has always been the domain of the rich, whether the rich are individual people or nations. Power – whether this is political power or economic power – has always been one of the major factors in the distribution of art around the globe. Although it is fashionable to talk of art being for all, this is a modern concept and in no way reflects reality. Those who have money can possess art; those who don't, usually cannot.

Some nations that have rich heritages, such as Italy and Greece, can build museums that depend almost entirely on art created in those countries. In northern Europe, perhaps because we have a less rich or younger cultural heritage, the universal museum was created. The theory of the universal museum grew out of the enlightenment. It was intended to be comprehensive, covering the arts, artefacts and cultures of the entire world.

An example of when restitution seems appropriate is when objects have a religious or spiritual significance. But within this there are still double standards: an item that might have a spiritual significance to a tribe in Africa would probably be returned in the current climate, but an altarpiece of a Madonna and Child that had a religious significance to an Italian village would almost certainly not be returned. Some cultures were quite happy to engage in commerce, and sold the goods. Shrunken heads, for example, were often made to order for Western collectors. The 'politically correct' issue here is not the legality of the exchange, but rather the concept that there was an imbalance of power when the items were acquired.

In May 2004 the Brooklyn Museum in New Yrok returned a collection of artefacts to an American Indian tribe, the Yurok. Members of the tribe expressed great delight at this, claiming that at last their ancestors could be put to rest and their crying could cease. Yet in 1905 when they had sold the artefacts to the Brooklyn Museum of Art, they had had no such worries about their ancestors failing to be at peace if the artefacts were in Brooklyn. It seems extraordinary that descendants could claim back something which their ancestors had sold. The artefacts were returned under the Native Americans Graves Protection and Repatriation Act of 1990. The Smithsonian in Washington DC was ordered to return all artefacts, bones and objects that were Native American to their 'rightful owners'. The curators wrote to as many tribes in America as they could locate. Out of some eighty tribes they contacted, just over a dozen wrote back. Most of these Native American groups quite happily accepted the return of various old artefacts, but none of them actively sought out their return, and most tribes didn't even bother answering the letters. The Smithsonian found that it was harder to return Native American artefacts than it sounds; the initiative to return these artefacts and the repeated pushes to do so came not from Native American communities themselves but rather from liberal politically correct white individuals in America.

Another argument put forward for restitution is that the objects can only be understood in the context for which they were produced. This is rather naïve. Since we are no longer pagans who worship the Olympian gods, neither we British nor the Greeks could ever fully understand the Parthenon and interact with it in the way originally intended. Although I live in Britain, I am far removed from the people who built Stonehenge. Modern Athens in the same way is not the context in which the Parthenon was produced; the city shares the coincidence of the same geography, but neither the same culture, nor the same religion. In fact, there is a group of revived pagans in modern Greece, who have returned to the worship of the Olympian gods; they have demanded access to the Parthenon for religious reasons, but been denied it by the Greek Ministry of Culture.

Our choice is quite simple. We either decide we believe in the concept of the universal museum, and we support those museums. We accept that these collections have been formed, and that these have now become great institutions in their own right, exhibiting works of art and cultural artefacts as well as encouraging education and research. Or we decide that they serve no purpose, and that their contents are returned to their countries of origin; the Louvre would thus display only French art, and so forth. This kind of cultural revisionism may sound ridiculous taken to this extreme but this extreme is in fact only a few steps along from the path of, say, returning the Elgin Marbles to Athens. We are either for enlightenment, the free trade of knowledge, or we are for a return to isolationism and nationalism.

In the summer of 2002 Constantine Simitis, then the Greek prime minister, met Silvio Berlusconi, his Italian counterpart, and they agreed that a small piece of the Parthenon east frieze in Palermo Museum would be returned to Greece. The Palermo fragment, a small piece of marble measuring some thirty-four by thirty-five centimetres, depicted a goddess's foot and part of her tunic. In a supreme act of spin, the Greek Ministry of Culture claimed the carving was of Peitho, the daughter of Mercury and Venus. Peitho was the goddess of Persuasion, and this led to countless headlines with puns on the word persuasion, and the idea that perhaps this generous Italian gift would persuade the British to do the right thing. This new interpretation came as a surprise to many scholars, as the figure is always thought to have been another goddess.

Had the piece been returned to Athens, this would have set a precedent, but in fact it was not returned. Although the proposed return received media attention around the world, the rest of the story did not. In Italy there was a huge outcry against this piece of restitution. The Italians wanted to keep their fragment of the

Parthenon frieze. The Director of the Palermo Museum also objected, and managed to gather a great deal of support around him. Finally, and rather quietly, Mr Berlusconi conceded and was persuaded to allow 'Peitho' to remain in Palermo.

In July 2003, Zahi Hawass, the head of the Supreme Council of Antiquities of Egypt, decided that the Rosetta Stone is also a special case, and demanded its return from the British Museum. To the Egyptians the Rosetta Stone is a unique part of their heritage. Hawass also asked for the statue of Hatshepsut from the Metropolitan Museum in New York, for the statue of Ramesses II from the Louvre, and for the Obelisk that has stood for some centuries in the Place de la Concorde in Paris. The Egyptians would also like the Bust of Nefertiti to be returned from Berlin. These are all items that have become iconic in Western museums, and which have come to represent Egyptian culture once they had left Egypt.

On purely technical grounds, the claim for the restitution of the Rosetta Stone to Egypt is much stronger than the claim for the restitution of the Elgin Marbles to Greece. The Rosetta Stone provided the key to deciphering hieroglyphics, and thus unlocking the writings of the ancient Egyptians and so their history. Although the Rosetta Stone records a rather banal decree of a Ptolemaic Greek king, in many ways it has been far more important than the Elgin Marbles in terms of archaeology. It gave us access to several thousand years of history and ancient culture in Egypt.

Hawass would like to see the Rosetta Stone returned to Egypt, but recently he has suggested that he too would be quite happy with a loan, perhaps for a few months for an exhibition so that the Egyptian people could see this icon of their culture. Obviously the same issue applies with the Rosetta Stone as with the Elgin Marbles loan. Would the Egyptian government return the Stone after the loan period had expired? One wag has suggested that perhaps we should ask for, say, the gold mask of King Tutankhamun to come to the UK in its place, to be held hostage and to ensure the Rosetta Stone does eventually come home to the British Museum.

The case of the Trojan Gold is another example of the redoubtable difficulties of restitution. Apparently Heinrich Schliemann found the gold treasure at Troy in the nineteenth century. He immediately declared that this was the jewellery of Helen, over whose honour the Greeks fought the ten-year Trojan War. This treasure, also known as the Gold of Priam, aroused suspicion almost as soon as it was found. Schliemann photographed his wife wearing it, but many suspected its provenance. After Schliemann, the Trojan treasure made its way to Berlin Museum where it remained until 1945. After the Russian liberation of the city, it vanished.

About a dozen years ago the gold was found in the basement of a Russian museum. Russian troops retreating from Berlin had taken it with them. Now of course we have the problem of where to return the gold – assuming of course that the Russians want to return it at all, and so far the Russians show every sign of wanting to hang on to the Trojan treasure. Berlin of course would like to display it in a museum. Turkey has also put in a claim arguing that Schliemann possibly didn't export it legally, although the Germans have managed to produce a receipt showing that he paid for it. If the jewellery did indeed belong to Helen of Troy, Helen in fact came from the city of Sparta, where her husband Menelaus was king, and so the city of Sparta has also put in a claim for the missing jewellery. The Greeks too claim the treasure is theirs, a surprising claim since even in antiquity the Greeks saw the Trojans as Barbarian foreigners, and Troy is today in the Turkish Republic. And how does one even begin to define these countries after a few thousand years? In the fifth century BC Athens and Sparta were two separate states; in the second century AD both Spain and Turkey were legally part of the same nation, Rome. In antiquity, modern-day Albania was seen as part of the Greek world, and Cyprus was more closely linked to Syria, yet contemporary Greeks claim an affinity to Cyprus but not to Albania. So to whom does the jewellery belong? It is an open question, and one that will probably never be resolved. Four nations are claiming the treasure, but for the foreseeable future it will probably remain in Russia.

One can ask who owns a nation's cultural heritage, but this can only be a rhetorical question. The idea of ownership of culture in many ways undermines the great achievements of culture. One could argue that nobody owns culture and that those, whether individuals or institutions, who have cultural artefacts in their possessions are merely custodians, looking after those artefacts for future generations.

The British Museum was founded in 1753, to house the collection of objects that had belonged to Sir Hans Sloane. It was designed to admit 'all studious and curious persons'. In 1759 it opened to the public in Bloomsbury. The Museum at the time had six curators, one librarian, a porter, a messenger, four maids and two watchmen. Although the British Museum has vast quantities of art amongst its holdings, education has always been part of its remit. Its main function is education, and the role of the curator is to educate the public as much as it is to preserve the objects under his care.

Museums are often a better place to study art because there, under one roof, are works from many countries and many periods, and one is able to compare and contrast them. Thus museum collections have greater value as a whole than the value of their individual pieces. The return of a few pieces thus threatens to undermine their integrity. The concept of the British Museum as a universal museum has become the foundation of its argument against returning the Elgin Marbles, but this is not the only argument for retention.

In my opinion, if seen in isolation, this could be a highly flawed and dangerous argument. The Museum would argue that trading a place in the universal museum for a place in a local museum would deny the Elgin Marbles a great deal of recognition. They argue that having great Greek works of art in other museums helps illustrate and promote the great glory of Greece's cultural heritage. These are all excellent points. But when people claim that only here can the worldwide significance of the Parthenon marbles be fully grasped, I disagree. The Parthenon marbles would be fully appreciated in almost any museum in the civilised world. I would be quite happy to see the Elgin Marbles in the Getty Museum if they were well cared for and well displayed; should Greece ever sort out a suitable museum display, it might be possible to appreciate them there fully one day. That they are in the British Museum because Elgin saved them is a happy accident of history. To say that the Parthenon sculptures can *only* be fully appreciated in the context of the British Museum is insulting.

The world is richer for having universal museums, and they are indeed far superior to many small, local museums. But the emphasis put on the concept of the universal museum suggests that great works of art cannot be appreciated on their own, but rather need to be put into a historical, chronological context. This supposes that, say, the frescoes in Saint Marco in Florence cannot be appreciated as well in the monastery for which they were created as they could be in a museum stuck between French, Flemish and Impressionist paintings, that Notre Dame in Paris cannot be appreciated on its own, needing a 'context' created artificially by surrounding it with items from different civilisations.

Greece by and large does a competent job of looking after much of its heritage and if we sometimes object to some of the things it destroys, one can always hope that in the future Greece will improve the quality and the care that it gives to its cultural heritage.

Conclusion

I came to oppose the Greek demands for the return of the Elgin Marbles when I was living and working in Greece. Although I worked with many wonderful Greek archaeologists, as a whole the Greek government's attitude to its history and culture leaves a lot to be desired. Although Athens was Muslim for almost four centuries, the only – and illegal – mosque was on the seventh floor of a hotel, and Ottoman-era buildings are still not preserved. Numerous archaeological sites were bulldozed to prepare for the 2004 Olympics, including the site of the battle of Marathon. The Parthenon sculptures in Athens remain in appalling condition.

The government of Greece has been unsuccessful in putting its own cache of surviving Parthenon marbles on display. It has been trying to build a new museum for them, but the project has been long delayed. Dozens of leading Greek archaeologists object to the site, not least because what lies beneath it, the remains of Athens' famous philosophical schools, has not been fully excavated. Greek authorities have unfairly attacked the way Britain has cared for its Parthenon treasures, yet their own track record is worse.

The Greeks of the nineteenth century, heavily influenced by the Germans, wanted to create a 'pure' Acropolis, one that was classical Greek and untainted by succeeding generations and cultures. They dug down to the bedrock, removing later monuments and the layers of earth that had always covered the surface of the Acropolis, turning it into a sterile mound. If Pericles were to return today, he would not recognise the Acropolis as it currently is.

The Parthenon and the other buildings on the Acropolis can no longer be seen as buildings with living, continuous histories; only the elements from the fifth century BC were allowed to remain. The sculptures on the Acropolis have fared badly under the independent state of Greece since 1831. Elgin had casts made of some of the sculptures he left in Athens. When one compares the casts made at the beginning of the nineteenth century with casts or photographs made in the later years of the nineteenth century and again in the middle years of the twentieth century with their condition today, it is quite clear that the sculptures have slowly but steadily declined in terms of their state of preservation. The Caryatids from the Erechtheion are the most dramatic example of this, but the Nike frieze from the small temple of victory that stood by the entrance to the Acropolis has also suffered badly.

The Greek government does not actively destroy its cultural heritage – except in preparations for the 2004 Olympic Games – but through its apathy and indifference it has allowed many of the sculptures and monuments in its care to become damaged. One can argue that the way the Greeks have been treating the cultural heritage currently in Greece is far from exemplary, therefore one can easily question why more sculptures should be returned to their care. The Greek government is abusing the cultural heritage in Greece, and so why should we allow them to acquire more sculptures?

The Elgin Marbles at the British Museum are well preserved, well cared for, and accessible to all free of charge. By contrast, the Parthenon sculptures in Athens are mostly in poor condition, continuing to disintegrate, and accessible only to specialists. The Elgin Marbles are quite happily housed in the British Museum, which saved them from destruction in the first place, and which has cared for them admirably ever since.

When the Greeks can demonstrate that they too have done an admirable job of caring for the marbles in Athens then, perhaps, we can discuss a loan.

Bibliography

General – Parthenon

There are several very good books on the Parthenon, though most tend
to concentrate on Antiquity and ignore the later period. Susan
Woodford, *The Parthenon*, Cambridge 1981; an easy, accessible introduction to the Parthenon. Mary Beard, *The Parthenon*, Profile Books
2002; is a short history of the building. Jeffrey M. Hurwit, *The Athenian
Acropolis*, Cambridge 1998; only covers antiquity, but is a wonderful
history of the Acropolis from Mycenaean to Byzantine times. P.
Tournikiotis, ed., *The Parthenon and its Impact in Modern Times*, Athens
1994; a lavishly illustrated Greek book covering many aspects of the
Parthenon, including its use in modern Greek advertisements. E. Berger,
ed., *Parthenon-Kongress Basel; Referate und Berichte*, Mainz 1984; the
main publication for much modern research on the Parthenon, including
its sculptures. V.J. Bruno, ed., *The Parthenon*, New York, revised edition
1996; slightly dated, this book has articles covering the entire history
of the Parthenon, with equal coverage given to the ancient and modern
periods. It is very good both for Ciriaco di Ancona's visits, and for the
explosion. Adolf Michaelis, *Der Parthenon*, Leipzig 1871; although very
old, this is still one of the best books on the Parthenon.

Prelude

The best source for this chapter's early history of the Acropolis is Hurwit's book, *op. cit.*.

Fifth-century Athens and the Parthenon

A.J. Podlecki, *Perikles and his Circle*, Routledge, London 1998; is the best and the most recent biography of Pericles.

Many books and articles have been published on the Panathenaic festival and the cult of Athena: J.A. Davidson, Notes on the Panathenaea, *Journal of Hellenic Studies* 78, 1958, pp. 23–41; Jennifer Neils, *Goddess and Polis: The Panathenaic Festival in Ancient Athens*, Princeton 1992; . Jennifer Neils, ed., *Worshipping Athena: Panathenaia and Parthenon*, Madison, 1996.

The building and funding of the Parthenon: A. Burford, The builders of the Parthenon, in *Parthenos and Parthenon*, Oxford 1963, pp. 23–35; R. Meiggs, The Political Implications of the Parthenon, in *Parthenos and Parthenon*, Oxford 1963, pp. 36–45; L. Kallet-Marx, Did tribute fund the Parthenon?, *Classical Antiquity* 8, 1989, pp. 252–66; L. Kallet, Accounting for culture, in D. Boedeker, K. Raaflaub, eds., *Democracy, Empire and the Arts in Fifth-century Athens*, Harvard University Press, 1998; R.S. Stanier, The cost of the Parthenon, *Journal of Hellenic Studies* 73, 1953, pp. 68–76; A. Giovannini, A, La participation des allies au financement du Parthenon: aparche ou tribut?, *Historia: revue d'histoire ancienne* 46, 1997, pp. 145–157; A. Giovannini, Le Parthenon, le tresor d'Athena et le tribut des allies, *Historia: revue d'histoire ancienne* 39, 1990, pp. 129–148; S.A. Pope, Financing and Design: The Development of the Parthenon Program and the Parthenon Building Accounts, in *Miscellanea Mediterranea*, Providence R.I 2000, pp. 61–70.

The architecture of the Parthenon

J.J. Coulton, The Parthenon and Periklean Doric, in *Parthenon-Kongress Basel, op. cit.* pp. 40–44, 368–369; F.E. Winter, Tradition and Innovation in Doric Design III: The Work of Iktinos, *American Journal of Archaeology* 84, 1980, pp. 399–416; M. Wilson Jones, Doric Measure and Architectural Design 1: The Evidence of the Relief from Salamis, *American Journal of Archaeology* 104, 2000; M. Wilson Jones, Doric Measure and Architectural Design 2: A Modular Reading of the Classical Temple, *American Journal of Archaeology* 105, 2001, p. 130 ff; M. Wilson Jones, Tripods, Triglyphs, and the Origin of the Doric Frieze, *American Journal of Archaeology* 106, 2002; M. Korres, Der Plan des Parthenon, *Mitteilungen des Deutschen Archäologischen Instituts (Athen. Abt.)* 109, 1994, pp. 53–120; W.B. Dinsmoor, How the Parthenon was Planned, *Architecture* 47, 1923, pp. 177–180, 241–244; P. Pedersen, *The Parthenon and the origin of the Corinthian capital*, Odense University Classical Studies 13, Odense 1989; a study of the capitals inside the Parthenon, which suggests that an early form of Corinthian capitals was used in the rear room.

The Parthenon Sculptures

There are countless books and articles about the Parthenon sculptures. These are those I consider the best, or are the most recent publications. J. Boardman, *The Parthenon and Its Sculptures*, London 1985; still one of the most solid recent studies of the sculptures, Boardman came up with the interpretation of the frieze as representing the Marathon dead. Ian Jenkins, A.P. Middleton, Paint on the Parthenon sculptures, *Annual of the British School at Athens* 83, 1988, pp. 183–207; a study of the little evidence for paint on the sculptures. M.R. Lagerlöf, *The sculptures of the Parthenon. Aesthetics and Interpretation*, Yale University Press 2000; the most recent English study. B.F. Cook, *The Elgin Marbles*, British Museum Press, London 1997; an accessible short book by the former Keeper at the British Museum.

The Pediments

O. Palagia, *The Pediments of the Parthenon*, New York 1993; the most complete recent study of the pediments, by a leading Greek archaeologist. B.S. Spaeth, Athenians and Eleusinians in the West Pediment of the Parthenon, *Hesperia* 60, 1991, pp. 331–362; B.F. Cook, Parthenon west pediment B-C.: The serpent-fragment, in Kanon, *Festschrift Ernst Berger*, Basel 1988, pp. 4–8; B.F. Cook, The Parthenon, East Pediment A-C, *Annual of the British School at Athens* 88, 1993, pp. 183–185, pl. 17–18; J.J. Pollitt, Patriotism and the west pediment of the Parthenon, in G. Tsetskhladze, A. Prag, and A. Snodgrass, eds., *Periplous. Papers on classical art and archaeology presented to Sir John Boardman*, London 2000, pp. 220–227; E.B. Harrison, Athena and Athens in the East Pediment of the Parthenon, *American Journal of Archaeology* 71, 1967, pp. 27–58. P. Schulz, *Poseidon's Nudity and the Iconography of the Parthenon's West Pediment*, Archaeological Institute of America 105th Annual Meeting Abstracts. Boston: The Archaeological Institute of America, (2004), pp. 22–23; to be published in full in a forthcoming volume of the *American Journal of Archaeology*; that Poseidon wore a cuirass is Schultz's new theory. W.H. Schuchhardt, Die eleusinischen Kopien nach Parthenonskulpturen, in *Festschrift Kurt Bauch*, Stuttgart 1957, pp. 21–28; publication of the small Eleusis copies of the Parthenon pediment. Peter Schultz, The Athenian Aprobates Race: Origins, Meanings, Transformations, in A. Choremi, O. Palagia, ed., *The Panathenaic Games*, Oxbow, forthcoming.

The Metopes

K.A. Schwab, The Parthenon north metopes. New approaches to reconstructing the 'Sack of Troy' – in: *Classical archaeology towards the third millennium. Reflexions and perspectives. Proceedings of the XVth International Congress of Classical Archaeology, Amsterdam, July 12–17, 1998*, Amsterdam 1999, pp. 367–369; C.C. Goulet, Theseus in South Metope 16 of the Parthenon, *Miscellanea Mediterranea*, Providence R.I 2000, pp. 71–76; I. Trianti, Neue Beobachtungen zu den Parthenon-Metopen, *Mitteilungen des Deutschen Archäologischen Instituts (Athen. Abt.)* 107, 1992, pp. 187–197; K.A. Schwab, Parthenon East Metope XI: Herakles and the Gigantomachy, *American Journal of Archaeology* 100, 1996, pp. 81 ff; M. Yeroulanou, Metopes and architecture: the Hephaisteion and the Parthenon, *Annual of the British School at Athens* 93, 1998, pp. 401–425.

The Frieze

Ian Jenkins, *The Parthenon Frieze*, London 1994; Ian Jenkins, The South
Frieze of the Parthenon: Problems in Arrangement, *American Journal of
Archaeology* 99.3, 1995, p. 445; Jenkins corrected previous mistakes in
the arrangement of the frieze. R.G. Osborne, The Viewing and Obscuring
of the Parthenon Frieze, *Journal of Hellenic Studies* 107, 1987, pp. 98–105;
J. Neils, *The Parthenon Frieze*, Cambridge 2001; B. Nagy, Athenian officials on the Parthenon frieze, *American Journal of Archaeology* 96, 1992,
pp. 55–69; M.B. Moore, Unmounted Horses on the Parthenon Frieze,
Especially West XII, *Antike Kunst* 46, 2003, pp. 31–43; J.J. Pollitt, The
meaning of the Parthenon frieze, in D. Buitron-Oliver, ed., *The interpretation of architectural sculpture in Greece and Rome*, Washington 1997, pp.
50–65; J. Boardman, The Parthenon Frieze, a Closer Look, *Revue
archéologique* 1999, pp. 305–330; T. Stevenson, Cavalry Uniforms on the
Parthenon Frieze, pp. 629–54, *American Journal of Archaeology* 107, 2003.
J.B. Connelly, Parthenon and Parthenoi: A Mythological Interpretation
of the Parthenon Frieze, *American Journal of Archaeology* 100, 1996, pp.
53–80; the theory that the frieze depicted the sacrifice of the daughters
of Erechtheus was not new, but this article gave it new publicity. The
theory is not accepted, mostly because one would have to have figures
change sex for it to work. C.W. Clairmont, Girl or Boy? Parthenon East
Frieze 35, *Archäologischer Anzeiger* 1989, pp. 495–496.

On the Nike temple, see most recently: Peter Schultz, History and Image
on the Nike Temple Frieze, in O. Palagia, ed., *The Timeless and the
Temporal: Art and the Peloponnesian War: 431–404 BC*, Cambridge, forthcoming.

The Statue of Athena Parthenos

N. Leipen, *Athena Parthenos: a reconstruction*, Toronto 1971; G.P. Stevens,
Remarks upon the Colossal Chryselephantine Statue of Athena in the
Parthenon, *Hesperia* 24, 1955, pp. 240–276.
Many inscriptions of the Treasures of Athena in the Parthenon survive:
L.J. Samons II, The 'Kallias decrees' (I.G I³ 52) and the inventories of

Athena's treasure in the Parthenon, *Classical Quaterly* 46, 1996, pp. 91–102; L.J. Samons II, A Note on the Parthenon Inventories and the Date of IG I³ 52B, *Zeitschrift für Papyrologie und Epigraphik* 118, 1997, pp. 179–182; M. Vickers, Persian gold in Parthenon inventories, *Revue des études anciennes* 91, 1989, pp. 249–257; W.E. Thompson, The Late Fifth-Century Inventories of the Parthenon. IG I³ 284/5, *Phoenix: the journal of the Classical Association of Canada* 18, 1964, pp. 262–271.

Athens in the Hellenistic and Roman periods

The best source for the later history of the Parthenon, with most written sources included, from the fourth century to the Turkish period, is: Anastasia D. Norre, *Studies in the History of the Parthenon*, Ph.D. Dissertation, UCLA 1966.

J. Frel, Ancient repairs of the Parthenon sculptures, in *Studia varia*, Rome 1994, pp. 47–62; Andrew Stewart, *Attalos, Athens and the Akropolis: the Pergamene 'Little Barbarians' and Their Roman and Renaissance Legacy*, Cambridge 2004; G.R. Culley, *The restoration of sacred monuments in Augustan Athens*, Ph.D. Dissertaion, University of N. Carolina, Chapel Hill 1973; William B. Dinsmoor, Jr., New Fragments of the Parthenon in the Athenian Agora *Hesperia* 43, 1974, pp. 132–155.

Byzantine Athens

V.R. Baydoun, *The Panagia Atheniotissa: The Parthenon as a Byzantine Church*, MA Dissertation NYU 2004; although an MA dissertation, this is one of the soundest articles written on the Byzantine Parthenon. Alison Frantz, From Paganism to Christianity in the temples of Athens, *Dumbarton Oaks Papers* 19, 1965, pp. 187–205; a study of when and how temples became churches in Athens. A. Frantz, Pagan philosophers in Christian Athens, *Transactions and Proceedings of the American Philological Association* 119, 1975, pp. 29–38; A. Frantz, Did Julian the Apostate rebuild the Parthenon?, *American Journal of Archaeology* 83, 1979, pp. 395–401; A. Frantz, *Late Antiquity: A.D. 267–700*, The Athenian Agora vol. XXIV, Princeton 1988; a brilliant study of the archaeological evidence for Christian Athens. P. Castrén, Paganism and Christianity in Athens and Vicinity during the Fourth to Sixth Centuries AD, in Brogiolo, G.P. and Bryan Ward-Perkins, eds. *The Idea and Ideal of the Town between Late Antiquity and the Early Middle Ages*, Leiden 1999; A. Cutler, The Christian Wall Paintings in the Parthenon: Interpreting a Lost Monument, *Deltion* 17, 1993, pp. 171–182; F. Gregorovius, *Geshichte der Stadt Athen im Mittelalter von der Zeit Justinians bis zur türkischen Eroberung*, Stuttgart 1889; C. Mango, The conversion of the Parthenon into a church, *Deltion* 18, 1995, pp. 201–203; H. Thompson, Athenian Twilight: A.D. 267–600, *Journal of Roman Studies* 49, 1959, pp. 61–72; K.M. Setton, Athens in the Twelfth Century, *Speculum* 22, 1944, pp. 181–5; J.-M. Spieser, La christianisation des sanctuaires païens en Grèce in *Forschungen in griechischen Heiligtümern*, Tübingen 1976, pp. 309–320.

Medieval Athens

K.M. Setton, *Catalan Domination of Athens 1311–1388*, Cambridge MA 1948; revised edition London 1975; K. M. Setton, Athens in the Middle Ages, *Variorum* 19, London 1975; K. M. Setton, The Latins in Greece and the Aegean from the Fourth Crusade to the End of the Middle Ages, in *Cambridge Medieval History*, Vol IV The Byzantine Empire: Part I: Byzantium and Its Neighbours, ed. J.M. Hussey, Cambridge 1966, 1967. My main source for Medieval Athens, Setton devoted his research to the period and has produced fascinating studies based on archival research.

J. Riley-Smith, *The Crusades*, Yale 1987; N. Cheetham, *Mediaeval Greece*, 1981; E. Zachariadou, The Catalans of Athens and the Beginning of Turkish Expansion in the Aegean Area, *Studia Medevalia* 21, 1980, pp. 821–838; D. Kleiner, B. L. Brown, Giuliano da Sangallo's Drawings after Ciriaco d'Ancona: Transformations of Greek and Roman Antiquities in Athens, *Journal of the Society of Architectural Historians* 42, 1983, pp. 321–335; M. Kazanaki-Lappa, Medieval Athens, in *The Economic History of Byzantium: From the Seventh through the Fifteenth Century*, A.E. Laiou, ed., Dumbarton Oaks Studies 39, Washington 2002; E.W. Bodnar, *Cyriacus of Ancona and Athens*, Latomus XLIII, Brussels 1960; E.W.

Bodnar, with C. Foss, *Cyriac of Ancona: Later Travels*, Harvard University Press 2003.

Turkish Athens

M. MacKenzie, *Turkish Athens, The forgotten centuries 1456–1832*, Reading 1992; an accessible study of the period. Michael Vickers, 'New' Parthenon fragments in Venice, *Antiquity* 62, 1988, pp. 718–723; Vickers has identified wall blocks built into Venetian structure. K. Reddemann, Die Zerostörung des Parthenon im Jahre 1687: zur Problematik des Tagebuchs Abraham Sobiewolskys, *Münchner Zeitschrift für Balkankunde*, 6, 1990, pp. 9–42.

Early travellers: The re-discovery of Antiquity and collecting

T. Bowie, D. Thimme, *The Carrey Drawings of the Parthenon Sculptures*, Bloomington Indiana 1971; F.-M. Tsigakou, *Thomas Hope (1769–1831) Pictures from 18th Century Greece*, Athens 1985; L. Beschi, L'acropoli di Atene in una veduta del 1670, *Numismatica e antichità classiche, Quaderni ticinesi* 31, 2002, pp. 347–358; M. Collignon, Le consul Jean Giraud et sa relation de l'Attique au XVIIe siècle, *Mémoires de l'Académie des Inscriptions et Belles Lettres* 39, 1913, pp. 373–425; J. Paton, *Mediaeval and Renaissance Visitors to Greek Lands*, Princeton, N.J., 1951. Jonathan Scott, *The Pleasures of Antiquity*, Yale 2003; a brilliant study of several centuries of British collectors of ancient sculpture.

The Elgins

A.H. Smith, Lord Elgin and his Collection, *Journal of Hellenic Studies* 36, 1916, pp. 163–372; the first publication of much of the material concerning the Elgins' acquisition of the Parthenon sculptures. This material and much more is covered by: W. St Clair, *Lord Elgin and the Marbles*, London 1967, revised edition 1998. Dr St Clair now owns much of the archive material, and has published a detailed study of Elgin's time in the East, and of how the Marbles came to the British Museum. Much of my text draws on his research, and that of Susan Wagel.

B.F. Cook, Lord Elgin and the acquisition and display of the Parthenon sculptures in the British Museum, in *Parthenon-Kongress Basel, op. cit.*, pp. 326–328, 453

J.P. Hamilton Grant, *The letters of Mary Nisbet of Dirleton, Countess of Elgin*, London 1926; S. Nagel, *Mistress of the Elgin Marbles: A biography of Mary Nisbet, Countess of Elgin*, New York 2004; Mary's letters and a new biography of Lady Elgin shed a great deal of light on her personality and her role in acquiring the Marbles.

The Marbles in the British Museum

J. Rothenberg, *Descensus Ad Terram: Acquisition and Reception of the Elgin Marbles*, Outstanding Dissertations in the Fine Arts, 1977; *Report of the Select Committee of the House of Commons on the Earl of Elgin's Collection of Sculpted Marbles*, London 1816; Ian Jenkins, *Archaeologists and Aesthetes*, London 1992; Ian Jenkins, Acquisition and supply of casts of the Parthenon sculptures by the British Museum, 1835–1939, *Annual of the British School at Athens* 85, 1990, pp. 89–114; Ian Jenkins, *Cleaning and Controversy: The Cleaning of the Parthenon Sculptures 1811–1939*, (Occasional Papers), British Museum Press 2001.

The Acropolis and the Modern Greek State

M. Korres, Wilhelm Dorpfelds Forschungen zum Vorparthenon und Parthenon, *Mitteilungen des Deutschen Archäologischen Instituts (Athen. Abt.)* 108, 1993, pp. 59–78; a study of the excavations on the Acropolis undertaken in the 19th century. R. Economakis, ed., *Acropolis Restoration: The CCAM Intervention*, London 1994; recent restorations. David Brewer, *The Flame of Freedom: The Greek War of Independence, 1821–1833*, London 2001; an evocative new history of Greek Independence.

The Restitution Debate

J.H. Merryman, *Thinking About the Elgin Marbles: Critical Essays on Cultural Property, Art and Law*, Kluwer Law International 2000; J.H. Merryman, Who Owns the Elgin Marbles?, *Art News* 85, September 1986, pp. 100–109; J.H. Merryman, Thinking About the Elgin Marbles, *Michigan Law Review*, 1986, pp. 1881–1923; J.H. Merryman, Two Ways of Thinking About Cultural Property, *American Journal of International Law* 1986, pp. 831–853; J.H. Merryman, A.E. Elsen, *Law, Ethics, and the Visual Arts*, Kluwer Law International, 4th edition 2002.

Index

Index

Index